THE POETICS OF CAVAFY

THE POETICS OF *Cavafy*
TEXTUALITY, EROTICISM, HISTORY

Gregory Jusdanis

PRINCETON UNIVERSITY PRESS
PRINCETON, NEW JERSEY

Copyright © 1987 by Princeton University Press

Published by Princeton University Press, 41 William Street,
Princeton, New Jersey 08540
In the United Kingdom: Princeton University Press,
Guildford, Surrey

All Rights Reserved

Library of Congress Cataloging in Publication Data will
be found on the last printed page of this book

ISBN 0-691-06720-1

Publication of this book has been aided by a grant from
the Paul Mellon Fund of Princeton University Press

This book has been composed in Linotron Janson

Clothbound editions of Princeton University Press books
are printed on acid-free paper, and binding materials
are chosen for strength and durability. Paperbacks, although
satisfactory for personal collections, are not usually
suitable for library rebinding

Printed in the United States of America by Princeton
University Press, Princeton, New Jersey

for V.
the dialectic of enlightenment

Contents

Acknowledgments, ix
Introduction, x

1. POET

   The Poet and the Nonpoet, 5   Inspiration, 8
   Imagination, 15   The Poet as Creator of His World, 19
   Alienation, 21   The Poet and Society, 24   The Poet as
   Expert, 31   The Poet as Aesthete and Decadent, 33

2. AUDIENCE

   Does the Audience Exist? 39   Dismissal of the Audience, 42
   Can the Audience Be Dismissed? 44   The Audience as
   Receiver and Interpreter of Texts, 48   Cavafy's Method of
   Distributing His Poetry, 58

3. POETRY

   The Early Poems, 64   Symbolism, 69   Formalism, 73
   Art and the Absolute, 80   Art as Redemption, 86
   Memory, 89   Art Preserves Essence, 92   Eroticism, 95
   Cavafy and Ruskin, 101   Modernism, 104   Toward a
   Postmodernism? 110

4. LANGUAGE AND WRITING

   Language as Object, 116   Literature and the Library, 119
   Literature as Written Language, 120

5. TRADITION

   Tradition as a Source of Knowledge, 137   Tradition as
   Source of Anxiety, 141   The Struggle in Tradition, 149

6. WORLD

   Mimesis, 157   Art and Guilt, 163

Afterword, 176
References, 181
Index, 191

Acknowledgments

The present work is based on my doctoral dissertation, completed in 1984 at the University of Birmingham. I had the good fortune to be supervised by Margaret Alexiou, a scholar with a rare command of the entire Greek tradition, who followed each stage of the thesis with dedication and rushed in a time of need to its defense. In the early stages the work was read by Dimitris Dimiroulis, Dimitris Tziovas, Marianna Spanaki, Maria Kakavoulia, Peter Baird, and Elsie Mathiopoulos. Each in his or her own way provided much comradely advice. I will always profit from the conversations I had with these friends. Donald Preziosi and Michael Herzfeld read the manuscript and emboldened me to seek publication. Alexander Nehamas helped in the final stages with his mastery of Cavafy and literary theory. The energetic Robert Brown of Princeton University Press was encouraging and admirably efficient from the initial submission of the manuscript to its publication. Vassilis Lambropoulos put Cavafy in perspective for me. I thank my parents for their moral and financial support and their understanding. My wife, Julian Anderson, went over each word of this book with tender care, often at the expense of her own work.

I am extremely grateful to the Social Sciences and Humanities Research Council of Canada for a generous three-year doctoral scholarship that enabled the research for this book. I would like to thank the Office of Research and Graduate Development of Indiana University for its financial assistance in offsetting copyright fees. I am indebted to Princeton University Press and Chatto and Windus for permission to reprint translations of Cavafy from *C. P. Cavafy: Collected Poems*, translated by Edmund Keeley and Philip Sherrard, edited by George Savidis; and to Harcourt Brace Jovanovich and the Hogarth Press for permission to quote verses from Cavafy's "rejected" and posthumous poems in *The Complete Poems of Cavafy*, translated by Rae Dalven.

Introduction

Modern Greek literature is of marginal concern to contemporary critical practice. It occupies a place of secondary importance with regard to the literary traditions of Western Europe and North America. It is the object of mild, if not patronizing, interest on the part of critics who wish to broaden their Anglocentric perspective. This study is written in the context of, and against, this xenophobia. It concerns the poetics of the Greek poet Constantine P. Cavafy. One of its aims is to see how Cavafy's poetics relates to the theories of art and literature of nineteenth- and early twentieth-century writers in Western Europe. Its method is necessarily comparative in that Cavafy, more than any other Greek poet of his time, worked within the context of European poetics. While his subject matter was Greek, either modern Alexandria or the Hellenistic world, his aesthetic assumptions have European sources. This perhaps partly accounts for the hostility his poetry inspired among his contemporaries and for the late acceptance of his work into the Greek literary canon. Cavafy is now celebrated as one of the preeminent poets of Greece, but during his own time his work was ridiculed or ignored by most critics and lay people.

Clearly, Cavafy presented to his reading public a poetry and poetics that was incompatible with the literary notions then current in Greece. Cavafy conceived of literature in formalist terms at a time when "literature" had not yet developed as an autonomous institution in Greece and the poem was not treated as a thing-in-itself. Literary texts were valued less for their own sake than for the uses they served in the linguistic controversy between purism and demoticism, and in the general discussions about Greek identity. In this respect, the development of literature in Greece differs radically from that in Western Europe. Literature had an ideological function; it was not conceived as pure form. Hence there was no receptive context for Cavafy's poetry. He was writing modernist, self-reflexive verse at a time when the Greek reader demanded a patriotic (if not nationalistic), romantic poetry. While his contemporaries in Greece were shunning the latest literary currents in

Introduction

Europe, he in Alexandria was cultivating a poetics derived largely from symbolism, aestheticism, and modernism.

Although poetics has gained wide currency in the literary criticism of the last few decades, it has been widely ignored in modern Greek critical discourse. Cavafian criticism is no exception. We have been offered the erotic, political, didactic, ironic, mythical, and countless other Cavafies, but no one has explored the poetic and aesthetic concerns in Cavafy's work. Indeed, some have even doubted their existence. Timos Malanos, one of the poet's first critics, peremptorily dismisses the presence of theoretical issues in his work: "I emphasize. He was not a theorist of poetry (in the sense we give to the word when we think of, for example, Mallarmé), rather he was so [theoretical] as was necessary to make his difference from others obvious" (Lehonitis 1942: 10). Although Cavafy, unlike Coleridge, Baudelaire, Mallarmé, and Eliot, did not devote himself to a consistent and methodical elaboration of his aesthetic views, both his prose and poetic work reveal a pronounced orientation toward poetics. Many of his essays, articles, and notes are devoted to such topics as poetic composition, the concept of the symbol, the nature of literary tradition, and language. Furthermore, many of the poems are concerned with these and other related themes. In this respect Cavafy's poetry may be characterized as self-conscious insofar as it is aware of itself as art and reflects on the problematics of art and literature. (This aspect of Cavafy's poetry will be discussed more fully in Chapter 3.) As Viron Leondaris states, Cavafy "speaks about poetry more than any other Greek poet" (1983: 27). Leondaris notes that one-third of the poems have poetry and art as their theme. Yet another third deal indirectly with poetics by treating related subjects such as inspiration, imagination, literary source, influence, writing, transgression, and reading.

In short, Cavafy's work is profoundly concerned with poetry—its production, function, and place in the world. It seems surprising then, that despite its prominence in Cavafy's work, poetics has been consistently neglected by Cavafian criticism.[1]

[1] This is so primarily because poetics has not existed as a serious object of inquiry in modern Greek critical discourse, and in this case Cavafian criticism is no exception. Even when Cavafy's critics referred to this concept, they meant not a theory

Introduction

Clearly Cavafy's early critics operated within a critical tradition that did not designate poetics as a noteworthy object of knowledge.

IT IS necessary to identify the terms I will be using. Generally I take poetics to mean a theory of literature that seeks a methodical knowledge of the principles underlying it. It defines literature and its subdivisions, as it also establishes the criteria and standards by which literature has meaning and value. As Tzvetan Todorov points out, poetics does not propose a close reading or a description of a particular work, nor does it promise to name the text's message; rather it explores the laws governing the production of literature (1981: 7). Poetics is concerned with the properties of literary discourse; it differentiates the codes specific to literature as opposed to those of other arts, such as painting, architecture, or dance. In other words, poetics represents the theory of a particular art—literature—in the system of arts.

But how can this definition apply to the work of a poet who did not record a systematic and self-conscious theory of literature

---

of literature, but poetic and stylistic techniques. Mihalis Peridis, for instance, devoting a chapter to Cavafy's poetics, defines the term: "Poetics is the art of incorporating the emotional and intellectual vision of poets in versification" (1948: 259). This formulation is ambiguous, but his discussion illustrates that by poetics he means Cavafy's poetic techniques, such as his manipulation of repetition, his use of apostrophe, and his dramatic mode of expression. Telos Agras uses the term similarly in his article on Cavafy; under the category "Poetics," Agras counts the number of metaphors, similes, metonymies, and adjectives, only to discover their virtual absence in Cavafy, although in his view they constitute the poet's chief tools. This finding compels him to ask how a poet can compose verse without these standard poetic devices. Such a question, however, does not relate to poetics (Cavafy's views on literature), but to style (how Cavafy's verses function poetically). Edmund Keeley also employs the term without rigorously defining it. When discussing Cavafy's changing perception of Alexandria, Keeley notes that the transformation of this symbol from a subjective, causal agent into a more objective metaphor coincided with an aesthetic purgation of his work. He adds: "A review of Cavafy's development in this regard gives us a particular insight into his poetics, because what emerged from the process was both the personal voice and the major preoccupation of his mature poetry" (1976: 24). Keeley then traces this development, which in his opinion involved the rejection of romantic imagery and the avoidance of aestheticism. But what insight into poetics is this? So formulated, this analysis concerns the evolution of Cavafy's mode of expression and the development of the symbol of Alexandria, but it does not address Cavafy's conception of these problems.

Introduction

and who sometimes employed the terms "art" and "literature" interchangeably? Clearly it cannot. Thus, when I refer to Cavafy's poetics, I mean Cavafy's view of the literary phenomenon and its underlying presuppositions. My aim is not to formulate Cavafy's theory of literature, but to highlight Cavafy's ideas on literature and art embedded within many tissues of writing—poems, essays, articles, letters, notes, and personal remarks. This, however, leads to a major obstacle, namely that of incorporating this material within a framework that would permit the discussion of those factors involved in the production, dissemination, and consumption of literature. In other words, an inquiry into Cavafy's poetics deals necessarily with those concepts that are implicated in the literary act. It must consider the image of the author, the conception of the poem, the effect on the audience, the function of language, the position of the audience, the role of tradition, the place of the work in the world. Two theoretical models open fresh possibilities.

The first is based on M. H. Abrams's schematization of the four different orientations of critical theories as formulated in *The Mirror and the Lamp*. In the introduction Abrams argues that all critical discourses differentiate four elements in a total situation of a work of art (1953: 7). First, there is the artifact itself—the *work*. The second is the *artist*, the creator of this product. The artist's work addresses an *audience*, the third factor, which may be composed of listeners, readers, or spectators. Fourth, the first three elements are located in the world, or *universe*, consisting of people, actions, ideas, feelings, material things, events, and supersensible essences (p. 6). Although any theory would take into account all four factors, almost all tend to explain, define, and classify the aesthetic phenomenon from the perspective of one coordinate only.

It is possible to borrow Abrams's four elements and devise a model for the examination of Cavafy's (or any other poet's) poetics. The model would consist of four factors: artist, work, audience, and universe. One could argue that for a theory of literature to be reasonably comprehensive, it must discuss all four elements. Similarly, when critics analyze the specific poet's poetics, they should examine that poet's ideas on, or conception of, each factor. The material would be organized on the basis of the four categories,

Introduction

and the poet's poetics seen as the synthesis of his or her views on these topics.

The second model is derived from Roman Jakobson's conceptualization of the act of verbal communication as outlined in his seminal paper "Linguistics and Poetics." In order to illustrate his argument that linguistics is connected to and embraces poetics, Jakobson schematizes the six factors involved in communication. According to Jakobson, a typical verbal act operates in the following manner: "The ADDRESSER sends a MESSAGE to the ADDRESSEE. To be operative the message requires a CONTEXT referred to, a CODE fully, or partially common to the addresser and addressee; . . . and finally, a CONTACT, a physical channel and psychological connection between the addresser and the addressee, enabling them to enter and stay in communication" (1981: 15). Although in a given linguistic situation one of these six factors may play a more prominent role than others, all six must be operative for effective communication. This last point must be emphasized, since meaning for Jakobson resides in the total act of communication, that is, in the process involving all six elements. Herein lies one of the main advantages of Jakobson's model: it distinguishes the individual function of each factor while emphasizing the totality of the act.

Jakobson's linguistically oriented conceptualization, which deals with the exchange of verbal messages, may be transferred to the field of poetics to explain the emergence of poetic meaning. In such a multidimensional context, poetic meaning may be seen as a result of the interaction of all six factors rather than one function only. That is, poetry could be conceived not simply as the poet's creation, or as a text on a page, or as the reader's reception, or as a copy of external reality, but as a complex process involving all six factors. Poetics, which studies those elements that govern the production of literature, should deal with all these factors. By the same token, Cavafy's poetics is not constituted solely of his conception of poetry, or the poet, or any other single element, but of the sum of his views and statements on the total act of poetic production, dissemination, and reception.

In comparison, Jakobson's model provides a more comprehensive view of the literary field than Abrams's and is a more suit-

Introduction

able guide for the classification of the material at hand. It incorporates two factors more than Abrams's schematization, and more important, it stresses the totality of the act in which all six factors are implicated. To devise a model for the study of a poet's poetics by utilizing the basis of Jakobson's model, one may substitute his six factors, derived from linguistics, with six roughly corresponding elements from the literary field. In such a translation of his model the addresser becomes the poet; the addressee, the audience; the message, poetry; the code, language; the contact, tradition; and finally the context, the world.[2] Thus a literary event may be described as an act that takes place in the *world* when certain *texts* are transmitted from an *author* to an *audience* and read according to certain linguistic *codes and conventions* and to reading practices provided by literary *tradition*—a cultural connection between the interlocutors that guarantees an effective contact.[3] By examining how Cavafy conceived of these six major elements, and a host of secondary concepts, I hope to provide a comprehensive account of Cavafy's poetics.

This, however, has the disadvantage characteristic of all synchronically oriented approaches. Although the model, through the incorporation of the concept of tradition, theoretically allows for a diachronic dimension in the system of poetics, it offers little scope for situating Cavafy's poetics as a whole in intellectual history. Such an omission would in effect render Cavafy tradition-less. To avoid this I will locate Cavafy's ideas on the relevant problematics within the context of European thought of the last two centuries. That is, I will provide a cross-section of each factor and compare Cavafy's ideas to similar theoretical concerns of other poets and writers, with particular attention to the literary dis-

[2] This proposed model is not intended to correspond faithfully to Jakobson's, since my aim is not to apply his theory to Cavafy's texts; rather his conceptualization is valuable in providing a structural framework for the classification of my material. Although I chose these interactive factors for my model on the basis of Jakobson's, I modified each element appropriately. This model may also be useful in the study of the poetics of other poets; it can help organize their ideas on art and literature into a system that in turn can be analyzed and also compared with the poetics of other authors.

[3] For a critique of Jakobson's model from a semiotic perspective, see my article "The Poetics of Roman Jakobson: Aesthetics or Semiotics," in *Semiotics 1984*, ed. John Deeley (Boston: University Press of America, 1985).

Introduction

courses of romanticism, symbolism, aestheticism, and modernism. My aim is not to uncover influences or to trace sources, but to map out relations, thereby demonstrating Cavafy's affiliation with this broader literary tradition.

This method introduces further problems, as the definition of these movements is not universally accepted. The most notoriously recalcitrant of the four is romanticism, a term persistently contested. The broad span of views concerning it ranges from Arthur Lovejoy's outright dismissal of romanticism as a single and unified movement to René Wellek's assertion of romanticism's common characteristics (Lovejoy 1975; Wellek 1975). This and other controversies remind us that the lines of demarcation between movements are not necessarily rigid or absolute, an idea often forgotten by Cavafian critics attempting to situate Cavafy in literary history. Cavafy's development has been seen as a process of maturation; insectlike the poet evolved through each movement, discarding, as he passed into a new one, the influence of the former, until he achieved his "mature voice." Typical of this approach is Mihalis Pieris's *Efodos sto Skotadi*, in which the author charts a map of Cavafy's "emotional and artistic adventure" by analyzing three posthumously published poems that, according to Pieris, represent the three stages of Cavafy's poetic career: "the first, the entirely early or romantic, the second, transitional or symbolist, and the third, mature or realist" (1982: 10). Similarly, Sonia Ilyinskaya sees a three-staged development in Cavafy through romanticism to symbolism and finally to realism (1983: 20).

Earlier critics, if less concerned with rigid patterns, adhered to the biographical approach. They saw changes in Cavafy's poetry or poetics as part of the poet's maturing process, during which he abandoned influences of certain movements and accepted those of others. Peter Bien, for instance, emphasizes Cavafy's rejection of the foreign romantics he cultivated during his youth, and his subsequent avoidance of "over-absorbing western European approaches" (1964: 33). Similarly, Edmund Keeley notes that Cavafy in his early work bypassed the dead end of nineteenth-century aestheticism, though he adds that Cavafy did return to it later in his life (1971: 25). Roderick Beaton in like manner dismisses the

Introduction

entire romantic movement, claiming that "Cavafy had no time for romanticism" (1981: 526).

Common to these authors' conceptions of the relationship between Cavafy and literary tradition are not only biographical but also organicist assumptions. That is to say, these literary movements are conceived as easily definable and self-enclosed organic entities, through which a poet develops in a logical pattern of perfectability. Yet to see Cavafy's poetics as a teleological evolution is ultimately rigid and reductive. I intend, therefore, to demonstrate the many-sidedness of Cavafy's poetics by foregrounding, not his growth toward poetic maturity, but the relationship between his ideas and those of other European poets and thinkers. In this way it will be possible to indicate the simultaneous presence of divergent and conflicting elements, and to examine inconsistencies and contradictions. Yet I should emphasize that despite my refusal to analyze Cavafy's poetics from the perspective of the poet's personal artistic development, I do not overlook Cavafy's rejection of some features representative of a particular discourse, such as the traditional concept of inspiration, or lyrically oriented modes of expression, or the notion of the symbol. Rather I hope my approach will avoid such a facile conclusion as that Cavafy had no time or simply transcended romanticism, and thus was alone able to bypass or disown an entire system of assumptions so fundamental to Western art and literature.

This, however, remains a common claim of Cavafian criticism. It is at variance with the current critical position that modern culture is either a triumph of romanticism or a continuity of it. Indeed the idea that modernism is more a succession to, than a revolt against, the reigning assumptions of romanticism has now become a platitude in critical discourse. As early as 1846 Baudelaire observed that "he who says romanticism means modern art" (1923: 90). Subsequent writers in diverse fields have underscored this. Renato Poggioli, in his *The Theory of the Avant-Garde*, often brings to light those features of romanticism that have survived in modernism. Malcolm Bradbury, in his introduction to *Modernism*, concludes that this literary movement developed from romanticism (1976: 26–29). In *Rhetoric, Romance and Technology*, Walter Ong emphasizes that we still live in the romantic epoch and will continue

Introduction

to do so through the foreseeable future (1971: 20). Writing on the subject of modernist painting, Clement Greenberg insists that modernism has in fact embraced tradition instead of revolting against it: "Nothing could be further from the authentic art of our time than the idea of rupture of continuity" (1973: 77).

In the light of these arguments it would seem rather extraordinary of Cavafy to have single-handedly discarded an entire movement and then to have marched onto the horizon of subsequent movements. Instead of trying to determine when and how Cavafy espoused or abandoned romanticism or symbolism, it would be more productive to trace his affiliation with these various movements with the aim of situating his work in its tradition. Cavafy's poetics becomes more explicable if it is seen as a convergence of certain literary and theoretical discourses rather than as a spontaneous and independent product of an isolated genius in a provincial city.

IN THE discussion of Cavafy's poetics I examine his various writings: the poems, essays, articles, letters, and notes. Unlike previous Cavafian criticism, however, I do not confer epistemological priority on any group of texts; I do not emphasize the published over the posthumous poems, nor do I value a poem more than a prose piece. Indeed, I regard all of Cavafy's texts as documents containing information on poetics and not as aesthetic masterpieces promising transcendental truths. A statement concerning the nature of literary tradition carries the same value whether expressed in a poem, an essay, or a note. Since I do not privilege his poetry, it follows that when commenting on specific poems I do not conduct a stylistic analysis. Instead of evaluating the aesthetic qualities of individual poems—to determine why they are beautiful—I examine them with respect to the subject of poetics. In so doing, I neither treat the poems as self-sufficient and autonomous entities nor do I feel bound to respect their alleged internal balance and unity. In this way, I often discuss only segments of poems, those relevant to the topic under examination (exactly as I do with a prose text). In many cases I analyze certain prose or poetic passages more than once, but in different contexts, and use the differing readings in my argument.

Introduction

My interest is neither in providing "new" and "original" interpretations of poems nor in constructing yet another "Cavafy" to join countless others we have inherited. I am not suggesting that we have finally arrived at the truth—*the poetic Cavafy*. Rather, for various epistemological reasons, the poetics of Cavafy has been neglected, and my aim is to investigate this overlooked dimension of his work. Since my theoretical orientation differs substantially from that of my precursors, I do not analyze or refer to their interpretations. Clearly, as this introduction has demonstrated, we address different problems. There exists little ground for a comparison of our readings; our goals, methods, and objects are incompatible.

Such a decision does not necessarily represent a dismissal of these readings, but simply means that they are not helpful in discussing poetics. Neither does it constitute a claim to priority, in absolute terms, of my own readings over those of other critics. On the contrary, I want to emphasize the specific and contingent nature of my observations, which arise from the application of a particular set of interpretive strategies to Cavafy's texts. It follows that, with another objective and using a different system of presuppositions, alternative, perhaps conflicting, readings emerge. Even a brief genealogical survey of Cavafian criticism reveals how the meaning of "Cavafy" depends on the context in which a critic situates his work.[4] Each discourse appropriates Cavafy's work in its own manner and uses it for its own ends. The interpretations that it generates are valid mainly for those critics who subscribe to its assumptions. For instance, the reading of Cavafy by George Seferis may not be considered normative by readers belonging to the Marxist community (such as Stratis Tsirkas), or to the structuralist (such as Massimo Peri), or to the emerging poststructuralist discourse, but they are accepted by the liberal humanist critics whom Seferis represents. It is from such a perspective that my readings here are contingent and context specific in that they result from interpretive methods and presuppositions that are in no way my own exclusive property and that are not necessarily accepted

---

[4] For one such examination, see Lambropoulos (1983b).

Introduction

as "true" by all readers. It is also in this sense that my own interpretations claim no universal validity over those of other critics.

WHAT follows is a summary of this study's six chapters. Chapter 1 deals with Cavafy's conception of the poet. It begins with an examination of the appearance of this notion with romanticism and then proceeds to examine it in Cavafy by exploring first the differences between poet and nonpoet and then those qualities, such as inspiration and imagination, that characterize him. I draw parallels between Cavafy's understanding of the imagination and that of Coleridge. The imagination permits the poet to create not only art, but also a world beyond his own subjectivity. But as in the case of Baudelaire, the poet's capacity to construct his own world (and his difference from others) compels him to reside in it alone. This leads to a discussion of both the solitary poet and his position in society. Cavafy's poems dealing with alienation reflect the tendency in European poetics of the last two centuries toward aesthetic isolation. I set this formalist discourse in the context of other authors, such as Schiller, Comte, Taine, Ruskin, William Morris, and Tolstoy, who either emphasized art's place in the world or condemned its aestheticism. The chapter ends with an analysis of the portrayal of the poet in Cavafy as aesthete and his position in the aestheticism of the fin de siècle.

Chapter 2 explores Cavafy's contradictory conceptions of the audience. On the one hand, Cavafy (faithful to aesthetics) sees the audience as superfluous to artistic creation and, on the other, regards it as an essential factor in the emergence of art. The chapter begins with a discussion of the dismissal of the audience by romanticism through an examination of texts from Shelley, John S. Mill, and then Gautier, Mallarmé, and Wilde. This position is related to Cavafy's own rejection of the audience in many of his poems. In other texts, however, Cavafy qualifies this elitist posture by admitting the audience first as a passive consumer of finished artistic works and later as an active participant in the production of aesthetic norms. At this point I analyze those texts in Cavafy that undermine the arguments for aesthetic autonomy and foreground the role of the audience, as a network of readers, students, teachers, critics, publishers, in the constitution of the current definition of art. The chapter ends with an exploration of Cavafy's political

Introduction

method of distributing his poetry, a method that attests to his understanding of art as a public event.

Whereas the first two chapters address the producer and receiver of art, Chapter 3 focuses on the object of aesthetic production. It begins with a discussion of the romantic view of poetry and poetic creation characteristic of Cavafy's first poems and then analyzes his dismissal of both this poetry (and the poetics that informed them) and his espousal of symbolist theory. This analysis reveals how Cavafy's interest shifted away from the object to the mode of representation, from content to form. Typical of nineteenth-century formalism, he tended to valorize and concentrate on form exclusively. The discussion of Cavafy's formalism is set in the context first of Kant's aesthetics, and then of the aestheticism of the nineteenth century. Cavafy, like many artists of this period, sacralized art since it provided the poet with a formalist sanctuary where he could escape from the sorrow, vulgarity, and ugliness of the world. This section demonstrates the theological dimension of the aestheticist view of art; it relates Cavafy's notion of beauty as the absolute to Flaubert's and Mallarmé's schemes for the composition, respectively, of a book about Nothing and of the *Grand Oeuvre*, which, like the Bible, would subsume all reality but remain autonomous and autotelic. The discussion of the redemptive and therapeutic powers of art is set in the context of Schopenhauer's philosophy. Art for Cavafy saves not only the artist, but also past experience; through the aid of memory it resurrects moments of plenitude and transfers them to the transcendental realm of beauty that exists beyond contingency and corruption. In most cases, the episodes preserved are visions of past eroticism. This leads to a discussion of Cavafy's modernist poetics and ends with an analysis of a postmodernist undercurrent in his work that strives to overcome the self-reflexivity, perfection, and autonomy of modernism, pointing to forces outside the work of art that fight for its appropriation.

Chapter 4 addresses Cavafy's conception of language and textuality. It begins with a discussion of the emergence of the notion of language as an object of knowledge during the eighteenth century and with the appearance of literary language. It then moves to an exploration of intertextuality. Cavafy, like so many poets of the last two centuries, is preoccupied with the textual dimension

Introduction

of literature. His poems are conspicuously permeated by tissues of other real and fictitious texts. By examining the intertextuality of his poetry, it is possible to demonstrate his concern with written language. This literary language is neither transparent nor a vehicle for communication, but an opaque and dense materiality that, by postponing and frustrating the act of representation, brings its own being to the fore and makes itself, rather than reality, the object of attention.

In Chapter 5 I explore the representation of tradition in Cavafy's poetics. I show that in Cavafy there exist two views of this notion, a traditional and a modernist one. The first sees tradition as a source of knowledge, a quarry to which the poet returns for thematic material and inspiration. In the second, tradition does not so much inform and enlighten the poet as threaten him. It is regarded as a source of anxiety. The belated poet perceives himself as confronting an intolerably vast accumulation of masterpieces. He sees his predecessors not as teachers, but as opponents against whom he must fight to win a place in history. The struggle is the central metaphor in this view of tradition, and originality its ultimate goal. I relate this conception of tradition to the discussion of belatedness that took place in Europe during the eighteenth century.

In the final chapter I am concerned with the relationship between art/poetry and the outside world. I begin with a discussion of Cavafy's rejection of mimesis as a means of conceiving artistic production. Art for Cavafy does not copy the phenomenal world. Much of his poetry expresses this radical and uncompromising repudiation of the world as subject for art. This separation of art from life, the rejection of purpose and use, resulted in a bad conscience since it deprived art of any seriousness. Art feels guilty because it is left with entertainment value only. I explore those texts in Cavafy that deal with both the consequences of aesthetic isolationism and Cavafy's attempt to overcome the dichotomies of art/action and theory/practice. The valorization of literature, its separation from society, lodges it in this oppositional taxonomy, which results in feelings of inadequacy, irrelevance, and insubstantiality. The implications of aesthetic autonomy return to haunt art and literature.

THE POETICS OF CAVAFY

1. POET

Western culture has regarded the poet as a source of poetry, or at least an essential component in the creative process. With romanticism a change occurred in the conception of the poet, manifested both in the enhanced social status he enjoyed as a purveyor of truth, and also in the increased reference made to him to explain and interpret poetry. In his influential study of romanticism, *The Mirror and the Lamp*, M. H. Abrams demonstrates that while previous ages in their conception of poetry foregrounded either the role of reality (which poetry copied) or the function of the audience (which poetry taught or pleased), by the late nineteenth century poetry came to be understood primarily from the perspective of the poet. The factors of reality and the audience forfeited their significance, as more emphasis was given to the creator. In short, with the rise of expression theory critical interest shifted away from these coordinates to the poet himself.

A passage that exemplifies this transformation and the one usually cited in this context comes from Wordsworth's preface to the *Lyrical Ballads* (1800), in which he alludes to poetry as the "overflow of powerful feeling." Wordsworth understands poetic creativity as a spontaneous gush of strong passion in the process of which the author pours forth his soul into verse. The source of the poem is the poet; it is he who both fashions the artistic product and renders it meaningful for others. The poet and his internalized microcosm emerge as the central factors in the explanation and judgment of poetry. This conception of artistic activity becomes an essential attribute of nineteenth-century critical discourse and marks the conceptual realignment toward the poet. Writing eighteen years after Wordsworth, William Hazlitt provides a parallel definition of poetry. For Hazlitt, poetry is the expression of the poet's feelings, it is "the language of the imagination and the passions" stemming from the bosoms of men (1930: 1). Terms such as "feelings," "passions," and the "imagination" are the key words by which poetry is discussed and analyzed. Their frequent recurrence in critical discourse—in his essay Hazlitt often repeats the passage quoted here—attests to the shift in thinking about the artistic act and brings to the fore the romantic preoccupation with the poet.

This change in theoretical orientation may be seen in many other critical writings of that and subsequent periods. A case in point is Carlyle's essay "The Hero as Poet" (1840), in which he refers metaphorically to Shakespeare's works as "windows through which we glimpse of the world in him" (1897: 110). But what view do the windows afford? They do not open out to the world, as poetry was expected to do, but reveal a picture of the poet himself; the work illuminates the inner soul more than it describes the universe. One can argue that, for Carlyle, poetry expresses the poet's mind rather than faithfully depicting nature or addressing itself to the experience of the audience. Carlyle's metaphor typifies the new conception of the poet, which gradually became the dominant explanation of poetic production.

Such pronouncements as those cited above constitute a juncture in the development of poetics inasmuch as they posit the poet at the center of interpretive reference. The artist sees himself (and is judged by others) as the triggering force in the act of creation. He emerges as the genius, as the freethinking subject who exists unconstrained by conventions and institutions, and who by his almost divine power fashions new forms. He alone bears the authority to confer upon an object the status of art; that is, an object is deemed to be artistic not because it faithfully represents nature, or because the audience designates it as art, but chiefly because it is produced by the artist. Edmund Wilson, in his study of late nineteenth- and early twentieth-century literature, perceptively points out the crucial difference between the romantic poet and his precursors. In his introductory remarks to *Axel's Castle*, he notes that while Racine, Molière, and Swift ask us to be interested in what they have created, Musset, Byron, and Wordsworth ask us to be interested in themselves (1931: 2).

Such perhaps was the generalized image of the poet that Cavafy inherited, albeit in modified form. In this chapter I explore the notion of the poet as it is represented in Cavafy's poetics, first, by examining the distinction made in his work between the poet

Poet

and the nonpoet, and second, by investigating the special attributes that are the characteristics of the poet.

THE POET AND THE NON-POET

One of the recurring features in Cavafy's poetics, which will be encountered throughout this study, is the segregation of the poetic from the nonpoetic dimension of life. The relationship between these two spheres of human activity is seen in terms of radical difference; the boundary dividing them is so vigorously defended by the poet that it becomes nearly impassable. Quite simply, one either possesses the qualities of the poet or one does not. The poets portrayed in Cavafy's work claim to be unique and distinctive beings isolated from the average person. They are preoccupied, if not obsessed, with their difference from the rest of the human race. Their self-image is informed by the notion of alterity, which, as shall be seen later in this chapter, manifests itself in diverse forms of alienation. In Cavafy's work the poet is an elitist who unabashedly proclaims his distinctiveness. Such is the theme of the early poem "Addition" (1897), in which the speaker argues that personal happiness is not the goal of his life:

> I do not question whether I am happy or not.
> But one thing I always keep gladly in mind;
> that in the great addition—their addition that I abhor—
> that has so many numbers, I am not one
> of the many units there. I was not counted
> in the total sum. And this joy suffices me.[1]

---

[1] The translation of this poem is taken from Rae Dalven (1976). Throughout this study I will make use of Keeley and Sherrard's (1975) translations. For posthumous or rejected poems not translated by Keeley and Sherrard, I will employ Dalven's translations. (For a discussion of the posthumous and rejected poems, see Chapter 3.) All translations from the French and German and from Cavafy's prose texts, unless otherwise stated, are my own and are meant to be as literal as possible. Transliteration from the Greek remains a confusing problem. Throughout this study I have tried to follow the guidelines as outlined in the *Modern Greek Studies Association Bulletin* 16, no. 1 (1984), which have also been adopted by the *Journal of Modern Greek Studies*. Keeley and Sherrard's translations appeared before the publication of this style sheet, though on the whole they attempt to approximate the actual sound in modern Greek except in the cases of classical names whose spelling is firmly established in English. Although their transliterations sometimes differ from my own—they write *Phernazis* and not *Fernazis*, for instance—I have repro-

Poet

What is paramount for him is maintaining his individuality and keeping a distance from the common rabble, for which he has only contempt. Redemption in life, the source of the only imaginable joy, stems from his successful evasion of the mediocre masses. Since the average man possesses none of the special talents and faculties of the poet, he remains for him uninteresting and uninspiring. Reconciliation between the poet and nonpoet is unwelcome. Indeed Aeschylus, in "Young Men of Sidon" (1920), is severely rebuked by a young man of letters for neglecting his tragedies when, in his epitaph, he refers only to having fought with the horde in the Persian Wars. (For a full analysis of this text see Chapter 6.)

In this poem, the composition of tragedies assumes supreme value and their author occupies a privileged position in the social hierarchy. The ability to write poetry rates as one of the most praiseworthy accomplishments. As Theocritus informs the novice Evmenis in "The First Step" (1899), even the "first step on the ladder of Poetry" deserves attention and respect:

> Just to be on the first step
> should make you happy and proud.
> To have reached this point is no small achievement:
> what you've done already is a wonderful thing.
> Even this first step
> is a long way above the ordinary world.

Theocritos's swift reply to his young poet's searching questions valorize the aesthetic experience. The ability to compose verse is deemed more valuable than any other human capacity. And the poet, who engages exclusively in this activity, ascends the steps of Poetry heading for his apotheosis as creator par excellence. Poetic discourse is divorced from ordinary discourse. This segregation of the poetic from the nonpoetic is, as we shall observe, not free of consequences, for the poet's celebration of his original voice eventually turns to a solipsistic monologue. Before examining the topic of poetic alienation in Cavafy, I wish to discuss those distinctive

---

duced their translations without change so that readers can turn to the poems in this volume without abruptly encountering divergent orthography.

Poet

features that allegedly differentiate the poet from all others and that bring about his ultimate isolation.

Chief among these characteristics is the poet's highly developed sensitivity, which, it is claimed, affords him a vision of truth. Poets were always thought to have access to privileged knowledge. Romanticism exaggerated this trait and created a distinct type of individual, one invested with an artistic personality. The romantic poet emerged as the uniquely gifted individual who in almost all respects differs from other human beings. In the preface to the *Lyrical Ballads*, Wordsworth enumerates these talents and skills: "A poet . . . is a man endued with more lively sensibility, more enthusiasm and tenderness, has greater knowledge of human nature and a more comprehensive soul . . . a man who rejoices more than other men in the spirit of life . . . delighting to contemplate similar volitions and passions as manifested in the goings on of the Universe, and habitually impelled to create them where he does not find them" (1966: 48). For Wordsworth the poet is an extraordinary individual endowed with refined senses that enable him to perceive those dimensions of reality to which common man is blind. Through his superior knowledge of human nature he creates for himself a more meaningful and happier existence, and most important, by his unique faculties he fashions beauty wherever it is lacking. Shelley echoes Wordsworth's eulogy of the unparalleled singularity of the poet as he too invests him with ontological priority: "the predominance of the faculty of approximation to the beautiful (taste) exists in excess among poets" (1977: 482). The poet, according to Shelley, is more delicately constructed than other men and is more sensitive to pain and pleasure, both his own and that of others. He is also "the wisest, happiest and best inasmuch as he is a poet" (p. 506). The use of such epithets becomes standard in the discourse on the poet. Novalis confers upon the poet the status of priest, while Carlyle gives him "infinitude" (Novalis 1945: 41; Carlyle 1897: 82). For Emerson, the poet is a "representative man" (1910: 82). Emerson goes on to say that the poet is superior in all ways; he is an inventor, a namer and language maker. "He unlocks our chains and admits us to a new scene" (p. 89). In short, he leads us to truth, we are richer for it, therefore we love the poet. Statements such as these point to the near unanimity in granting the poet superior cognitive and emotional faculties, which distinguish him from nonpoets.

Cavafy shares many of these views, particularly in his early poems. For instance, the posthumous "Correspondence according to Baudelaire" (1891) claims that the poet possesses a discriminating sense of perception: "The glance of the poet is sharper."[2] He alone has access to an unmediated vision of the world: "Only the chords of the lyre / know the truth, and in this life / they are the only certain guides" ("The Poet and the Muse," 1886). The poet's work provides a knowledge of the world that serves as a guide in life. He is also closer to the vital currents in life, more intimately connected with nature, coexisting with her: "Nature is a familiar garden for them [the poets]" ("Correspondence according to Baudelaire"); "The singer's Nature is divine" ("The Singer," 1892). In these verses the poet has been elevated to a transcendental state, but paradoxically, he seems to be nearer to things, enjoying a beneficial relationship with nature, whose secrets he alone uncovers. The image of the poet common to these poems is that of an exceptional individual who leads a much more authentic existence; his senses remain receptive to all stimulation, while his intellectual faculties enable him to apprehend the truth. In the later poems the notion of the poet as an uncommon individual is retained and is in fact reaffirmed; it is purged, however, of hyperbolic epithets and sentimental clichés so typical of the verses cited above. This modification of the figure of the poet can be observed microscopically in the development of one of the poet's special attributes—the faculty of inspiration.

INSPIRATION

In the early and rejected poems inspiration is conceived in the traditional sense as the spontaneous and unconscious factor in cre-

---

[2] G. W. Bowersock (1983: 183), in his article "Cavafy and Apollonios," draws attention to this line and compares it to relevant verses from "Correspondances" in order to illustrate a relationship with Baudelaire, a link that, he says, is crucial for understanding the aesthetic ideals of Cavafy in the 1890s. This relationship is no doubt important, but the attribution of a "heightened perception" to the poet is not a feature unique to Baudelaire (as the argument implies), nor is it limited to Cavafy's ideas of the 1890s. Rather, it represents, as a more comparative approach to the topic demonstrates, one characteristic of the general conception of the poet quite common to nineteenth-century poetics and shared also by Cavafy.

ation. Excerpts from three rejected poems illustrate the romantic overtones inherent in this notion as it appears at this stage:

> Far from the world poetic magic intoxicates him. . . .
> Friend, be quiet;
> meditate and sing. Be of good heart, mystic apostle.
> "Singer"
>
> Honest inkwell, sacred to the poet
> from whose ink a world emerges—
> "The Inkwell" (1895)
>
> Mellifluous song
> drops from your lips, and you are a treasury of myrrh—
> "The Poet and the Muse"

A feature common to all three examples is the exaggerated and affected language employed to describe the poet when under the spell of inspiration. Prior to and during the act of composition, he surrenders his conscious will, having been overcome by poetic intoxication. The whole process seems to occur without the intention of the poet, since from beginning to end he is borne away by poetic enthusiasm. The "sweet melodies" flowing from the lips of the "mystical apostle," or through the sacred ink pen, are triggered independently of his design. This view of inspiration is also found in Cavafy's essay "A Few Words on Versification," written in 1891: "Imagination, style, great ideas, in other words, divine inspiration are gifts flowing directly from nature" (Cavafy 1963b: 28). Inspiration, Cavafy believes, arises from nature, beyond the control of the poet's consciousness. During the process of composition, his will is suppressed and the muse's mystical powers take control.

Cavafy eventually renounces this romantic account of composition, as indeed he questions the very necessity of inspiration. The poem "Kaisarion" (1918) illustrates the emergence of a different understanding of composition in that it dramatizes the process of poetic creation. (For another reading of this poem see Chapter 3.)

> Partly to verify the facts of a certain period,
> partly to kill an hour or two,

Poet

> last night I picked up and read
> a volume of inscriptions about the Ptolemies.
> The lavish praise and flattery are much the same
> for each of them. All are brilliant,
> glorious, mighty, benevolent;
> everything they undertake is full of wisdom.
> As for the women of their line, the Berenices and
> > Cleopatras,
> they too, all of them, are marvelous.
> When I'd found the facts I wanted
> I would have put the book away, but a brief
> insignificant mention of King Kaisarion
> suddenly caught my eye . . .
>
> There you stood with your indefinable charm.
> Because so little
> is known about you from history,
> I could fashion you more freely in my mind.
> I made you good-looking and sensitive.
> My art gives your face
> a dreamy, appealing beauty.
> And so completely did I imagine you
> that late last night,
> as my lamp went out—I let it go on purpose—
> I thought you came into my room,
> it seemed you stood there in front of me, looking just as you
> > would have
> in conquered Alexandria,
> pale and weary, ideal in your grief,
> still hoping they might take pity on you,
> the scum who whispered: "Too many Caesars."

One immediately notices in this poem the disciplined language used to describe the poet: gone are the excessively lyrical and hackneyed metaphors and expressions. The poet is not wreathed in garlands or overcome by poetic intoxication, but quite soberly consults a volume of Ptolemaic inscriptions to verify some facts. The subject matter for poetry is found in texts, inspiration is sought in lists of ancient inscriptions. But is this notion of inspi-

Poet

ration similar to that represented in the early poems? Superficially this appears to be so, for at a point halfway through the poem the line is terminated with a series of dots, indicating perhaps that at this juncture, after the discovery of the reference to Kaisarion, the poet abandons his will to the mysteries of creation: "I would have put the book away, but a brief / insignificant mention of King Kaisarion / suddenly caught my eye. . . ." This impression is confirmed by the emergence of a fanciful atmosphere in the poem's second half. Under these conditions, the poet seems to lapse into reverie as he fashions the figure of the young king from the scant information provided by the text. But does the poet yield to inspiration? Not really, since there exist statements in the poem that foreground the awakened mind of the poet and his conscious control over his work. Indeed, it is the poet's will that predominates as the governing presence in the poem's composition. It is he who triggers the whole process, since he chooses to consult the volume, read it, dim the light, imagine, and fashion Kaisarion. Or, as he claims, it is his craft that is responsible for the creation of this figure: "I made you good-looking and sensitive. / My art gives your face / a dreamy, appealing beauty." This experience is not induced upon him spontaneously in the form of poetic madness, but is the result of his own conscious decision to verify certain facts out of which he produces Kaisarion, as both mental image and poem. In this process the poet activates his intellectual faculties and suppresses the emotional impulses that might impede the deliberate act of writing. Poetry no doubt stems from the poet, but not as an "overflow of powerful feeling"; rather it comes into existence as an artistic construct of his awakened mind. Inspiration, the unconscious principle in creation, is thus abandoned as an essential agent in composition. The poet claims exclusive responsibility for this achievement.[3]

In order to appreciate fully the emergence of the poet as self-conscious artist, it is necessary to examine the traditional concep-

---

[3] Cavafy's posthumously published notes include the remark "He who is excessively filled with enthusiasm cannot do good work" (1983a: 39), which illustrates the hostile attitude toward inspiration. In this passage (1907), while acknowledging the role of the emotions in creation, Cavafy emphasizes that they must be brought under control.

Poet

tion of inspiration, which, as Abrams notes, constitutes the oldest and most persistent account of poetic invention (1953: 189). According to Abrams, inspiration differs from the normal cognitive experience in four distinct ways: (1) it is sudden, effortless, and unanticipated; (2) it is involuntary and automatic; (3) under its effect the poet feels excitement, elation, and rapture; (4) the completed poem is unfamiliar to the poet, as if it had not been composed by him.[4] Cavafy's "Kaisarion" represents a repudiation of the concept as defined above. Although the poet finds himself in an excited state, the creative process is nevertheless anticipated and willed and its result is quite familiar to him, since it was executed according to his plans and intentions. Inspiration is not a prerequisite for writing; it is neither valued as an experience nor privileged as an agent in creativity. Hence that typical romantic fear that "when composition begins inspiration is already on the decline" loses its threatening force, since writing begins with the poet's volition.[5] There occur no lapses into poetic madness, no preliminary privileged moments that are somehow debased at the onset of writing.

[4] This notion of inspiration as the spontaneous and subconscious agent responsible for artistic creation became widespread with the romantics. Shelley's "Ode to a Skylark" provides a typical illustration within the context of English literature: "Hail to thee blithe Spirit . . . / that from heaven or near it / Pourest thy full heart / in profuse strains of unpremeditated art."

[5] The quotation is taken from Shelley's "Defense of Poetry." This poet's work serves to demonstrate once more the contrast between the romantic and modernist positions. The complete passage runs as follows: "But when composition begins, inspiration is already on the decline, and the most glorious poetry that has ever been communicated to the world is probably a feeble shadow of the original conception of the poet. I appeal to the greatest poets of the present day whether it is not an error to assert that the finest passages of poetry are produced by labor and study." Implicit in this quotation is the privileging of what Derrida calls the moments of presence and the debasing of artistry and writing. Shelley valorizes the divine state of inspiration during which the poet allegedly lies closer to true being. The act of writing disrupts this plenitude of ecstasy, it is external to and a departure from it. Hence, for Shelley, written poetry is a feeble representation of the original instant when his feelings and thoughts were embraced with nature. Shelley views artistry and composition with skepticism, since they threaten to enervate the natural, immediate, and authentic process of artistic creation. As a point of contrast, compare these ideas with those of Poe's in the discussion that follows.

For an analysis of the Derridean notion of writing as it relates to the modern Greek context, see my paper "The Politics of Criticism: Deconstruction, Kazantzakis, 'Literature,' " *Journal of Byzantine and Modern Greek Studies* 9 (1984–85). 161–86.

Poet

The conclusions emerging from the analysis of "Kaisarion" can be situated in the postromantic poetic/theoretical discourse that sought novel ways to delineate the notions of the poet and poetry. A noteworthy attempt to depict the poet as an artist fully conscious of the intricacies of composition is Poe's "The Philosophy of Composition" (1846). In this essay Poe explains with wit and hyperbole the method by which he wrote the poem "The Raven." He insists that, unlike other poets who allege to compose unconsciously, in a state of frenzy, he writes according to the disciplined direction of his conscious mind. By arguing that in the creative process the poet is dominated not by subliminal forces, but by his own cognitive faculties, Poe projects an image of the poet that contrasts with its romantic prototypes. Poe's poet does not abandon himself to an oneiric trance, but remains awake, cautiously selecting, rejecting, and erasing (Poe 1899: 267). Poe strives to demystify composition and to expose its secretive rites. He refers to the inception of "The Raven," insisting that "no point of its composition is referable either to accident, or intuition, that the work proceeded step by step to its completion with the precision and rigid consequence of a mathematical problem" (p. 268). In this passage Poe uncompromisingly repudiates the idea that writing is necessarily executed under the spell of poetic intoxication. Indeed, Poe's position in the entire essay, although often ironic, is unyielding as he sets out to deconstruct the romantic approach to writing.

Cavafy's "Kaisarion" may be situated in the theoretical context of Poe's essay in that it also signifies a shift in the conception of poetic composition. In this poem the poet's intellect is foregrounded and is given responsibility for composition. The poet as craftsman draws attention to his role in the writing of the poem. Seen in these terms, the poem expresses not so much a moment of vision—of the king Kaisarion—as it records the production of an artistic artifact. Even the idea of the dream, or *rêve*, which seems to overcome the poet in the latter part of the poem, is in fact summoned by him. In "Kaisarion," as in other poems, the dream is closely connected with the evening, candlelight, and above all with the formation of images.

The speaker of "Since Nine O'Clock" (1918) lights a candle and begins recalling the past; an image of himself as a young man

Poet

emerges, reminding him of both tragic and joyful experiences. Similarly, the speaker of "To Call Up the Shades" (1920) strives to fulfill these required conditions in order to create the atmosphere for the appearance of images:

> One candle is enough. Its gentle light
> will be more suitable, will be more gracious
> when the Shades come, the Shades of Love.
>
> One candle is enough. Tonight the room
> should not have too much light. In deep reverie,
> all receptiveness, and with the gentle light—
> in this deep reverie I'll form visions
> to call up the Shades, the Shades of Love.

At the end of the poem, the speaker is free to indulge in reverie and yield himself to the visions of love. Yet this *rêve* and its association with sleep do not compromise his rational faculties, since he induces the experience upon himself, he is the creator of the images. Indeed *rêve* is linked with the idea of art making, as "I've Brought to Art" (1921) demonstrates:

> I sit in a mood of reverie.
> I've brought to Art desires and sensations:
> things half-glimpsed,
> faces or lines, certain indistinct memories
> of unfulfilled love affairs.
> Let me submit to Art:
> Art knows how to shape forms of Beauty,
> almost imperceptibly completing life,
> blending impressions, blending day with day.

The dream implies that poetic images are created not, as it seems, in a state of slumber, but through the awakened mind of the poet. Such is the meaning of *rêve* common in symbolist poetry, particularly in the work of Baudelaire. A. G. Lehmann, in *The Symbolist Aesthetic in France*, states that for Baudelaire *rêve* does not suggest sleep, but on the contrary, it means staying awake to write poetry; Baudelaire does not regard reverie as a passive act, but as a state under his conscious control in which he searches for images, met-

Poet

aphors, and words (Lehmann 1950: 86).[6] During this process the rules of mimesis are abandoned, since, no longer bound by the conventions of realistic art, the poet has to organize and synthesize the stream of visions and sensations according to his own aesthetic principles. It is this or a similar activity that is enacted in the above-mentioned poems, especially in "I've Brought to Art," where the relationship between *rêve* and writing is most apparent. The poet indulges in reverie, not simply for the sake of pleasure, but with the aim of facilitating accumulation of raw materials (images, sensations, memories), which, through the intervention of the imagination, he transforms into forms of beauty.

IMAGINATION

Imagination plays a crucial role in this transmutation of sense perception, since in a nonmimetic conception of art it is indispensable as that creative force enabling the artist to modify and shape into patterns nature's rough material. This faculty accounts for originality; it is responsible for the emergence of new objects. Hence, it is generally regarded as the poet's supreme gift, which, since romanticism, has been conceived as one of the chief attributes of poetry.[7] The significance of imagination in romantic aesthetics is emphasized by John Keats in one of his letters: "I am certain of nothing but the holiness of the Heart's affections and the truth of imagination—what the imagination seizes as Beauty must be truth—whether it existed before or not" (letter to Benjamin Bailey, 22 November 1817; Keats 1970: 37). The imagination can perceive truth and also fashion it in new ways. This double function of seeing reality more sensitively and also of inventing it is exploited by the poet in his attempt to understand the world and to change it. For the poet this faculty becomes indispensable. It is, in

---

[6] With regard to Baudelaire, note the following verses from his poem "Paysage," which incorporate in poetic form his ideas on the dream and composition: "For I shall be plunged in this pleasure / Evoking the Springtime with my will / And drawing the sun from my heart, and forming / From my burning thoughts a warm atmosphere."

[7] I am referring here to Wellek's article "The Concept of Romanticism in Literary History" (1975), in which he contends that the concept of the imagination constitutes one of the three inherent features of romanticism, the other two being that of the organism and the symbol.

Poet

the words of Wallace Stevens, one of the great human powers, its only genius (1951: 138).

For Cavafy, imagination serves as the poet's chief tool in the creation of art and as the main conciliator in the gulf between a fragmentary reality and desire. By means of this faculty the poet may overcome the absence of experience both in art and in his own life, as is shown in the first half of Cavafy's "Ars Poetica." In this part of the essay, where, among other topics, imagination is discussed, Cavafy argues that personal experience is not absolutely necessary for artistic creation. A poet need not have direct knowledge of, or practical acquaintance with, certain facts or events in order to incorporate them thematically into his poetry. "By the imagination (and by the help of incidents experienced and remotely or nearly connected) the user can transport himself into the midst of the circumstances and can thus create an experience" (Cavafy 1963c: 38–40). According to Cavafy, want of an experience can be overcome, although some relationship with phenomenal reality must be maintained. Thus, while he affirms the capacity of imagination to invent, he also stresses the necessity of basic materials in this process.[8] Imagination acts as a creative force on nature's rudimentary patterns to unite or reorganize them into new forms, or as in this example, to create an experience that was missing in life.

A concrete example of this function is found in the posthumous "Half an Hour" (1917), in which the artist temporarily transcends the discontinuities of existence by evoking, through his mind, sensations equal or superior to those felt by the nonartist. The absent experience in this poem is physical pleasure. The artist cannot possess, as he needs, the person sitting next to him, so he begins to fantasize a sexual encounter with him, an event triggered by his desire, the influence of alcohol, and by the close proximity of the real body. At the end he induces upon himself an experience of such acute intensity that it becomes almost tangible but "totally erotic."

---

[8] See Chapter 3 for an additional analysis of the relationship between imagination and nature, as well as a comparison of Cavafy's ideas with those of other poets and thinkers.

Poet

> But we who serve Art,
> sometimes with the mind's intensity
> can create pleasure which seems almost physical
> but of course only for a short time.

The "mind's intensity" functions much in the same way as "imagination" does in the poem "In Despair" (1923). It is through his *fantasia* that the poem's anonymous subject hopes to re-create the lover who has now abandoned him:

> He's lost him completely, as though he never existed.
> Through fantasy, through hallucination,
> he tries to find his lips in the lips of other young men,
> he longs to feel his kind of love once more.

Imagination mediates between physical need and reality, acting to overcome absence and satisfy desire. Often, as was suggested in "Half an Hour," the experience it has conjured is perhaps cherished more than real pleasure. The speaker of "On Hearing of Love" (1911) states this emphatically:

> On hearing about great love, respond, be moved
> like an aesthete. Only, fortunate as you've been,
> remember how much your imagination created for you.
> This first, and then the rest
> that you experienced and enjoyed in your life:
> the less great, the more real and tangible.
> Of loves like these you were not deprived.

This poem leaves no doubts as to the value of the imagination. The aesthete clearly considers more valuable the erotic sensations perfected by his imagination than "the more real and tangible" pleasures. The poet prizes his imagination, since by promoting invention it facilitates his confrontation with an ostensibly hostile reality. Imagination also serves as the most crucial factor in the creation of art, where it functions as an active agent transforming nature's base material into novel forms. In this process imagination does not copy reality, but rather synthesizes its raw substances into aesthetic designs, as described in the poem "I've Brought to Art":

Poet

> Art knows how to shape forms of Beauty,
> almost imperceptibly completing life,
> blending impressions, blending day with day.

Imagination possesses associative and aggregative qualities through which it transforms perceptions into forms of beauty.

Such a view shares many features with the Coleridgean conception of the imagination. Coleridge is usually cited as one of the earliest critics concerned with this topic. In his *Biographia Literaria* (1817), he draws his influential distinction between fancy and imagination. Fancy for Coleridge is nothing other than a "mode of memory emancipated from the order of time and space"; it receives "all its materials ready made from the law of association" (1975: 167). In short, fancy acts as a mechanical and passive faculty, operating on the principle of reflection by repeating or mirroring nature's forms. Imagination, on the other hand, emerges as an organic, living power capable of generating and creating new form; it is, according to Coleridge's "Dejection Ode," primarily a "shaping spirit." Against the mechanical and passive fancy, Coleridge sets up the organic and active imagination, which "dissolves, diffuses, dissipates, in order to re-create, . . . it struggles to idealize and to unify. It is essentially *vital*, even as all objects (as objects) are essentially fixed and dead" (p. 167).

Romantics such as Coleridge granted to the imagination a primary position in the scale of their poetics, which is not surprising in light of the privileged status they gave the poet as autonomous and creative genius. As long as recourse was made to the poet to explain poetry, the notion of imagination was indispensable. As such, this recalcitrant term can be found in the poetics of symbolist poets such as Baudelaire, who valorized it as much as the romantics, although, it is argued, he stressed its intellectual rather than its emotional powers. Baudelaire hailed it as the "reine des facultés," insisting further that all faculties of the human mind be subordinated to it ([1859] 1923: 274, 283). For Baudelaire the universe exists as a storehouse of images and signs to which the imagination assigns their relative place and value; the world serves as a sort of food, which it digests and transforms (p. 283). This faculty does not simply rearrange elements, but transmutes them, impart-

Poet

ing upon them something of itself. Indeed, this is, according to Baudelaire, what a poet should stive to do: "I want to illuminate things with my mind and to project this reflection upon other minds" (p. 284). The poet is seen here metaphorically as an illuminating lamp, which casts upon objects its own particular light.

Cavafy's conception of the imagination rests within the tradition delineated by Coleridge, which runs through the nineteenth century to our own time. For Cavafy this faculty acts as an energetic force that synthesizes objects into original entities. These new patterns are all the more cherished, since they have not been copied but brought into existence by the poet's creativity. With "intensity of mind" the poet blends and fuses aspects of reality to produce distinctive dimensions. Not bound by the principles of representational art, he fashions beauty according to his own aesthetic standards. For Cavafy the imagination is the active agent in the process of artistic innovation and is a means by which the poet may alter his reality when he finds it deficient. In other words, the poet does not limit his energies to the creation of beautiful patterns, but extends his vision to mold a world beyond himself. This idea is also of romantic origin for, as Coleridge argues, images faithfully copied from nature do not themselves characterize the poet; they become proof of original genius only after they have been modified by passion, or "when a human and intellectual life is transferred to them by the poet's own spirit" (1975: 177). The romantic and postromantic poet creates his own living universe, or rather this world stems from his own subjectivity. He selects the raw materials and then imparts to them the vitality of his soul to fashion his own personal microcosm. The poet, as the following lines from Wordsworth's "Prelude" imply, emerges as the masterbuilder of reality: "I have made a world around me—twas my own / I made it: for it only lived to me" (1805: III, 142–43).

THE POET AS CREATOR
OF HIS WORLD

The universe outside the poet's self is his own insofar as he invests it with meaning by converting it into a vision revealed exclusively to himself. The poet's mind, to return to the metaphor of the lamp, illuminates the world and in this way provides it with

Poet

existential signficance. This is the sense of Cavafy's "In the Same Place" (1929):

> The setting of houses, cafés, the neighborhood
> that I've seen and walked through years on end:
>
> I created you while I was happy, while I was sad,
> with so many incidents, so many details.
>
> And, for me, the whole of you has been transformed into
>   feeling.

The outer environment (the houses, the neighborhood) that the speaker has inhabited is his own individual achievement, produced from his own personal experience. The phrase "I created you" unequivocally affirms the poet's intrinsic capacity to fabricate the world around him. The poetic imagination actively generates meaning, forging out of a core of phenomena an independent and exclusive reality. But in Cavafy, the mind of the poet does not merely act on material objects, nor does it simply transfer upon them "human and intellectual life"; rather it renders them pure sensation. This "feeling" does not correspond to the actual world, since the poet does not realistically render what his senses perceive, but internalizes this vision, imparting to it the distinctiveness of his own subjectivity. Eventually, as in the case of "Morning Sea" (1915), the transmutation of nature reaches such a degree of abstraction that the poet begins to doubt its existence. As he preoccupies himself more with this esoteric reality, his own invention, he runs the risk of irrevocably severing himself from the world.

A similar notion of poetic creation appears in Baudelaire's "Le Cygne," in which a corresponding transformation occurs in the poet's mind as the distant though familiar environment is aestheticized into allegory:

> Paris changes but in my grief nothing has stirred.
> New palaces, and scaffolding, blocks,
> Old suburbs, all turn for me into allegory,
> And my dear memories weigh more than rocks.

Like Cavafy's "In the Same Place," these verses, structured on the inside/outside polarity, concern the relationship between the in-

Poet

terior poetic self and its external surroundings. Yet the emphasis falls on one pole of the dichotomy, on the poet's subjectivity as expressed by the "pour moi" (like Cavafy's "yia mena" and Wordsworth's "to me"), which actively assimilates his environs and bestows upon them an aesthetic representation. While the material surroundings outside undergo change, they are saved by the poet, who sensuously turns them into allegory, inscribing their image on his memory as a private but transcendent truth. In both poems, nature in its raw and unmediated state ceases to concern the poet; indeed the natural object becomes valuable to him only after it has been modified by his imagination. What is evident in both instances is the rejection of nature as a subject for poetry and the consequent valorization of the poet's self as the central theme. Increasingly, attention is directed toward the poet's inner realm of experience. As Baudelaire himself insists, it is no longer sufficient to depict things as they are: "Nature is ugly and I prefer the monsters of my imagination to the triteness of reality" (1923: 273). Indeed, one of the salient features of postsymbolist poetry is its tendency to foreground these manifestations of the imagination—the fantasies, memories, sensations, and desires to which Cavafy ceaselessly alludes.

ALIENATION

As mentioned earlier, the poet's uncompromising repudiation of the real, the ordinary, and the common gives rise to an aesthetic isolationism and, ultimately, to the divorce of the poet and his poetry from the wider cultural realm. Although this image of the artist in isolation can primarily be located, as Frank Lentricchia says, in the post-Mallarméan poetic, its prototype lies in the earlier nineteenth century in the various self-portraits of artists "who even while they suffer the painful alienation of difference from other human beings, receive the special dispensation of such a difference by being granted (at least this is the common rationalization of their unhappiness) a unique vision of truth" (1980: 216).[9] This alienation-oriented mode of thought represents one of

---

[9] For an influential such prototype the name of Hölderlin comes to mind, perhaps one of the first romantic poets to incorporate the topics of alienation and the flight of the gods in his work. "Der Wanderer" presents the image of the isolated poet who once was blessed with an all-unitive vision, but is now left with a sense of ab-

Poet

romanticism's chief legacies to the modern poetic, especially to its conception of the poet. The postromantic poet increasingly casts himself in the role of the misunderstood and maligned outsider. Yet paradoxically he actively seeks this isolation since he considers it indispensable to his creativity. It was only through a solitary and miserable life that he could prepare (and pay) for his art. Few men, confessed Flaubert, had or will have suffered as much as he did for literature (letter to Mme. Leroyer de Chantepie, November 1857; Flaubert 1974: 612).

In Cavafy no such self-afflicted pain (and the inner satisfaction derived from it) occurs; the theme of alienation, however, is quite prevalent. It manifests itself in many modes; the sexual, aesthetic, social, and political. A poem that articulates well the poet's feeling of estrangement from his environment is "Morning Sea":

> Let me stop here. Let me, too, look at nature a while.
> The brilliant blue of the morning sea, of the cloudless sky,
> the shore yellow: all lovely,
> all bathed in light.
>
> Let me stand here. And let me pretend I see all this
> (I actually did see it for a minute when I first stopped)
> and not my usual day-dreams here too,
> my memories, those sensual images.

What is noteworthy about this poem is the near absence of nature from the poet's vision. The speaker is so preoccupied with his own internalized realm of experience that he cannot comprehend the open, available world. Despite his efforts, and apart from a fleeting but unsatisfactory glimpse, the natural landscape eludes him. Instead of the sea and sky, he senses only manifestations of his own opaque subjectivity—fantasies, memories, and visions of pleasure—with which he becomes increasingly obsessed. The poet verges on sollipsism since, as it seems, nothing exists save his experience, or rather, nothing can come into being without first being perceived by him. The poet encloses himself within an aes-

---

sence and loss: "Father and Mother? And if friends still live, / they have found other gains and are no longer mine . . . / I seem dead to them and they to me. / And I am all alone."

Poet

thetically detached space where he contemplates his art. Furthermore, convinced that his sensibility is somehow superior to that of others, he severs the already precarious bonds with his audience, so that ultimately he becomes isolated from both natural and social reality.

This double estrangement is particularly noticeable in the earlier poems, which are permeated by a feeling of angst. "Walls" (1897) for instance, depicts the individual as a captive who has been "imperceptibly" imprisoned by anonymous agents. Much like Kafka's beleaguered protagonists, he lies prostrate, unable to combat further the malevolent though unidentifiable forces: "With no consideration, no pity, no shame, / they have built walls around thick and high." Finding no way out through the walls erected by his oppressors, he resigns himself to his fate, overcome by desperation. In the related poem "The Windows" (1903), the speaker attempts unsuccessfully to locate the opening of the darkened cell:

> In these dark rooms where I live out empty days,
> I wander round and round
> trying to find the windows.
> It will be a great relief when a window opens.
> But the windows aren't there to be found—
> or at least I can't find them. And perhaps
> it's better if I don't find them.
> Perhaps the light will prove another tyranny.
> Who knows what new things it will expose?

The futile search for the windows leads perhaps to the realization of a more terrible truth; the failure to find them could be a blessing since they might reveal a vision more dismal than the present one. The melancholy mood of "Walls" is transformed here into one of total despondency and pessimism. No communication can take place between the individual and the world beyond the walls; he is confined within the bounds of his loneliness.

The atmosphere of gloom pervading these and other early poems is characteristic of much of the poetic discourse of the late nineteenth and twentieth centuries. Alienation and its attendant feeling of anxiety emerge as central features in the thematic preoccupation of modern art, becoming, in many cases, its catchwords.

Poet

Yet in Cavafy, apart from the early manifestations, the "fear and trembling" brought about by isolation along with the themes of victimization and self-hatred almost completely disappear later. In fact solitude is not bewailed but actively sought, and since isolation acts as a guarantee of poetic creation, the corresponding image of the lonely artist is cultivated. The poet in Cavafy does not, like the romantic nightingale, sing alone in the darkness to cheer his own solitude; he wears a different plume, that of the self-conscious individualist, aesthete, and hedonist who asserts and triumphs in his dissimilarity from (and superiority to) other human beings.

THE POET AND SOCIETY

The poet feels threatened by the community and regards society as a constraint on his artistic expression. We have seen how the poet insists on his difference from others and claims this uniqueness as an essential condition for his creativity. In order to guarantee this difference, he seeks to break any bonds to the social group that might compromise his aesthetic beliefs. Indeed, he pushes the notion of nonconformism to its extreme. As an artist, he aims not only to ridicule public taste, but to transgress society's laws. The poet thus maintains an antagonistic relationship with society. Although he rejects the need for a general audience and substitutes it with a select group of acolytes, he cannot successfully avoid the demands of the public around him.

The poem "Theater of Sidon (A.D. 400)" (1923) brings to the fore this confrontation between social norms and poetic license. The son of an honorable citizen writes "highly audacious verses in Greek," poems that deal with a "special kind of sexual pleasure, / the kind that leads toward a condemned, a barren love." Because of the provocative nature of his subject matter he fears the censorship of the conservative authorities, those who "prattle about morals" and who may be offended by the licentious verse. Yet, despite their censorial demands, he does not stop writing and chooses to circulate his poems surreptitiously. As a poet he could neither tolerate any interference with the sacrosanct act of creation nor abide society's demands for moral discretion. Art, as Oscar Wilde proclaimed in the preface to *The Picture of Dorian Gray*, is immoral and the artist necessarily assumes the role of an immoralist. This aph-

Poet

orism holds true for the portrait of the poet in Cavafy's work, in which the poet, as a nonconformist, is eager (and finds it necessary) to subvert society's aesthetic conventions and violate its moral norms.

Indeed, the unacknowledged motto of the poet in Cavafy may be the argument articulated in the posthumous "Growing in Spirit" (1903), which openly advocates resistance to the imposition of rules:

> He who hopes to grow in spirit
> will have to transcend obedience and respect.
> He'll hold to some laws
> but he'll mostly violate
> both law and custom, and go beyond
> the established, inadequate norm.
> Sensual pleasure will have much to teach him.
> He won't be afraid of the destructive act:
> half the house will have to come down.
> This way he'll grow virtuously into wisdom.

I return to this poem in Chapters 3 and 5, but here I examine it as a statement of the poet's hostility toward closed systems, such as that of society in general and of his inherited poetic tradition in particular. The speaker essentially sees himself as a rule breaker, as one who exhorts the transgression of laws and customs, although he envisages a partial emancipation of the poet. He calls for the destruction of "half the house," arguing that the self can primarily be realized outside the bounds of obedience and respect and beyond the norms and barriers established by authority. One can attain self-knowledge only when one accepts the liberating powers of the destructive act. This polemic of defiance becomes very relevant to the poet of "Theater of Sidon (A.D. 400)," who strives to thwart society's demand for moral integrity. It provides as well a message for the poet Temethos of the poem "Temethos, Antiochian, A.D. 400" (1925), who also faces the state's imminent censorship, but manages to circumvent it.

This poem, like "Theater of Sidon (A.D. 400)," dramatizes the disjunction between literary and nonliterary discourse. The poet Temethos has little contact with the audience at large. But he still

Poet

feels threatened by it, so in order to avoid the public's censure of his immoral verses, he also circulates his poetry privately:

> Lines written by young Temethos, madly in love.
> The title: "Emonidis"—the favorite
> of Antiochos Epiphanis; a very good-looking young man
> from Samosata. But if the lines come out
> ardent, full of feeling, it's because Emonidis
> (belonging to another, much older time:
> the 137th year of the Greek kingdom,
> maybe a bit earlier) is in the poem
> merely as a name—a suitable one nevertheless.
> The poem gives voice to the love Temethos feels,
> a beautiful kind of love, worthy of him. We the initiated
> know about whom those lines were written.
> The unsuspecting Antiochians read simply "Emonidis."

Temethos has composed a poem about his lover, but fearing that such an overtly homosexual theme will shock Antiochian society, he has decided to give the text a historical perspective by entitling it "Emonidis," the name of an imaginary friend of an ancestor of the current king. The Antiochians, believing that the poem is about this figure, will not be offended and will not intimidate its author. The poet does not care about their opinions, since he has not written the poem for them but for a much more limited, though enlightened, audience, an inner circle of friends who are initiates to the rites of poetic composition. The inclusion of false clues and misleading information in the text does not compromise the poet's sincerity, however, since his true audience—those who understand art—will be able to decipher the poem's hidden meaning.

The arguments raised in these poems concern the artist's reaction to what he felt was society's relentless encroachment on his own autonomy. They may be related to broader social developments in Europe, such as industrialization and the accompanying rise of the bourgeoisie. The appearance of the middle class brought with it a wider public for art, which wanted to be represented aesthetically. The artist, as we shall see here and in the following chapter, resisted this popularization of his craft, seeing this tendency as a potentially corrupting threat. In an age of democratization he dreamed of remaining an aristocrat. Thus he took a more aggressive posture against bourgeois manners. When he insisted on his difference it was from these philistines that he strove to distance himself, since they embodied the attributes antithetical to his poetic taste: the commonplace, common sense, crassness, insensitivity, conservatism, and puritanism.

Furthermore, the aesthetic isolationism espoused by Cavafy's poetry, and by much of postromantic art, stands in contrast to those discourses in the nineteenth century that sought to combat art's tendency toward formalism and autonomy by emphasizing its relationship to society and life in general. Many late nineteenth-century thinkers, under the influence of the new social sciences, directed their inquiries to the social aspect of art in order to determine its place in the world and to define its responsibilities. Of course something of this sort was attempted before, in works such as Shelley's "A Defense of Poetry (1821)," and particularly in Schiller's *On the Aesthetic Education of Man* (1794–95). Shelley, as the title of his essay implies, sought to defend poetry against charges of uselessness and to explore the role of art in human life. Poetry, he argued, contributes to the happiness of man, communicates pleasure, and is indispensable in the pursuit of the highest values in life. Schiller's letters and Shelley's essay constitute two of humanism's most noteworthy endeavors to confirm the role of the imagination in life. Schiller undertook to reestablish the connection between art and politics that had been severed since Kant. He brought to the fore those qualities of art that were, in his opinion, essential to the well-being of humanity. The prime mission of art, as he saw it, was to edify and to civilize (1967: IX,7). Art ennobles our character, since through beauty we realize our humanity. Indeed Schiller claimed that beauty offers us perhaps the sole possibility of attaining our human potential (XXI, 6). Art, for Schiller, represented an urgency in our lives, since it is ineluctably tied to our ability to achieve our very humanness.

Schiller's main purpose was to plead for the necessity of art in life by linking beauty with the realization of ourselves as social and cultural beings. But this aim differs from the goals of nineteenth-century theorists such as the positivists, who investigated art in terms of its social context. Auguste Comte, one of the most influential of the positivists, included among his writings on the organization of society his reflections on the ideal role of art. In a chapter of his *A General View of Positivism* (1830–42), he outlined the artist's contribution to the progress and welfare of man. Comte conceived of art as primarily a didactic enterprise with the mission to "charm and elevate human life," to cultivate man's instincts for perfection, and in so doing to enhance the path of social progress (1880: 205). The chief function of art lay in constructing types "of the noblest kind," which, through our contemplation of them, would uplift our thoughts and emotions (p. 209). Comte incorporated the aesthetic experience into his view of society. Indeed he fought strenuously against the isolation of the imagination, which he saw as leading ultimately to the corruption of manners and the decadence of the state. Art for Comte had a purpose to fulfill, and it called on the artist to concentrate on more virtuous subject matter, to speak of noble values, and to contribute to the education of man.

After Comte, Hippolyte Taine continued the sociological inquiry into the basis of art. Although, as Wellek states, Taine was not a true positivist because he did not exclusively privilege the methodology of the natural sciences, he did emphasize art's social source (Wellek 1955–65: IV, 46). Indeed he is credited with the founding of the sociological study of literature. In the introduction to his *History of English Literature* (1864), he expounded the new method of literary research by posing novel questions: "Given a literature, philosophy, society, art, group of arts, what is the moral condition that produced it? What the conditions of race, epoch, circumstance that are most fitted to produce this moral condition?" (1887: 19). Taine proceeded to show that literature, being one of the arts, has its own moral condition, which is dependent on its milieu—the physical, social, and political circumstances that fashioned it. The task of the critic is to relate literature to its own social and political environment, and in this sense to provide its background. The author performs a similar task, since by virtue of his deep insight he is capable of depicting not only the psychology of his own soul, but that of his time and even of his race. In other words, the writer not only expresses his own thoughts and even "rallies round him the sympathies of an entire age and an entire nation" (p. 20). For Taine, literature has a social source as well as a social function.

In England, John Ruskin similarly conceived of art as a product of society and as a measure of its moral stature. As we shall see in Chapter 3, in a detailed comparison of Ruskin's and Cavafy's thought, Ruskin strove to posit art in its social and moral context, since for him art, society, and morality were inseparable. As with the positivists, the value of art lay in its edification of man, in its capacity to communicate the fundamental moral worths; humanity could profit from art because it embodied the greatness of past ages. In this respect, as George Landow explains, Ruskin was one of the first thinkers in England to emphasize that art is a matter of public concern (1971: 10–11). For Ruskin, art no longer was the possession of a privileged caste, but the inheritance of every member in society. William Morris fashioned such nascent populist ideas into the framework of his writing on art. In an essay with the revealing title "The Art of the People" (1879), he condemned such aesthetic doctrines as art for art's sake, which sought to isolate art from its social milieu. He insisted that it is not possible to disassociate art, morality, politics, and religion, and he pleaded for an art "made by the people and for the people" (1948: 533). He repeated these arguments in "The Beauty of Life" (1880), in which he declared that the great cause for humankind is to support the "Democracy of Art" and the ennobling of common work (pp. 63–64). He called for the resurrection of a popular art, the handicrafts, which, unlike contemporary high art, would grant people pleasure in things they use. "Nothing can be a work of art," he stated in "The Lesser Arts" (1877), "which is not useful . . . which does not . . . amuse, soothe, or elevate the mind in a healthy state" (p. 512).

The democratic view of art was expounded with uncompromising force and vigor by Leo Tolstoy in *What Is Art* (1898). In this work Tolstoy completely repudiated the notion of art for art's sake and indeed the entire formalist tradition. In so doing he denounced almost all of the art of the past three hundred years as elitist, immoral, and decadent. Instead of transmitting the highest feelings to which humanity has attained, contemporary art, Tolstoy argued, had impoverished itself by becoming unnatural, superficial, and the property of a privileged class (1930: 149). Being far removed from the working people, this high art was incomprehensible to them and, as such, afforded amusement only to the wealthy few. In contrast to this aristocratic art, Tolstoy advocated an art that would communicate one person's feelings to other people, which would spring from religious values and which could be employed as a propagandist tool in the amelioration of the human condition. Tolstoy's theories, and those of Comte, Taine, Ruskin, and Morris, illustrate that alongside the formalist discourse on art, to which Cavafy belonged, there existed other, antithetical approaches that sought to locate art in a social, moral, and even religious context. These theorists regarded the artist as a citizen in society and hence expected of him ethical responsibility. But the artist resisted this missionary call, believing, as he did, in his independence from social conventions. He struggled against all attempts by others to impose upon him the role of moralist, scientist, philosopher, and propagandist. It was in protest against the employment of his talents for nonaesthetic ends that he polemically asserted art's autonomy, uselessness, and immorality.

Cavafy's conception of the poet, exemplified in the poems examined so far, and his position on art for art's sake (analyzed in Chapter 3), is situated in these cultural developments of the nineteenth century. That is, they may be seen as a reaction against both social pressures and the theoretical demands for a morally and socially responsible art. The artist in Cavafy renounces his social duty in order to devote himself exclusively to his craft, which he regards as the supreme human activity. This attitude is best expressed by the way the artist of "For the Shop" (1913) views and treats his work:

> He wrapped them up carefully, neatly,
> in expensive green silk.
> Roses of rubies, lilies of pearl,
> violets of amethyst: according to his taste, his will,
> his vision of their beauty—not as he saw them in nature
> or studied them. He'll leave them in the safe,
> examples of his bold, his skillful work.
> Whenever a customer comes into the shop,
> he brings out other things to sell—first class ornaments:
> bracelets, chains, necklaces, rings.

Poet

The artist in this poem, much like the poets of "Theater of Sidon (A.D. 400)" and "Temethos, Antiochian, A.D. 400," asserts his independence from popular aesthetic taste. Note that he withholds from public view his more skillful and prized creations, selling instead only ornaments and trinkets. For potential customers he plays the role of artisan, but is an artist only for himself. His most daring work, executed according not to current and celebrated norms but to his own conception of art, he reserves for himself and locks up in a safe. The public is not permitted access to it. Real art, it seems, is not exhibited in the marketplace lest it be corrupted by the crass expectation of the mass consumer. True art has no exchange value; it cannot, or should not, be sold for a wage or a price. Craftsmanship is mercenary; it works for its livelihood. Fine art does not enter commerce; its essential value is greater exactly because it does not have any market value. The artist creates, he plays, but he does not partake in any mercantile activity. He has no patrons or clients. (Ironically, as this poem suggests, high art depends for its existence on the mercantile art that sells its products, thereby allowing art the illusion of independence from the audience. I return to this in the second part of Chapter 2.) The artistic process becomes an intense private and solitary affair, and its justification stems not from public recognition and acceptance, but from values intrinsic to art itself.

THE POET AS EXPERT

In his belief that he emancipated himself from social constraints, the poet withdrew to the elevated heights of his ivory tower to pursue the solitary composition of his poetry. In the aesthetic sanctuary the poet could polish his verses, weighing each syllable so as to render his work perfect. The increasing emphasis given to novelty in literature had the effect of conferring privilege on not only original thought, but linguistic form as well, which had hitherto been neglected, since language was considered unproblematical and common property. But as language came to be conceived of as an opaque subjectivity and as its expressive function began to be doubted, form emerged as a value in poetry and became a focus of the poet's concern. (For a discussion of the change in the conception of language, see Chapter 4.) Related to this development, according to Roland Barthes, is the appearance

Poet

of the image of the writer as expert, "who shuts himself away in some legendary place, like a workman operating at home, and who roughs out, cuts, polishes and sets his form exactly as a jeweller extracts art from his material, devoting to his work regular hours of solitary effort" (1968: 63). The example of the artist in "For the Shop" comes immediately to mind as an appropriate description of creative activity. As practical illustrations of the above observation, Barthes points to Flaubert "grinding away at his sentences," to Valéry "at his room at the crack of dawn," and to Gide "standing at his desk like a carpenter at his bench." To this list one may certainly add Cavafy, consulting ancient sources, verifying obscure historical facts, tracing the etymologies of words, and devoting himself unflinchingly to drafts of poems over an exceptionally long period of time.[10]

The poet of the latter half of the nineteenth century came to see himself as a specialist in his field and not as bard or sage, as in former ages. He was a practitioner of literature, that is, a gifted individual who put language to a particular (literary) use. As a specialist it was essential for him to master the techniques and methods, the criteria and norms, inherent in his field. In poetry (and art in general) the dominant value came to be form. And since the writing of poetry was conceived of as an autonomous act, the message grew progressively more redundant. As art gradually withdrew into itself, mastery of its rules manifested itself in terms of technical proficiency and conscious artistry. The artist pursued excellence in form. Perhaps it was with this in mind that Poe, in "The Philosophy of Composition," exhorted poets never to lose sight of the object—"supremacy or perfection at all costs" (1899: 27). Similarly, Baudelaire, writing on the painting of Delacroix, noted that although the artist had the precious gift of the imagination, this faculty would have remained sterile had it not had the service of skill (1925: 9). Baudelaire referred to the mutual interdependence of skill and imagination in another essay: the more imagination one has, he argued, the more one needs technique to accompany it; it is folly to have one without the other (1923: 262).

---

[10] The longest period of revision for a poem is perhaps that of "If Actually Dead," the first version of which was begun in 1897; the poem was eventually published in 1920, twenty-three years later.

Poet

With the increasing valorization of skill and technique, clearly attention was directed away from the "what" and toward the "how" of art. Writing turned into a technical triumph. Self-aware artistry became highly valued, while inspiration was denounced; precision and economic expression were admired qualities, while sentimental, affected, and sloppy verse was despised. The poet as craftsman and specialist devoted himself intensively to the creation of pure form; he displayed an unquestioned faith in his craft. A youth of "Young Men of Sidon (A.D. 400)" is mad about literature; the poet Phernazis of "Dareios" (1920) is so committed to writing that despite the invasion of his country by the Romans, he persists in finishing his epic; the poets appearing in "Theater of Sidon (A.D. 400)" and "Temethos, Antiochian, A.D. 400" continue to circulate their poetry in spite of the risk of public persecution. With the elevation of the aesthetic experience to the pinnacle of the human value system, the creation of beauty came to be regarded as one of the highest of all cultural activities, and one to which the artist religiously committed his energies. Yet, as the example of the poets in the two latter poems illustrate, obedience to art did not imply an ascetic abstention from the pleasures of life; on the contrary, life was perceived from the perspective of beauty and lived as art. The devotee of art was simultaneously an aesthete and a hedonist, combining both beauty and pleasure in a unique style of life.

THE POET AS AESTHETE
AND DECADENT

One remembers that the poet's senses were thought to be acutely refined and receptive to almost any stimuli so that it was possible for him to pursue the pleasures of both eros and art. Such is the case of the artist in "Craftsman of Wine Bowls" (1921), who is about to incise on a silver crater the image of his former lover. There is a deliberate emphasis on the erotic aspect of this representation: the subject is a "beautiful young man," his body is naked and sensual, the setting is artificial and hermetic. The decorative details of the bowl are elegant and graceful. The work is intended for those few who can appreciate art; it will be exhibited in a house where "good taste is the rule." The five youths of "Young Men of

Poet

Sidon (A.D. 400)" convey a similar image of style and hypersensitive refinement. They are portrayed as overcivilized creatures, the last products of their culture, who exist on the geographical fringes of civilization at its historical demise. The young men renounce reality, fleeing into the felicitous world of poetry and perfume:

> The room opened out on the garden
> and a delicate odour of flowers
> mingled with the scent
> of the five perfumed young Sidonians.

The scent of the flowers outside blends with the sweet smell of the young men, who, like the plants in the garden, have developed their sensitivity to the point of corruption. The five youths are representative of many of the aesthetes, poets, and artists who inhabit Cavafy's aesthetic microcosm. A typical example is the central figure in "Of the Jews (A.D. 50)," who perhaps epitomizes the Cavafian notion of the artist. He not only possesses a beauty as fine as Endymion's, but as painter, poet, runner, and discus thrower, is also uncommonly talented. Furthermore, he submits himself equally to "aesthetic pursuits" and to "hard Hellenism," with its devotion to faultlessly conceived but perishable white limbs: "The Hedonism and Art of Alexandria / kept him as their dedicated son." Art and pleasure coexist as the poet's primary objects of concern and desire. They are inseparably bound and capture within their parameters the poetic attitude.

This dialectical relationship between pleasure and poetry is an important feature of late nineteenth-century poetics, as an extract from one of Rimbaud's letters tellingly expresses: "I am debauching myself as much as possible. Why? I want to be a poet" (1966: 302-303). This passage raises the issue so common to that elusive literary movement known as a decadence, namely, the necessity of debauchery as a precondition for the creative process. At the heart of poetic identity is embedded a feeling for the antisocial, exotic, and perverse. The decadent poet is so susceptible to outside stimuli that he is almost exhausted by life and history. Unable to sustain the vulgarity and pain of reality, he escapes into secluded villas to fashion art and to experience pleasure, if only intellectually. The poet surrenders himself to pleasure; he drinks, as

Poet

the speaker of "I Went" (1913) proclaims, from the potent wines of love:

> I didn't restrain myself. I gave in completely and went,
> went to those pleasures that were half real,
> half wrought by my own mind,
> went into the brilliant night
> and dark strong wine,
> the way the champions of pleasure drink.

The sexuality of the decadent is abnormal, in keeping with his revolt against nature and with the cultivation of his self-portrait as outsider. Erotic anomaly became a ubiquitous theme in the literature of the fin de siècle, a fact observed by Cavafy. In a posthumous note (1905), he alludes to this phenomenon, remarking that in recent years many French novels "courageously take into consideration the new phase of love." Not that this is new, he adds, it has just been repressed for centuries, as it is now neglected by English writers (Cavafy 1983a: 35). In Cavafy's poetics a perverse eroticism is essential for poetic self-identity, and many of his poems take as their dominant theme the idea of sexual difference. The speaker of "To Sensual Pleasure" (1917) openly proclaims his rejection of acceptable sexual practice:

> My life's joy and incense: recollection of those hours
> when I found and captured pleasure as I wanted it.
> My life's joy and incense: that I refused
> all indulgence in routine love affairs.

The speaker's hostility toward the conventional mode of love is reminiscent of familiar statements regarding the difference between the poetic and nonpoetic. The juxtaposition of natural and unnatural erotic pleasure is a manifestation of that ostensibly more fundamental difference. With the adoption of an unorthodox sexuality, the speaker undertakes yet another violation of social norms, freeing himself in this way of any vestiges of normality.

The poet in Cavafy, as noted earlier, recognizes neither many of society's moral laws nor its distinctions between good and evil. "The true artist," writes Cavafy, "does not have to choose, with regard to the hero of his myth, between Virtue and Vice . . . ; but both will serve him and he will love both equally" (Cavafy 1971: 238). Writing for Cavafy often is, as I show in Chapter 3, associated with transgression. In order for the ephebe of "Passing Through" (1917) to become worthy of poetry, to develop into a poet, he must submit unreservedly to unlawful erotic ecstasy, "as is right (for our kind of Art)." After he fulfills these requirements, the simple boy "becomes something worth our looking at, for a moment / he too passes through the exalted World of Poetry, / the young sensualist with blood fresh and hot." An anomalous sexuality is a precondition for initiation into the lofty "World of Poetry." The adoption of an unconventional erotic orientation serves a dual advantage to the poet: it assures his isolation and enhances his self-image as transgressor, both of which he considers essential for creation. The artist avoids the rooms where with decorum "they partake of the celebrated pleasures" and enters those chambers others condemn as shameful. But for the poet of "And I Lounged and Lay on Their Beds" (1915) this deliberate choice does not result in disgrace or dishonor, since poetry commands it:

> But not shameful to me—because if they were,
> what kind of poet, what kind of artist would I be?
> I'd rather be an ascetic. That would be more in keeping,
> much more in keeping with my poetry,
> than for me to find pleasure in the commonplace rooms.

This candid confession explicitly illustrates the poet's conscious attempt to cultivate the image of the nonconformist, in this case of the homosexual artist, which of course comes as the logical outcome in the poet's vehement struggle to differentiate and isolate himself from the typical, the common, the ordinary. Homosexuality, as George Steiner points out, is indispensable in postsymbolist literature for the poet's creative solitude (1978: 116). In the writing of Verlaine, Rimbaud, and Wilde, Steiner adds, homosexuality overlapped with the image of the artist as outsider. Cavafy undoubtedly belongs to this lineage, since in his work the homosexual poet is a recurring theme. Homosexuality perhaps represents the poet's ultimate strategy to alienate and thereby emancipate himself as much as possible from society's constraints, in

Poet

order to pursue, unrestrained, life's foremost goal—art.[11] It has been suggested that the ubiquity of the homosexual Greek boy in fin-de-siècle literature in a sense epitomizes the spirit of decadence (Stephan 1974: 42).[12] The glorification of this theme in Cavafy's work puts him solidly, in this respect at least, within this literary tradition of the late nineteenth century.

[11] I am not at all suggesting that these poets attained such a degree of emancipation or that it is possible for someone to work unrestrained by social conventions. I am simply arguing that this was one of the goals of fin-de-siècle artists. In Chapter 2 I discuss another attitude toward art in Cavafy that sees art as a product of norms and standards of taste.

[12] The following passage from Gerald Moore's *Confessions of a Young Man* (1888) lends support to this observation. Each century, says the novel's narrator, has its special ideal, and the ideal of the nineteenth century is the young man. "The position of a young man in the nineteenth century is the most enviable that has ever befallen to the lot of any human creature. He is the true bird, and is fêted, flattered, adored. The sweetest words are addressed to him, the most loving words are poured over him" (1972: 177).

2. AUDIENCE

I referred to the audience indirectly in the preceding chapter, when I argued that since romanticism the dominant literary discourses have taken little account of the audience as a factor in the production, transmission, and analysis of poetry or art in general. Poetry has been primarily conceived of in terms of the poet, from whom it was thought to flow, and who conferred upon it the status of art. The artist has come to be viewed as the sole creator of art, fashioning forms of beauty out of nature's raw materials, which—independently of cultural restraints and social institutions—he endowed with meaning, and which he designated as timeless aesthetic artifacts. Artistic creation was understood as a private and autonomous act transcending the specificity of time and place. Hence little notice was taken of the receiver and his historical situation.[1] As will be recalled, artists like Cavafy vehemently repudiated all attempts of those theorists to situate art in a moral, political, or social context. For these artists the writing of poetry was an autonomous act in which there was no place for the nonaesthetic. But the audience, at least in Cavafy, was not completely dismissed from the poetic domain. It reappeared in another approach to aesthetics, according to which art came to be regarded less as an esoteric preoccupation of the artist and more as a public event. That is, although the role of the artist in aesthetic creation was acknowledged, more attention was given to the audience's presence as receiver, judge, and interpreter of a work, and by extension, contributor to the emergence of art. Such a theoretical framework recognizes the capacity of the audience—as a broad public network of readers, students, teachers, critics, publishers—to influence the constitution of the current definition of art. Under this view, art is removed from the exclusive confines of the

---

[1] As was shown in Chapter 1, there existed other theorists who insisted on the social source of art, arguing that the artist resides in a community and has certain responsibilities to it. Art was created not to amuse the artist or please his coterie, but to serve the interests of the audience as a whole. Implicit in these sociological theories is the recognition of the public as an audience for art.

Audience

artist's imagination and situated in its sociocultural context, where it functions as an act of aesthetic exchange.

In this chapter my aim is to examine these two conflicting views of the audience implied in the equally contradictory conceptions of art. On the one hand, the role of the audience in aesthetic creation is considered superfluous, if not counterproductive, while on the other, it is seen as an essential factor accounting for the emergence of the current aesthetic. Both positions are active in Cavafy's work, although I should stress that the former is far more dominant, especially in the published poems, while the latter, appearing largely in posthumous texts, in a way subverts the prominence of the first view. Whereas the one claims eternal and universal value for art, the other undermines these aspirations by relentlessly reminding one of art's historicity. A more precise delineation of these conflicting points of view may clarify these differences and highlight the tensions between them.

DOES THE AUDIENCE EXIST?

The first position, as we saw in Chapter 1, is oriented toward the poet who conceives of himself as an alienated bard incapable of communicating meaningfully with his listeners. Shelley recorded this schism between poet and reader in that often-quoted passage from his "Defense of Poetry," where he emphasizes both the isolation of the poet and the audience's inability to comprehend him: "A poet is a nightingale, who sits in darkness and sings to cheer its own solitude with sweet sounds; his auditors are as men entranced by the melody of an unseen musician who feel that they are moved and softened, yet know not whence and why" (1977: 486). In the light of Shelley's metaphoric formulation, the addresser and addressee are not aware of each other's presence, and indeed, the poet speaks forth, irrespective of his auditors' existence or intentions; he continues to write poetry though it may be read by only a few. Shelley's description points to one of the most persistent features of romanticism, alienation that comes to be associated with the very possibility of poetry. Indeed poetry is increasingly seen as the soliloquy of an estranged poet. John S. Mill emphasized this aspect of poetic composition in his essay "What Is Poetry" (1833), in which he proposed that poetry is unconscious of

Audience

listeners since it constitutes feeling confessing itself to itself in moments of solitude (1897: 209). Poetry, according to Mill, does not direct itself toward the public, since it stems from an intensely private experience; only eloquence, he says, presupposes an audience. In distinguishing poetry and eloquence Mill alludes to the widespread discussion of his day concerning the attempt to differentiate the new romantic conception of poetry from its previous rhetorical basis. Poetry comes to be seen as the pure expression of the poet's feelings untainted by such extra-aesthetic factors as the wishes and demands of the audience (whereas in the operations of rhetoric, the audience occupies the central position, and is the target of language's power and strategies). Wanting to protect the autonomy and immaculateness of poetry, Mill banishes rhetoric and the audience.

Yet it is through rhetoric, through the text's capacity to move or influence—Horace's *prodesse* (to teach) and *delectare* (to please)—an audience that poetry was primarily conceived and analyzed from Aristotle until the eighteenth century. But with the advent of romanticism, this mode of literary study and appreciation fell out of favor, being replaced by a discourse that designated the poet as the principal agent of poetic creation, and hence the object of critical examination. In such a context, the audience came to be regarded as unwelcome interference in the poetic process. The passage from Mill expresses the apprehension that the listener may somehow corrupt the pure process of creation. Wordsworth similarly saw composition as a solitary act. Indeed, as he said of his own poems, they "are either absolute inventions of the author, or facts which took place within his personal experience or that of his friends" (1966: 11). The reader receives little attention here, since he is superseded by the figure of the poet, who begins to dominate the discourse of poetry.

In the latter half of the nineteenth century the poets' attempts to exclude the audience from poetry's realm became more uncompromising and often dramatic. Theophile Gautier underscored the new development by repeating Shelley's image of the alienated poet who sings and plays his lyre alone (1877: 866). Mallarmé also made reference to this motif in his description of the extraordinarily unique miracle that was taking place in the history of poetry:

Audience

"Each poet goes to his corner to play on his flute all on his own the melodies that he likes; for the first time since the beginning the poets do not sing from the lectern" (1945: 866). The poet does not address his audience publicly, but withdraws into his own chambers to compose verses for and by himself. In the same essay Mallarmé further foregrounds the irreversible separation of poet from his audience by comparing the poet (whom society does not permit to live) to a man who isolates himself in order to carve out his own tomb (p. 869). But the poet does not bewail his alienation; indeed, as we saw in the preceding chapter, he actively seeks it. In his contempt for his audience the poet removes himself to the ivory tower, where, to paraphrase Oscar Wilde, he can pursue the *Bios Theoreticos*, the theoretical life (1945: 83). In this ethereal sanctuary, where the commonplace was banned, the poet could free himself from what Whistler called that vulgarity "under whose fascinating influence the many have elbowed the few" (1979: 28). Here he could devote his energies to life's most cherished task, the creation of art. Both Wilde and Whistler through polemical positions rendered the audience redundant insofar as it had little to contribute to the artistic process. Quite simply: "Art seeks the artists alone" (Whistler 1979: 29).

Mallarmé, equally implacable in his elitism, peremptorily revoked the public's prerogative to read poetry, believing this would eventually lead to poetry's dissolution. Man can be democratic, but an artist should remain an aristocrat, he insisted, adding with a contemptuous tone: "Let the masses read works on morality, but please do not allow them to ruin our poetry" (1945: 260). The English novelist Gerald Moore echoed Mallarmé's aristocratic sentiments. "Art is the direct antithesis to democracy," he insisted provocatively in his novel *Confessions of a Young Man*. "The mass can only appreciate simple and naive emotions, puerile prettiness, above all conventionalities." These two passages from Mallarmé and Moore foreground the ironic elitism of the nineteenth-century artist and bring to attention the antithesis between their own exclusive aesthetic doctrines and those of writers such as William Morris and Tolstoy. Morris, it will be recalled, pleaded for the democracy of art, for its popularization through the resurrection of the applied arts. It would be a shame, he warned in "The Lesser

Audience

Arts," for the artist, or for a privileged few, to horde and enjoy art for themselves (1948: 514). Yet this is what aesthete, symbolist, and decadent artists took delight in doing. As far as they were concerned the hoi polloi could occupy themselves with moral questions, but they had to keep away from poetry. There was no room for democracy at the altar rail of poetry.

DISMISSAL OF THE AUDIENCE

In Cavafy the rejection of the addressee serves as the theme of many poems. The audience is prohibited from entering the "exalted World of Poetry," and hence its function in the production, transmission, and appreciation of art is ignored. This is a position held by various artists and poets residing in Cavafy's aesthetic sanctuary, such as the artisan in "For the Shop." This poem presents an explicit and uncompromising repudiation of the notion of aesthetic reception:

> He wrapped them up carefully, neatly,
> in expensive green silk.
> Roses of rubies, lilies of pearl,
> violets of amethysts: according to his taste, his will,
> his vision of their beauty—not as he saw them in nature
> or studied them. He'll leave them in the safe,
> examples of his bold, his skillful work.
> Whenever a customer comes into the shop,
> he brings out other things to sell—first class ornaments
> bracelets, chains, necklaces, rings.

The artist of this poem, in taking an eccentric attitude toward his finished products, represents perhaps the most extreme case in Cavafy of aesthetic isolationism. He fashions two types of products: art and trinkets; the first, created according to his own notion of beauty, he keeps hidden in a safe, while the second, made perhaps on the basis of popular mimetic norms, he sells to his customers. By withdrawing from public view the most cherished examples of "his bold, his skillful work," and allowing only secondary articles to be sold, he demonstrates his contempt for the market as far as art is concerned. He offers the audience what it wants, as the ironical "first class ornaments" suggest, but he does not introduce his "real" work into the cultural distribution system. Art clearly has

Audience

no place there, nor does it require the audience's recognition for its existence. It is art insofar as it has been created by the artist. To him art is a private, self-sufficient, and self-consuming activity; it derives its value from itself and not from a wider system of norms and conventions, which would be implied by the acknowledgment of the audience.

In like manner, the poet of "Temethos, Antiochian, A.D. 400" regards the act of writing poetry as a self-justifying task, although this poem does intimate an audience—a select and limited number of initiates blessed with poetic knowledge. (See Chapter 1, "The Poet and Society," for the text.) The poetic field is expanded to include a few disciples who understand the "real" theme of Temethos's recently completed poem, the fact that though it deals ostensibly with Emonidis, an imaginary character, the real subject is Temethos's actual lover. These few initiates hold the key to the poem's "correct" interpretation. The "unsuspecting" Antiochians, the broader reading public, fail to grasp the poem's essential meaning, believing in their ignorance that Emonidis is its subject. They misinterpret the poem because they are excluded from the practices of literary discourse. As the poem's concluding verses indicate, the Antiochians are not qualified to read poetry since such knowledge belongs exclusively to the poet and his acolytes: "We the initiated / know about whom those lines were written. / The unsuspecting Antiochians read simply 'Emonidis.' " Temethos and his friends, like the artist of "For the Shop," strive for the same end, to prevent the work of art from being read and appreciated, and from being subjected to public interpretation. Because they are certain that the masses corrupt art, they endeavor to save it from misreadings and eventual ruin. The poet belongs to an aristocratic class that sees the composition of poetry as an elitist activity. This is exactly what Theocritos in Cavafy's "The First Step" reminds the novice Evmenis, namely, the aesthetic experience is superior to all others; to climb the "ladder of Poetry," Theocritus contends, is a privilege bestowed only on a few worthy individuals:

> To stand on this step
> you must be in your own right
> a member of the city of ideas.

Audience

> And it's a hard, unusual thing
> to be enrolled as a citizen of that city.

There is perhaps no more appropriate way of expressing poetry's exclusiveness than by comparing it to a republic of ideas, citizenship in which is conferred only on those who can meet its stringent requirements. Access to literature and its interpretation is denied the public at large. Art remains the sole property of the poet and his initiates; it belongs to the sensitive and perfumed youths of "Young Men of Sidon (A.D. 400)," to Cavafy and his chosen devotees, to Gautier's Petit Cénacle, to Mallarmé's Tuesday evening gatherings, and to Stefan George's literary circle.

CAN THE AUDIENCE BE DISMISSED?

Despite all the rhetoric concerning the necessity of aesthetic isolation, ultimately the arguments were not convincing; since the poet did not succeed in banishing his readers from his republic, they continued to infiltrate it. In poems where the poet professed to have gained independence from all nonaesthetic elements, the audience was present even in a negative manner, as an object of contempt and derision. For instance, the existence of the "unsuspecting Antiochians" serves as a repeated reminder to the poet Temethos of factors that function beyond his own direct sphere of influence. In the same way, the hostile public of "Theater of Sidon (A.D. 400)" compels the poet to take precautionary measures in the circulation of his poems in order to circumvent the censorship of the church and the state. But here again the poet is obliged to recognize the role of the audience, albeit as an inimical force. From these poems there emerges a different attitude regarding the audience, which becomes more apparent in a prose passage titled "Independence" (1907). In this text Cavafy explores the implications that success and public recognition have for the poet. The audience here becomes an object of inquiry even though, as in the examples above, it is treated as a violator of the poet's independence. The lack of general success, Cavafy argues, is really a blessing in disguise; it guarantees the poet's freedom of expression by relieving him of the necessity of taking public taste into account

Audience

when he is composing verses. He can remain faithful to his own personal ideals and not be swayed by the standards and demands of the audience:

> An author who is very certain that he will sell each edition of his work and later perhaps more editions, such an author is sometimes influenced by this future success. No matter how sincere he is and that he has convictions, moments will come—without wanting and perhaps without realizing it—when recognizing how the public thinks, what it likes, and what it buys, he will make some minor sacrifices—he will express one passage differently, and he will omit another. And there is nothing more disastrous for Art (I shudder even at the thought) than to express this passage differently and to omit another. (Cavafy 1963b: 192)

The poet regards the reader as a potential threat, which may interfere with the process of versification by causing unjustified compromises. This tendency toward self-imposed segregation from the audience constitutes, as illustrated in the previous chapter, one of the central characteristics of the Cavafian conception of the poet. Indeed, the arguments proposed in this essay could have been uttered by any of Cavafy's poets, not least the artist of "For the Shop," who could employ them as a rationalization for his eccentric habit of withholding his most valued creations while selling trinkets to the public. In both examples the audience intrudes as a foreign agent upon the poem's autonomous space, and the poet strives to expel it in order to preserve his work's pure essence. In a way, the absence of an audience guarantees the full presence of art. It is for this reason that the poet alleges not to interest himself in publication, and circulation, or the wider issue of public taste.

Although in "Independence" the audience's existence is implicitly acknowledged, it is still mistrusted. There exist instances, however, in which the poet seems to dispense with this apparently uncompromising attitude. He emerges from his sanctuary to enter the *agora*, having accepted both the reality and morality of the marketplace. In this context of exchange, the conception of the artwork undergoes a transformation; in other words, it is seen not as an essence of pure form to be protected from the corruption of the

Audience

buyer, but as a commodity. The "Sculptor of Tyana" (1911) exemplifies this different awareness of both art and the audience, for unlike the previous artists, who were essentially engaged in an interior monologue, he admits spectators into his workshop and openly addresses them in order to convince them of his accomplishments and reputation:

> As you'll have heard, I'm no beginner.
> I've handled a lot of stone in my time,
> and in my own country, Tyana, I'm really quite famous.
> Actually, a number of senators here
> have also commissioned works of mine.
> Let me show you a few of them.

The sculptor has not only permitted the nonartist into his studio, but hopes to interest him in his products. However, the admission of the audience into the once segregated domain necessarily terminates what the artist considered an autonomous existence as it implicitly compels him—in direct antithesis to the arguments of "Independence"—to take the audience's aesthetic preferences into account.

Similarly, the isolationist view of poetry is undermined by the way the poet of "That's the Man" (1909) approaches his craft. In his view the composition of poetry is not solely justified by the activity itself, but is derived as well from such nonaesthetic sources as the fame that a poet may acquire. This foreign poet in Antioch has become exhausted after the completion of his eighty-third hymn, yet unlike the poet of "Pictured" (1915), who seeks relief from the fatigue of writing in art itself—"And it is in art that I recover from the effort of creating it"—he is rescued from his depression by the thought that one day he will be known, and that people will point at him admiringly with the phrase "that's the man":

> But a thought suddenly brings him out of his dejection:
> the sublime "that's the man"
> which Lucian once heard in his sleep.

The mention of Lucian refers to that sophist's dream in which a personification of Education appeared to him, promising that one

Audience

day he would become so famous that everyone would be able to identify him immediately. Likewise, it is the hope of such future prominence and renown that induces the anonymous poet to return to his hymns despite his fatigue. Recompense for his effort does not entirely come from the pleasure of composition, since it also depends on the wider public recognition of his art. For this poet, poetry ceases to be solely an esoteric experience. Both he and the sculptor acknowledge the function of the audience in the public reception of their work.

In "The Retinue of Dionysos" (1909) the presence of the audience is foregrounded, and its legitimate role as interpreter is emphasized. Damon, the poem's principal figure, is introduced as the most gifted and able sculptor in the Peloponnese, a craftsman enthusiastically devoted to his art. Yet, however much he strives to execute realistically the frieze of Dionysos's procession, his mind is not satisfied with aesthetic perfection, but wanders off to contemplate the wealth he will accrue and, not least, the honor he will acquire in his city:

> Damon carves all these. And as he works
> his thought runs now and then
> to the fee he's going to receive
> from the king of Syracuse:
> three talents, a large sum.
> Adding this to what he has already,
> he'll live grandly, like a rich man,
> he'll even be able to enter politics
> —what a marvelous thought:
> he too in the Senate, he too in the Agora.

Damon neither fears nor avoids his patrons; on the contrary, he actively seeks to sell them his sculptures and to please their aesthetic tastes. His understanding of art seems to contradict the credo of the artist as expressed in "Independence," namely, that the artist should eschew consideration of such extra-aesthetic elements as publication, circulation of texts, fees, and public recognition, since they would compromise poetry's purity. Damon, for his part, dismisses these arguments, as well as the aesthetic assumptions held by the artist of "For the Shop" and "Pictured." He

Audience

becomes a public figure in the world of art. Having deserted the holy sanctuary of autonomous and autotelic art, he enters the marketplace to partake of its operation of exchange. In contrast to those other artists, his work will be circulated, consumed; in other words, it will be bought, sold, displayed, analyzed, criticized, taught, and interpreted. It will enter fully the cultural distribution system and the public discourse on art. This fact, of course, affects the way the work is conceived, that is to say, the work's meaning will not depend solely on its point of origin, the artist, but will be produced in its transmission through the economy of art. The poem acknowledges the crucial role of the audience in this economy.

THE AUDIENCE AS RECEIVER AND INTERPRETER OF TEXTS

The poems "The Sculptor of Tyana," "That's the Man," and "The Retinue of Dionysos," demonstrate that another conception of art exists in Cavafy, one that incorporates the function of the addressee in the reception, evaluation, and canonization of an artistic artifact. It follows that a work assumes its status as art not at its inception, but in its public dissemination. The idea of the public reception and interpretation of a text is introduced by the poem "Very Seldom" (1913). Such a reading of this particular poem is suggested by Cavafy himself in a note on this text found in *Self Comments*: "The title constitutes a commentary on the poem. The time span during which a work of art inspires one generation after another is not a sign of accidental but of exceptionally good art, a case which appears 'very seldom' " (Lehonitis 1942: 28). According to Cavafy, the poem has as one of its themes the effect a work of art may generate in its readers. Again the emphasis falls on the addressee. This means that artwork is not conceived solely with respect to its creator, but to the audience as well, which it "moves" or influences. Essentially the passage raises the issue of a work's fate, but sets this in the context of the receiver. While in previous poems an artwork was thought to survive because of qualities endowed by the artist, aesthetic continuance is seen here as depending more on the audience that receives the work and incorporates it within the discourse on poetry. The audience confers upon it a

Audience

meaning it would not have were it to remain unpublished in the poet's dossier. A work of art cannot be beautiful or have aesthetic worth in itself, nor exist for the artist alone, since in order to survive it must be canonized and culturally reproduced, be pleasing or valuable to a wider audience, which, having been "moved" by the work, endorses it and passes it on to the next generation. Such is the import of the poem.

In the first stanza of "Very Seldom" the subject is an old poet who is said to be "wasted by the years" and who is unable to contribute anything new or substantial to art. Although he is about to die, he will not be forgotten, since his poetry has been accepted by a new generation of young men:

> His verse is now quoted by young men.
> His visions come before their lively eyes.
> Their healthy sensual minds,
> their shapely taut bodies
> stir to his perception of the beautiful.

What is presented in this second stanza is an instance of aesthetic reception, the circulation of a text in the public domain and its transmission to a new generation of readers. These not strictly aesthetic factors largely govern the survival of the poet's work inasmuch as his readers quote his verses, are moved by his vision, and thereby enable the poem to be categorized as an aesthetic artifact and to circulate as art. Whereas the poet eventually dies, his work outlives him, for having been designated as an object in the discourse on poetry, it is read, studied, and criticized by subsequent generations, and thus reproduced. The prominence of the receiver in the transmission and hence the survival of poetry is foregrounded to a greater extent in this poem than in "The Sculptor of Tyana," "That's the Man," and "The Retinue of Dionysos." Yet, he is characterized as a passive consumer of the author's finished products and serves primarily in the role of carrier of his poems. Furthermore, the audience is still limited to a group of sensual young men. Two posthumous texts of Cavafy's, however, the poem "The Enemies" (1900) and the corresponding essay "The Reflections of an Old Artist" (c. 1894–1900), depict the audience in a different light, portraying it less as a servile receiver of com-

Audience

pleted works and more as an active participant in the production of literary meaning.²

The main figure in the essay, as in "Very Seldom," is a renowned but very old poet who in his declining years begins to witness public dissatisfaction with his once universally acclaimed poetry. He observes the gradual waning of his dominance over his readership and forebodes the inevitable loss of his authority over it. He discerns the emergence of new schools of poetry that are capturing attention and favor. "He observes that beneath the formal admiration of the many there exists a slight coldness of the few. His works are not so much admired by the young. His school is not their school, and his style is not their style" (Cavafy 1971: 101).³ The new school poses a threat to the poet's own in the sense that by striving to appropriate the audience's aesthetic tastes to its own advantage, it may eventually replace its rival's privileged position in literary discourse. The poets of these schools do not concern themselves solely with the creation of pure form, but also take into consideration the reading public, whose recognition they endeavor to win. This struggle over the audience is, of course, an implicit acknowledgment of the public rather than private nature of literature. That is, literature comes into existence not solely through the wishes of the author, but is a public activity involving extra-aesthetic elements. It is the outcome not of personal decisions, but of social agreement.

The poet proposes such a notion of literature (and art) when he admits that "art is a vain thing with its fashions [*sirmus*] that change often." The noun *sirmus*, with its connotations of habits, customs, and fashions, foregrounds art's social nature and suggests that art is an institution; that is, art is not viewed as a timeless form, but as a human construct situated in its own finitude and thus always subject to constant modification. This historical aspect of art receives further emphasis in another passage of Cavafy's written as a commentary to a text of Ruskin's: "But Beauty is

---

² I return to both texts in Chapter 5. For an examination of these and other texts from the perspective of poetic politics, see "Cavafy and the Politics of Poetry" (Jusdanis 1985).
³ The translations of "The Reflections of an Old Artist" and "The Enemies" are mine.

Audience

sometimes contradictory (truth they want positive and affirmative) and is often the result of opinions and habits" (Tsirkas 1971: 241). Cavafy's priorities shift here from idealized and immutable aesthetics to a historical awareness of the nature of beauty. He regards beauty as a relative concept, a product of customs, habits, and tastes of a particular community, and not as a metaphysical quality that preexists and survives this community. It follows, then, that art in general is also viewed as the subject of social debate, as a category emerging from the current aesthetic, the network of rules and standards according to which a work is judged to be artistic or not. This aesthetic system cannot be controlled or validated by one member, such as the artist, but depends on the negotiation between interested participants of society (including the artist), such as students, teachers, readers, critics, publishers, and distributors. The changes that the old artist observes are the result of their struggles as some fight to preserve the status quo while others attempt to call attention to their own seemingly eccentric and radical positions.

The artist constitutes one member of this debate who, like the other participants, acts in order to redirect public taste to his own advantage as much as possible and to guarantee his work's survival. His aim is to write in a "different manner," to gain access for his work to the distribution network, to introduce new modes and standards, and have them recognized and legitimized by the wider community. As Howard Becker points out in his *Art Worlds*, only those changes survive that succeed either in capturing existing cooperative networks or in developing new patterns of common work. It is these innovations that win organizational victories, that convince sufficient numbers of people to believe in it and to maintain it by accepting these new assumptions as a basis for a new activity (1982: 301–310). The point of the struggle, the old poet of the essay asserts, is the competition for space in the public economy of art, the appropriation of the audience's taste, and the consolidation of new criteria for the judgment of art: "He was one of some fifty young men who created a new school, wrote in a new style, and changed the mind of those millions who respected a few predecessors and a few old artists" (Cavafy 1971: 102). The poet is concerned less with inspiring his audience, as was the case in

Audience

"Very Seldom," than with influencing its aesthetic preferences. He and his associates established new schools of poetry; they introduced a novel style of writing with the intention of so altering the taste of the reading public as to dislodge the established poets. By working to transform the overall context from which all works take their meaning, they could bring to the fore their own marginalized works and highlight the conservative and hackneyed texts of their rivals. The task facing each successive generation is the successful appropriation of the evaluational criteria shared by the community of readers on which the fate of the work depends. It is over these standards that the struggles between the old established and recently developed literary schools are waged. The old poet sees the relationship between successor and precursor as a conflict in which one triumphs over the other. In this regard, directly after the passage cited above (1971: 102), the poet adds that his objective was the "victory" over public opinion, facilitated by the death of his forerunners, when for a period of time he could consolidate unchallenged his newly won position and succeed in identifying his work with that of the public category of "art."

This category and the cultural norms and values on which it is based are not stable, but are always subject to change. For this reason the old poet resignedly admits that the work of art is "temporary," and that "art with its fashions . . . change often," and that "the Enthusiasm and Poeticity of each author begin to appear strange or ridiculous as soon as they become 40 or 50 years old" (Cafavy 1971: 102). The quality of "poeticity" or literariness is a historical concept, that is, literature does not exist as a predetermined, eternally valid *Ding an sich*, but as a notion that emerges under specific applications of aesthetic codes. The old poet understands art as a social event, one that is based on conventions and dependent on public interest, norms of taste, and rules of interpretation. An artist who holds such a view does not hide his work from public examination, as the artist in "For the Shop," since this act could rob his creations of any aesthetic meaning; they would remain empty texts and not be understood as art. On the contrary, the poet of the essay advocates through his own practice that the artist openly display his products in his shop window and promote them actively in the agora. Such was the strategy of the poet and

Audience

his associates when they founded a new school of poetry and introduced reading practices antithetical to those in the past; their purpose was to redirect the taste of the audience. Instead of retiring peacefully to the library to contemplate pure form, these poets fought over public opinion, having recognized that the community as a whole and not the artist alone determines the current definition of art. It is in the context of the community that the poems will be either enjoyed by the millions or mocked as "strange" or "ridiculous," "démodés" or "ancient."

Herein lies the difference between the two positions as represented by the hermeticism of "For the Shop," "Pictured," and "Independence" and the active engagement of "The Reflections of an Old Artist" and "The Enemies." On the one hand, art is conceived as the private expression of the artist, who exclusively confers upon the object he creates the status of the artistic; on the other, it is understood as a matter of social negotiation dependent on certain cultural conventions that emerge under specific historical conditions. The first emphasizes isolation and distance from the outside world, while the second is characterized by conflict and the artist's involvement.

The notion of the power struggle between successive generations of poets introduced in the essay becomes a central theme in "The Enemies." This poem, as George Savidis has noted (in Cavafy 1971: 104), closely resembles the essay in content and may be considered a subsequent versification of the essay's main arguments:

>   Three sophists came to greet the Consul.
>   The Consul had them sit close to him.
>   He spoke to them politely. And then jokingly
>   he told them to take heed. "Fame
>   provokes malice. Your rivals keep on
>   writing. You have enemies."
>   One of the three answered with solemn words.
>
>   "Our present day enemies will never do us any harm.
>   Later will our enemies the new sophists come.
>   When we in our old age will lie wretchedly
>   and some of us will have gone to Hades. Our present

Audience

> words and works will appear strange (and
> ridiculous perhaps) since the enemies will change
> sophistics, style, and tendencies. Like me and them
> who so much transformed the past things.
> What we portrayed as beautiful and proper
> the enemies will reveal to be foolish and useless,
> repeating the same things differently (without much effort).
> Just as we spoke the old words in another manner."

The main figure of the poem is a sophist who is acutely aware of his fate as author, as well as that of his work in the discourses of the future. He predicts that his texts and those of his colleagues will appear "strange" and "ridiculous" once they themselves die. Succeeding generations will invert the literary conventions to such a radical extent that what contemporary sophists regard as beautiful and proper will be revealed by the younger ones to be foolish and useless. The deconstructive sophists of the future are regarded as real enemies, since they subject the inherited texts to violence by disregarding their "original" meaning. Furthermore, they fundamentally alter the evaluational standards for the analysis of texts so as to affect the destiny of their precursors' work negatively and to influence the reception of their own positively. In the end, the enemies gain dominance over their predecessors, but only till new enemies appear and repeat the same violation upon the texts of their forerunners.

This is the model of literary change that is also formulated in "The Reflections of an Old Artist." The poet achieved his "victory" over his precursors by modifying the context in which texts are read. By introducing a novel form of poetry, his school (and presumably other literary groups sharing his objective) instigated a change in public taste and a revision of the rules in the evaluation, appreciation, and interpretation of poetry. As a result, where formerly the texts of the established poets were admired as masterpieces, under the new conditions these same works are ridiculed for their conservative and "démodés" tendencies, and contrarily, while the poems of the once radical authors were misunderstood or dismissed as nonpoetic, they are now held to be exemplary works of art. This historical pattern of events is dram-

Audience

atized in the poem "A Byzantine Nobleman in Exile Composing Verses" (1921):

> The frivolous can call me frivolous.
> I've always taken important things
> extremely seriously. And I insist that no one knows
> the Holy Fathers, or the Scriptures, or the Canons of the
>   Councils
> better than I do.
> Whenever he was in doubt,
> whenever he had any ecclesiastical problem,
> Botaniatis consulted me, me first of all.
> But exiled here (may she be cursed, that viper
> Irini Doukaina), and incredibly bored,
> it's not altogether unfitting to amuse myself
> writing six- and eight-line verses,
> to amuse myself poeticizing myths
> of Hermes and Apollo and Dionysos,
> or the heroes of Thessaly and the Peloponnese;
> and to compose the most strict iambic,
> such as—if you'll allow me to say so—
> the scholars of Constantinople don't know how to compose.
> It may be just this strictness that provokes their disapproval.

Although now in exile, under the rule of Botaniatis, the noble was employed as adviser to the emperor in matters of the Scriptures and canons. He was delegated the responsibility of interpreting texts of fundamental importance to the administration of the state. The noble and the other scholars possessed the right to study texts, establish their meaning, and deliver it to those in power. Presumably, as one would surmise from the first and last lines, he also engaged in the composition of poetry. When the noble enjoyed the support of the emperor, both his interpretation of texts and his conception of a good poem constituted the accepted standard and the authoritative view.

However, with the overthrow of Botaniatis by his rival, Alexios Komnenos, not only the power of the emperor, but also the entire substructure of his rule were usurped, with the result that the noble forfeited his authority as adviser and was replaced by

Audience

others who had been until now prohibited from participating in the dominant interpretive and literary discourse. These scholars introduced their own standards and rules for reading and writing texts that are imcompatible with those of the noble. As in the essay and in "The Enemies," the criteria by which a text or an interpretation of it was judged to be either "good" or "bad" had been appropriated by others.[4] The poetry of the noble (and his analyses of religious documents) is no longer held to be acceptable and does not receive the same circulation and exposure; quite simply, it has fallen out of fashion and is dismissed, like the old poet's work, for being "strange, ridiculous, and démodé." Indeed, the noble reacts to this change in a similar though less conscious manner to that of the old poet of the essay, by accusing the other scholars of being unable to compose verses of such high quality:

> and to compose the most strict iambics,
> such as—if you'll allow me to say so—
> the scholars of Constantinople don't know how to compose.
> It may be just this strictness that provokes their disapproval.

The old poet of "The Reflections of an Old Artist" likewise believes that his poetry is better than that written by the younger generation: "The old artist reads and studies their words conscientiously and he finds them inferior, or at least not better than his own" (Cafavy 1971: 102).

Yet, although both the noble and the poet insist on their poetry's inherent value, what is at issue here—as the old poet implies

---

[4] Michel Foucault, in his essay "Nietzsche, Genealogy and History," records the following appropriate observation on the power struggle, implicit in this poem—but more obvious in "The Enemies" and "The Reflections of an Old Artist"—over the appropriation of the rules of discourse: "The successes of history belong to those who are capable of seizing these rules, to replace those who had used them, invert their meaning and redirect them against those who initially imposed them; controlling this complex mechanism, they will overcome the rulers through their own rules" (1977: 151). This passage, which reads as if it were a paraphrase of "The Enemies," is relevant to the three texts under discussion in that it contextualizes the power struggle that serves as a subject in each one. The aim of the poets, sophists, and scholars was to alter irreversibly the literary criteria and codes in their favor so as to establish themselves in the dominant position of the literary community. Success represented consolidation of this position and the identification of their local view of literary value with the global concept of literature.

Audience

and the sophist insists—is not simply quality, but the public standards by which poetry is judged to be good or bad. Herein lies the difference of the sophist's position, for unlike the noble, he does not conceive of literature as an immutable and autotelic object endowed with universal and global qualities. Rather than concerning himself with the notion of good poetry, the sophist emphasizes the cultural conventions on the basis of which a text is thought to possess attributes of "impeccable iambics." These standards are subject to change and so are the interpretations of the poem. Thus the characteristics of a good poem that held true in the noble's literary discourse are not necessarily the same as those operating in the discourse of his rivals; what was portrayed as "beautiful" and "proper" is shown to be "foolish" and "useless." We return once more to the old poet's dictum, namely, that "art is a vain thing with its fashions which change often." Seen from this perspective, the reason behind the scholars' censure of the noble's poems is not necessarily the metrical "strictness," but the failure of the noble's theories to correspond appropriately to the latest notion of good poetry, as practiced by those currently in authority.

The position of the noble in this poem bears some similarities to that of the poet Phernazis in "Dareios," whose main concern is the completion of his epic poem. He strains to imagine how King Dareios reacted when he seized the Persian throne—was he overwhelmed by feelings of arrogance and intoxication, or did he have an understanding of the vanity of greatness? These are the questions preoccupying Phernazis. As soon as he learns of the imminent Roman invasion, he turns his attention away from the poem's aesthetic qualities to its future reception. For as Phernazis realizes, the present King Mithridatis will not have time for poetry in the midst of a war, and what is worse, the Romans will probably be victorious and overthrow the king, leaving Phernazis in the same predicament as that of the noble in the previous poem. The Romans will introduce a foreign state apparatus as well as a new order with regard to the composition, distribution, and consumption of literature. For example, not only will the king—for whom the epic was probably intended—no longer be in authority, but the other scholars and Phernazis's critics, whom he hoped to silence and above all impress, will also have forfeited their positions in the new

Audience

literary discourse. In short, Phernazis fears that he will not win the fame he desires by composing a celebrated epic:

> Phernazis gets all worked up. What a bad break!
> Just when he was sure to distinguish himself
> with his *Dareios*, sure to make
> his envious critics shut up once and for all.
> What a setback, terrible setback to his plans.

Phernazis will never succeed, since his plans depend on a particular context for their realization. But this context will change in the future under the invaders, and the poetic conventions according to which his poem was written will no longer be considered valid. The new critics, patrons, and readers will examine his epic in a completely different light; perhaps they might not show any interest in an epic dealing with King Dareios, an ancestor of the vanquished king. Phernazis is left speechless by the sudden turn of his fortune; he frets over the probable destiny of his work, which will remain a text without an audience. It will not enter the public discourse on poetry as a work of art to be consumed, circulated, stored in libraries, sold, taught in schools, and criticized. It will likely be retained as a private possession of Phernazis, much like the work kept by the artist of "For the Shop," but it will be aesthetically meaningless.

CAVAFY'S METHOD OF DISTRIBUTING HIS POETRY

Up to this point I have drawn attention to those texts in Cavafy that contradict the isolationist and hermeticist view of art. There remains, however, an example of another order that lends support to this position and foregounds the audience's role in the emergence of the current aesthetic, namely, Cavafy's own method of "unpublishing" or circulating his poetry. First I must emphasize that in discussing Cavafy's methods of circulating his poems I am not entering on a biographical study; I am not interested in exploring his life, personal wishes, plans, and dreams, nor am I lending support to the view of authorial omnipotence and omniscience, that the author possesses ultimate authority and control over the fate of his work. Rather, the examination of this strictly nontextual

Audience

data further confirms the position outlined so far, that the poet represents one member, albeit a very powerful and interested one, in the public struggle for the definition of the aesthetic category. Cavafy's peculiar method of releasing his poems into the public domain, and his unwillingness to publish them in a definitive edition, provides an example of an author's energetic involvement in this debate. It should be seen as evidence of Cavafy's recognition of the audience's function as receiver and interpreter of a text, and also of the poet's attempt (much like the poet in the essay) to influence the audience's reception of his work and thereby enhance the chances for its survival.

Cavafy resisted the publication of his work in a complete volume. The first such text appeared two years after his death, under the supervision of his heir, Alexander Singopoulos. During his own lifetime, Cavafy pursued a unique, if not eccentric, procedure of introducing his poems into the public sphere, which can be characterized less as publication than as strategic distribution. George Savidis, in his *Cavafy's Editions*, has mapped out three distinct modes of distribution employed by Cavafy; subsequently, in collaboration with Edmund Keeley, he returned to this topic in the introduction to *Passions and Ancient Days*.[5] Between around 1891 and 1904, the poems were printed individually on broadsheets and distributed to close friends and associates, much in the manner of the poet in "Theater of Sidon (A.D. 400)." During this early phase Cavafy also published thirty-nine poems in various journals in Egypt and abroad, though he later rejected much of this material.[6]

Between 1904 and 1910 two pamphlets, both privately distributed, appeared. The first (1904) contained fourteen poems and was issued in one hundred copies; the second, which represents an enlarged version of the first, included twenty poems. These two pamphlets, as Peridis points out, constitute the only "books" that

---

[5] My own analysis of this subject is based on the information found in these two sources.
[6] These poems were published collectively in the journal *Ta Nea Grammata*, no. 1 (Jan. 1936). In 1983 all were reissued as a book by Savidis. For a translation of these "rejected" poems see Dalven 1976.

Audience

Cavafy ever published (Peridis 1948: 130, cited by Savidis 1966: 35).

Then, between 1911 and 1932, Cavafy circulated his poems in folders, which by 1933, the year of his death, totaled ten. He arranged the poems in each collection either thematically or chronologically. When a new poem was printed on a broadsheet, Cavafy distributed copies of it individually, or more often, he inserted them in folders.[7] Each new sheet was added to the last page of the folder and the new title was written by hand in the table of contents. By this method, as Keeley and Savidis point out (1971: X), the folders could not be transfixed as a "definitive edition" or a permanent collection; they could be expanded, altered, and revised constantly. In 1917, when one folder could no longer accommodate any further sheets, some of the earlier poems were withdrawn and sewn into booklets, a process Cavafy repeated several times. Thus by 1933 Cavafy's work consisted of two sewn booklets of sixty-eight poems organized in chronological order.

These then, according to Savidis, were the three methods Cavafy employed for the distribution of his poems. He used the folders for the longest period (nearly twenty years) probably because they afforded him the most freedom to manipulate the circulation of his poems. Indeed, in the light of these strategies, it is not possible to speak—during Cavafy's lifetime at least—of a fixed oeuvre, a formation that was established much later by mechanisms beyond the poet's control:[8] for instance, through the publi-

---

[7] Before inserting them in a folder Cavafy distributed off-prints of poems to friends after, or sometimes prior to, publication.

[8] Here indeed, according to Foucault, lies the impracticability of the notion of the oeuvre, which he sees as a unity imposed on a series of discontinuous and heterogeneous elements. An oeuvre is normally recognized as a collection of texts belonging to one author, but this designation, Foucault says, cannot be considered a simple exercise. For, he asks, what should be included within this category: the texts published by the author under his name, or under a pseudonym; unfinished texts; collections of jotting, sketches, corrections, notebooks, letters, rejected versions, abandoned drafts? (1972: 23-24). This problem becomes very apparent in Cavafy, who himself resisted the totalization of his texts into a singular mode of existence with a beginning and an end. Under the name "Cavafy" one now understands a continuity embracing the poems of the 1963 definitive edition, the prose pieces issued by Papoutsakis (1963), the posthumous poems (1968), unfinished drafts, personal notes, and letters. This oeuvre did not emerge from the poet's mind, but is, as Foucault points out, the result of an operation that is necessarily interpretive. It

Audience

cation in 1935 of the collected poems by his heir, Singopoulos; the collective reissue of the rejected poems in *Ta Nea Grammata* (1936); the appearance in 1963 of the definitive edition of his poetry, and the publication during that year of his prose work in a single volume, and of his previously unpublished prose texts; the issue in 1968 of the posthumous poems; the subsequent release from Cavafy's archive of unpublished poems, essays, articles, notes, and letters; and the publication of new editions of the works cited above.

Prior to his death in 1933, before the critical and philological techniques began to form and canonize his work, Cavafy's "collection" of poetry existed to a certain extent in an open form, under constant revision and in a state of flux, or "in progress," as Seferis characterized it (Seferis 1974: 238). The term "in progress" may be misleading, however, since it suggests a teleological development. What takes place here, however, is not a progression toward a final goal, such as Keeley's metaphorical city,[9] but the opposite, the refusal of unity, the frustration of homogeneity, and the delay of permanence. Publication of a fixed and definitive edition was eschewed in order to avoid the resulting constancy and inflexibility. For Cavafy publication of such a collection would have entailed the imposition upon the poems of a stable order, which would have led to their irrecoverable surrender to the audience, and the cession of his control over them to history. It would seem that Cavafy was unwilling to submit his poetry to the hazards of public interpretation without his prior intervention.

---

is a unity imposed on the texts—this study not excepted—to organize them into a coherent order, an act that, ironically, goes against the "intentions" of the poet as exemplified in his practice.

[9] Keeley's enterprise, as mentioned in my preface, is based on the alleged principle of unity that informs Cavafy's work: "The reader of his work benefits by discerning and accommodating the unifying element, the unifying mythology, that relates one poem to another" (1976: 186). Keeley's goal is to trace "the poet's aesthetic development, as he perfected his mature voice, and to delineate the expanding contours of his central myth" (p. 12). Yet, in the light of the present discussion of Cavafy's attempts to "unoeuvre" his work, the following question arises: is Keeley's concept of a "central mythic structure" a conscious product of Cavafy's "aesthetic perfectionism and critical intelligence" (p. 186)—at a time when the work was in no way uniformly structured—or is it a result of the reader's unity-imposing strategies, as Keeley himself suggests in the quotation above?

Audience

This peculiar practice suggests Cavafy realized that there exist factors outside of the text that influence the fate of the work and that its aesthetic features do not alone guarantee its survival and its possible entry into the canon. This position bears some similarities to that held both by the poet in "The Reflections of an Old Artist" and by the sophist in "The Enemies," and it implies political overtones. In all three cases the author sees himself as pinned in a battle of negotiation with other writers and readers over control of his texts. By forbidding a permanent publication of his poetry and the emergence of a fixed oeuvre, it could be argued that Cavafy tried to guarantee, at least during his own lifetime, his effective intervention in his work's progress, and thus exercise his authority over its meaning. The open state of his poetry's arrangement enabled him to exert his will over his work's fate even though it was circulating within the public sphere. In Cavafy's case, the "enemies" were the critics and readers (and no doubt other poets) who did not have at their disposal a single collection containing all of his poems on which they could comment.[10] Cavafy made every possible attempt to prevent the reader from achieving closure and to preempt his final and ultimate interpretation. Indeed, some individual pamphlets and folders contained poems absent from the others, or arranged in a different sequence. Furthermore, the addition of each new poem to the pamphlet prompted the structural and thematic reappraisal of the whole set, inasmuch as it modified the relationships of the poems within each group. It would seem that through these various tactical moves Cavafy strove to manipulate some of the mechanisms operating in the public consumption of art.[11] Seen from this perspective, such a practice does not repre-

[10] Critics and readers could have, of course, interpreted or criticized individual or groups of poems, but they did not have the benefit of an up-to-date collection of all the then published poems, such as one usually finds with the work of other poets, and of Cavafy after his death.

[11] The degree to which this stragegy was successful is at present impossible to determine, since it requires research into the reception of Cavafy's work by his contemporaries. The following relevant questions may be posed, however: to what extent did Cavafy's method of distributing his poems influence the reception and understanding of his work during his lifetime, and to what extent did this initial interpretation affect future readings of his work, including our own? Even if such a strategy is not capable of achieving the intended results, it highlights Cavafy's

Audience

sent Cavafy's "aesthetic asceticism," as Keeley and Savidis propose (1971: XI),[12] but the opposite, namely, his recognition of poetry's public nature, and of its exchange in the economy of art.

This view of art and the audience differs substantially from that characterized as aesthetic isolationism and analyzed in the first half of this chapter. In Cavafy there exist two conceptions of art and of the audience. The first and most dominant view stresses the independence of art from its social milieu; the second foregrounds the public and relative nature of the aesthetic category. The former arises from the formalist preoccupations of the last two centuries; the latter, by drawing attention to the institutionality of art, shatters the notion of self-reflexivity and self-sufficiency—two of the hallmarks of modernism—and begins to point to postmodernism's involvement with the modes and conditions of the production of art.

---

astuteness to intervene as much as possible in the circulation of his work. This position could hardly be characterized as isolationist or aestheticist.

[12] The initial stage, characterized by the distribution of poems to friends, relatives, and associates, does suggest an element of asceticism and romantic perfectionism, but it should be noted that Cavafy was simultaneously publishing poems in journals and magazines.

3. POETRY

I argued in the last chapter that the two different conceptions of the audience in Cavafy reflect two conflicting approaches to poetry or art;[1] the one draws attention to art as the private concern of the poet and his initiates, and the other stresses the position of art as a social entity in the broad context of an extra-aesthetic reality. Without limiting my analysis to the perhaps restrictive dichotomy of private and public art, I want to examine, in all its diversity, Cavafy's concept of poetry, which ranges from the conventional denotation of verse composition, to an all-embracing connotation of a life-style or *Weltanschauung*. In this broad spectrum of signification, no single meaning or function emerges as absolutely dominant, so it is not possible to draw any hard conclusions as to the primary definition of this term. There exists no ultimate meaning of "poetry" or "art" in Cavafy; what one sees is a series of unities, each representing separate concerns and sharing different relations with various literary and theoretical discourses. In analyzing the concept of poetry I hope to highlight the many dimensions of this term.

THE EARLY POEMS

Cavafy's early and rejected poems vividly emphasize the poet, rather than poetry, as an object of thematical consideration, no doubt reflecting a romantic preoccupation with the artist. As argued in Chapter 1, with the advent of romanticism, the poet was elevated to the center of critical reference, and poetic creation began to be conceived from its source—the poet. Many of these poems orient themselves toward their creator, as some of the titles indicate: for example, "The Poet and the Muse," "Singer," "The Inkwell" (as a synecdoche for the poet). In many instances the poet is portrayed as a divinely inspired man who expresses his feelings through his melodies. Indeed, he thinks of his creations as songs:

---

[1] As I pointed out in the preface, I use the terms "poetry" and "art" interchangeably, since Cavafy employs both concepts without rigorously distinguishing one from the other; often they refer to the same idea.

Poetry

> My songs are a beguiling image of the world.
> I sing of love and joy.
> > "The Poet and the Muse"

> "Friend, be quiet;
> meditate and sing. Be of good heart, mystic apostle!"
> > "Singer"

> The sea intones for us a tender song,
> a song composed by three great poets
> the sun, the air, and the sky.
> > "Voice from the Sea," 1899

The poem as song is that unconscious manifestation of the poet's inner soul. Like sweet sounds, it flows effortlessly from his lips ("The Poet and the Muse"); like ink from the inkwell, it simply issues from the poet, brought forth by forces beyond his control and requiring no work or expertise. In these texts the poem itself does not arise as a problem to the poet, that is, as an object of theoretical and imaginative concern. As the corresponding conception of language, it is transparent, accepted with blind faith and defended against any doubts or questions. When the novice of "The Poet and the Muse" voices his uncertainty about the authenticity of poetry, the muse quickly reassures the skeptic and reaffirms the ability of the harp's chords alone to perceive the truth. The poet, she adds, should not fear the darkness covering the world, since nature will compensate him with genuine and privileged knowledge:

> It is only a light mist that frightens your vision.
> Under the veil, gracious nature prepares for you
> garlands of roses and violets and noble narcissus,
> sweet-scented rewards for your songs.

The images of this stanza, as of the entire poem, depict an uncomplicated world, but more important, they embody an innocent—in comparison with that in later poems—conception of the poet and his craft. In this poem the poet's conviction of the superiority of his art remains resolute, unaffected by self-criticism.

The poet of "Singer" resorts to similarly naive and simplistic arguments (again in comparison with ideas found in subsequent texts) in refuting the critics of poetry. Those who attack poetry, the speaker insists, employ the strategies of logical thinking, which is foreign to the mystical and emotive mode of the muse. The poet's nature is divine, "for him beautiful verses are the whole world." In this sanctuary, which is fashioned for him by imagination out of "magic emeralds," the poet, crowned with garlands of roses and narcissi, listens to the whispering voices inviting him to sing. His song inspires others with its sweet melodies, but also soothes the bard himself, as demonstrated in "Good and Bad Weather" (1893):

> It does not bother me if outside
> winter spreads fog, clouds, and cold.
> Spring is within me, true joy.
> Laughter is a sun ray, all pure gold,
> there is no other garden like love,
> the warmth of song melts all the snow.

The poet remains unaffected by the wintry conditions outside, since he is warmed by his verses and invigorated by the flowers of spring, which have been presented to him by the muse.

Such, then, is the hyperbolic language and unrestrained imagery used to describe poetry and its creator in these early published poems, most of which were subsequently renounced by Cavafy. The other surviving poetic texts of this period, having been posthumously published, indicate a perceptible shift in the conception of poetry. In this regard, "Nous n'osons plus chanter les roses" (1892) occupies a prominent position insofar as it illustrates a contrasting understanding of the art of poetry, one based not on the principles of the "lyrical imagination," but on the poetics of self-conscious craftsmanship. This becomes apparent even in the title by which the poet announces that he no longer dares to sing of roses, or indeed, of narcissi, garlands, or emeralds (in contrast to "Singer" and "The Poet and the Muse"). Conspicuously absent from "Nous n'osons plus chanter les roses" is the previously dominant conception of the poem as inspired song. Here, in one of the earliest instances in Cavafy of a self-conscious poem, verse making becomes problematized. No longer taken for granted, it is themat-

Poetry

ically incorporated as one of the poem's subjects. The speaker considers a critical attitude essential in composition; poetry is not a transparent expression of his passions, but an object of his conscious concern:

> Fearing the commonplace
> I leave many words unuttered.
> Many poems are written in my
> heart; and those interred songs
> are the ones that I love.

The poet now judges critically the new poems he composes. Even though he loves those poems inscribed in his heart, he leaves them unspoken. Indeed, it is to avoid that dreaded commonplace that he decides not to sing of roses (or even to sing at all), and to withhold those countless poems that risk the accusation of being unoriginal, hackneyed, and trite.

It is perhaps in this context of self-appraisal and self-criticism that the note written by Cavafy in October 1906 is to be understood, since in retrospect it applies to the proposals set out in this poem. "By my postponing, and repostponing to publish," Cavafy states, "what a gain I have had!" He goes on to list a series of "Byzantine poems" that would disgrace him now. "And all those poems written between 19 and 22 what wret[c]hed trash" (Cavafy 1983a: 64). The "trash" probably refers to those texts that Cavafy subsequently disclaimed or destroyed. One may postulate here that he rejected them because of what he retrospectively saw as their mannerist style and the naive poetics that informed them. This may be deduced from notes and comments that Cavafy wrote on certain later poems, in which he draws attention to—in order to avoid—those stylistic and theoretical infelicities that were so emblematic of the "Byzantine poems."

One such instance occurs in the *Self-Comments*; discussing the device of "emphasis" in "Ithaka," Cavafy notes that the emphasis "did not happen accidentally or due to the influence of lyricism" (Lehonitis 1942: 26). Yet it is such abandonment to lyricism that, from Cavafy's perspective, constituted one of the main defects of the early poems and led to their rejection. By his comment on "Ithaka," Cavafy no doubt wished to show, like Poe writing on "The

Poetry

Raven," that the poem's composition did not result from inspiration, nor was the poem itself characterized by unfettered lyricism or unchecked emotion. Exaggeration of any sort in poetry is now considered a serious aesthetic failure. This attitude becomes clear in a passage of a letter from Cavafy to his friend Periklis Anastasiadis on the subject of the poem "In the Same City" (the first version of "The City"):

> "In the Same City" is from one point of view perfect. The versification and chiefly the rhymes are faultless. . . . But I have "parakamei" [overdone] it and somehow got cramped on the exigencies of the meter; and I am afraid I havn't [sic] put in the second stanza as much as should have gone in it. I am not sure that I have drown [sic] in the 2nd, 3rd and 4th lines of the second stanza an adquetly [sic] powerful image of ennui—as my purpose was. It may be however that by trying to do more, *I should have overdone the effect and strained the sentiment, both fatal accidents in art.* [my emphasis] (Peridis 1948: 312)

As in the example above Cavafy draws attention to the dangers of hyperbole and mannerism, two common features of the "Byzantine poems," which he now regards as possibly fatal to art. Implicit in both passages is a conception of poetry that contrasts with that found in the rejected texts. For instance, Cavafy makes no reference to song or singing and he avoids using sentimental language to describe the poet and poetic composition. The poet thinks critically about the text before him, which is his own creation and not a gift from the muse. The development of this new conception of poetry is no doubt related to the mid-nineteenth-century appearance of the image of the poet as craftsman (discussed in Chapter 1). During the emergence of such literary movements as symbolism, the notion of the author underwent a transformation from bard or wise man to a specialist in literature. It was natural, then, that the craftsman would conceive of the product of his labor differently from what the bard regarded as his song. With the appearance of symbolism there arose a novel poetic style and poetics. The passage from Cavafy quoted above may be seen in such a context in that it indicates a change in his conception of poetry and an orientation toward other literary discourses. Indeed, the use of the

Poetry

French *ennui* (one of many such instances in the texts to be examined) points to the relationship between Cavafy's poetics and certain elements of symbolist theory. It is to symbolism that I turn now, though I repeat that the object of my analysis is poetics and not poetic style.

SYMBOLISM

Symbolism is a very elusive term, since it is often used interchangeably with decadence and sometimes in parallel with aestheticism. Originally it denoted a self-conscious literary school in Paris, dating from between 1885 and 1895, which published its manifesto in *Figaro* (1886) and which attracted to the French capital poets and intellectuals from all over the world. By the late 1890s it became, as René Wellek points out in his "The Concept of Symbolism in Literary History," a blanket name covering recent developments in French poetry (1970: 95). This general meaning of the term came to be accepted in the Anglo-Saxon world particularly after the intervention of Arthur Symons and T. S. Eliot (Balakian 1977: 3). For Anglo-Saxon critics symbolism suggests the poetry and poetics of the major French poets writing in the second half of the nineteenth century: Baudelaire, Rimbaud, Verlaine, Mallarmé, Laforgue, and Corbière. When I employ the term "symbolism" here, it is to this extended sense I refer, since this is the way it was used by Cavafy as well. One of the chief characteristics of symbolism is the emphasis it gives ambiguity and indirect communication. Symbolism implies the opposite of literal representation, since meaning is thought to be communicated not by words referring directly to reality in a one-to-one relationship, but indirectly through association and suggestion. As Mallarmé put it: "To name an object is to conceal two-thirds of the pleasure of the poem which is made to reveal itself bit by bit: suggestion that is the *rêve*. This is the perfect usage of the mystery which constitutes the symbol: to evoke an object little by little in order to show a state of the soul, or, inversely, to choose an object and to free a state of the soul through a series of decipherments" (1945: 869). Symbolist writing banishes description and literalism. As Mallarmé stated in another passage, the poet evokes images in a

Poetry

shadowy atmosphere; he expresses the object not directly, but through allusions (p. 400).

Language can no longer faithfully represent nature, the signifier cannot transport the reader to the signified; meaning becomes problematic.[2] It is in such a climate of linguistic skepticism that poets such as Mallarmé sought a new literary language that would not depict the object, but highlight its effect (Mallarmé 1959: 137). Since poetic language is unable objectively to render, define, or describe its subject, communication takes place through the use of unexplained symbols. In symbolism priority is given not so much to the direct expression of ideas, as to the evocation of a mood or the creation of a certain atmosphere; enigma and mystery are the end products of such writing. The poet does not fear mystery and vagueness, but seeks these qualities as literary values. The poet should prefer uneven rhythm, wrote Verlaine in his famous poem "Art Poétique"; there is nothing more dear than a gray song in which the undefined and the exact combine; never the color, but always the shade. Meaning in this context of ambiguity loses its certainty and coherence, since the reader does not hold the keys to interpretation; the symbols do not necessarily correspond to a predefined code that permits their decipherment. The absence of such information from the poem frustrates the reader's attempts to reach a conclusive interpretation and thus gives rise to polyvalent and dissonant readings.

It is primarily this aspect of symbolism that appears both in Cavafy's early published poetry and in his theoretical scholia on these texts.[3] In a comment on "Theodotos" (1915), Cavafy refers to the role that the symbol plays in representing another concept or idea. He characterizes the whole poem as symbolist, adding that the "symbol (Julius Caesar) is found in the first part of the poem, the poet leaves it in the second part where he addresses himself to everyone. Alexandria symbolizes happiness, success" (Lehonitis 1942: 30). In this passage Cavafy attempts to interpret the

---

[2] For a discussion of the crisis in language, see Chapter 4.
[3] Many of Cavafy's early published poems illustrate the theoretical concerns of symbolism discussed here. An analysis, however, of Cavafy's use of symbols in such poems as "The City," "Ithaka," and "Candles" would extend beyond the scope of this study, since it would deal with poetic style, not poetics.

Poetry

poem by deciphering the two symbols that remain unexplained within it. "Theodotos" is symbolist in that it conceals its meaning through the incorporation of the two symbols, which, by nature, lend themselves to more than one reading. They act as interpretive fields, allowing the reader many ways of decoding them. In a symbolist text it is the reader's responsibility to interpret the symbols according to the poem's context, and also on the basis of his or her own strategies and assumptions. As Cavafy wrote in the "Ars Poetica": "Very often the poet's work has but a vague meaning; it is a suggestion; the thoughts are to be enlarged by future generations or by his immediate readers" (1963c: 42).[4] In another passage he adds: "Luckily poems are sometimes cryptic; and in this way it is possible to add to them other related emotions or emotional states" (1983a: 44).

The symbolist poem eschews literal representation and foregrounds ambiguous expression, leaving the field as open as possible for the reader. The adjective "vague," used by Cavafy in the passage above, reappears in a letter to his brother, John, concerning "The Windows," which his brother had translated: "The 'up and down' gives a vague idea (certainly very vague, and it is for this reason that I did not consider the words faulty)" (1963b: 237). In composing "The Windows," Cavafy reveals that he sought a vague, enigmatic mode so as to create an effect rather than to describe concrete objects. The aim of the poem was to evoke a mood of pessimism and desperation, as is indeed outlined later in the letter: "It is a high degree of *pessimisme* when 'things' are considered fearful only because they are 'new.' "

At this point it would be useful to recall Cavafy's observations on "The City," that by emphasizing certain elements of the poem, he would have exaggerated the effect. In this poem, as in "The Windows," his ostensible aim is to elicit "a powerful image of ennui," to induce an effect of hopelessness rather than to portray a particular city. The choice of this strategy underscores the symbolist orientation of Cavafy's poetics at this stage, since it corresponds to one of the tenets of symbolism best expressed by Mal-

---

[4] This means that Cavafy's reading of "Theodotos" represents one—the poet's—of many possible interpretations. The "immediate readers" or the "future generations," however, are not compelled to accept this reading as definitive.

Poetry

larmé in a passage quoted earlier, namely, that an artist should strive to paint not the object, but the effect it produces. From Cavafy's perspective, the effect of "The City" is the evocation of despair in the reader. As Cavafy observes: "There is a class of poems whose role is 'suggestif.' My poem comes under that head [*sic*]. To a sympathetic reader—sympathetic by culture—who will think over the poem for a minute or two my lines, I am convinced, will suggest an image of the deep, the endless 'désespérance' which they contain 'yet cannot all reveal' " (Peridis 1948: 312).[5] Poems such as "The City" are *suggestif* insofar as they elicit an ambiguous atmosphere that envelops the reader. Since the poem does not offer a definite and single message, but only elusive and ambiguous hints, it invites the reader to participate actively in the deciphering of the symbols. Yet, as Cavafy maintains, the symbolist poem cannot reveal all its secrets; it always conceals a part of itself and thereby thwarts the reader's attempts to grasp its meaning unequivocally. Unable to extract a conclusive message from the verses, the reader withdraws with only an enigma, a feeling, or simply an impression of something.

This word "impression" appears in another of Cavafy's letters (1898), in which he comments on the poem "Absence":[6] "The poem is in itself strange, but it is better that this strangeness flow only from the *impression* created by the verses rather than be expressed emphatically" [my emphasis] (Cavafy 1963b: 245). As in the previous examples, Cavafy foregrounds veiled suggestion as opposed to direct and unambiguous expression. In "Absence" the quality of "strangeness" is not explicitly announced to readers, but is communicated through the impression it creates in them. The poem allows readers to draw their own conclusions from a field of ambiguous references.[7] The poet's task is not to solve the enigma

---

[5] The recurrence of French words in these passages, such as *suggestif, désespérance, ennui,* and *pessimisme,* emphasizes Cavafy's interest in French poetry and poetics of the late nineteenth century.
[6] Only the English translation of this poem survives. (See Cavafy 1963b: 145 for the text.) Cavafy reworked this initial version and published it under the title "If Actually Dead" (1920).
[7] In an article titled "Shakespeare on Life," Cavafy writes that he prefers the observations of great men to their conclusions, since by prescribing no fixed answers

Poetry

in his poem, but simply to describe "a possible and an occuring state of feeling—sometimes very transient, sometimes of long duration" (Cavafy 1963c: 32). The symbolist poem is composed of shifting, mobile elements, of feelings, impressions, memories, hints, gestures, and symbols that resist the reader's desire to comprehend them permanently. The passages of Cavafy's examined here indicate a prominent preoccupation with symbolist theoretical concerns and distinctly situate his ideas in the context of symbolist poetics.

FORMALISM

What these extracts also reveal is a marked orientation toward form. In nearly all the passages examined so far poetry has been primarily conceived from the perspective of form. That is, it is understood and discussed with reference to the mode of representation rather than the object it represents; importance is given to the "how" as opposed to the "what" of poetic discourse. In his comments Cavafy shows less interest in the faithful depiction of his subject, and more in the poem's devices and the resources that could be employed for the desired effect. This characteristic is not unique to Cavafy, but reflects a more or less fundamental shift in the aesthetic values of the second half of the nineteenth century—a crisis manifested in the widening rift in the duality between form and content. A majority of the literary and discursive writing of the period opts for the former element of this conceptual dichotomy. The primacy given to form can be witnessed in many authors (Poe, for example) who stressed the supremacy of the poem itself, in Wilde's claim that art finds perfection in itself, in Gautier's assault on utilitarian art, in Mallarmé's aspirations toward the *Grand Oeuvre*, in Valéry's quest for pure poetry, not to mention the emergence of language as object of poetic and theoretical concern, a circumstance that underlies much of the literary development of the age.

Cavafy, as the ensuing discussion will show, shares this general tendency to emphasize form at the expense of content. A case

---

they permit readers to form their own interpretations from the information available (Cavafy 1963b: 30).

in point is the comment written by Cavafy on a passage from John Ruskin concerning language. In the text Ruskin argues that although language is "invaluable as the vehicle for thought," by itself it is nothing, since for him what is significant is not the mode of representing, but what is represented (Ruskin 1893: 121) [*Modern Painters* I, I, 1, §4]. Cavafy disputes this claim and insists that form can exist without the message: "Form can have beauty independently of the idea, and having been freed [from this] it incites the imagination of the spectator or reader. Not having its own distinct and specific ideas, it suggests ideas" (Tsirkas 1971: 228). Cavafy adds further that many works of art exist exclusively on the basis of the "mode of representing or of language" and draws attention to a type of art that has form as its main referent. Such an art, according to Cavafy, is liberated from the constraints of realism, since it is no longer bound to represent reality faithfully. Having cast off the burden of mimesis, form may propose or suggest a variety of possible hypotheses. The verb "suggest," recalling the previous discussion on symbolism, stresses an art that operates indirectly and seeks to involve the receiver in the interpretation of itself. This type of art, as will be shown later, is conscious of itself as art and highlights its own aesthetic devices while supressing the ostensible object of its representation.

Historically, "art for art's sake" (or aestheticism) was one of the earliest artistic schools to privilege form consciously and elevate it above all other considerations. Aestheticism isolates the concept of beauty, segregates the aesthetic from other human experiences, and presents art as an autonomous free play of the imagination that requires no extra-aesthetic justification. The theoretical context usually cited to illustrate the emergence of nineteenth-century aestheticism is that of Kantian and post-Kantian idealism. Kant, in his seminal *Critique of Judgement* (1790), played an influential role in the constitution of aesthetics as a mode of philosophical analysis whose sole object is the beautiful. Through the Third Critique Kant sets out to establish the autonomy of the aesthetic and to designate its distinctive qualities by differentiating it from the discourses on pleasure, emotion, morality, and knowledge.[8] In his examination of the aesthetic, Kant

---

[8] On the emergence during this period of Art as an autonomous institution that

Poetry

gives primacy to the judgment of taste, which he considers a disinterested faculty. For Kant, the contemplation of a beautiful object, though characterized by pleasure, is based on the formal purposefulness of the object, distinct from individual needs and tastes. In the experience of the beautiful our intellectual faculty is in free harmonious play and continues to exist in that state, not through our will or interest, but through the purposefulness of the formal properties of the objects themselves—"the lawlike manner in which the formal qualities of the object appear to us when we freely reflect upon them" (Crawford 1974: 50). Aesthetic contemplation is as purposeless as it is disinterested and has no aim other than the prolongation of this state.

This idea is succinctly summarized by Kant's paradoxical phrase "Zweckmässigkeit ohne Zweck" (purposefulness without a purpose), which is usually taken to mean that the object does not have a purpose, although its formal harmony leads us to think that it has been purposed as a result of a plan or rule. But the beautiful, Kant asserts, is not based on a rule or concept (Kant 1928: § 217). It is a synthesis of sensory data that does not depend on a concept and cannot provide knowledge of the object. Rather the experience of the formal properties evokes the free play of the cognitive faculties of the subject, resulting in disinterested pleasure. This pleasure has no practical end—such as the desire to acquire food or seek shelter—other than the maintenance of itself. Without any purpose or goal, the judging subject is incited to remain in that state, observing the beautiful object. As Kant himself formulated it: "*Beauty* is the form of *finality* in an object, so far as perceived in it *apart from the representation of an end*" (§ 236). Kant divorced beauty from utility, desire, and knowledge, as he also separated it from morality. "The interest in beauty gives no evidence of a mind

---

comprehends all the fine arts under one unified and distinctive domain, see Raymond Williams (1960), M. H. Abrams (1981), Christa Burger (1977), Martha Woodmansee (1984), and Peter Bürger (1984). Kant, of course, did not invent either the concept or the field of aesthetics; the term itself goes back to Alexander Baumgarten's *Reflections on Poetry* ([1735] 1954: § 116), in which it appears for the first time. Kant simply systematized the discourse on aesthetics that existed before him. In this regard, Karl Mortiz's article, with the very instructive title "Versuch einer Vereinigung aller schönen Kunste und Wissenschaften unter dem Begriff des in sich selbst Vollendeten" [Attempt at a Unification of All the Fine Arts and Sciences under the Concept of Self-sufficiency] ([1784] 1962), contains many of the ideas on aesthetic contemplation found in Kant's treatise written six years later.

attached to the morally good but is the mark of a good soul" (§ 299). Kant isolated beauty and sought to analyze its inherent properties. In this respect his theory is formalist; it privileges form over concept and bars the aesthetic experience from the worldly. Kant's valorization of aesthetic form was very influential on subsequent thinkers, making him one of the philosophical sources of a formalism that led ultimately to the movement of art for art's sake.

One of the intermediaries in this development was Friedrich Schiller, who accepted Kant's notion of beauty's autonomy. For Schiller as well art is not subservient to the nonaesthetic—political, social, or moral. Although Schiller did not completely isolate beauty from life, in that he wished to examine the relationship between art and culture, he valorized the aesthetic and extolled its function in life by identifying it with humanness. Beauty, he stated in *On the Aesthetic Education of Man* (1794–95), offers us the possibility of becoming human beings (1967: XXI, 6). Freedom, the harmony of laws, which for Schiller constitutes one of man's noblest values, resides in the aesthetic form (XXII, 5). One of the fundamental tasks of *Kultur* (education) is to expose man to form, to encourage his aesthetic sense since morality develops out of the aesthetic itself. Beauty, for Schiller, mediates between man and nature; it exercises a civilizing force and in a sense gives meaning to life. It promises no particular result and accomplishes nothing practical, intellectual, or moral (XXI, 4). But the aesthetic impulse is at work, introducing harmony into society and making man whole, happy, and forgetful of his limitations. The aesthetic mode of communication unites society, whereas all others divide it (XXII, 11).

Although Wilkinson and Willoughby, in their introduction to *On the Aesthetic Education of Man*, and Wellek, in his "Kant's Aesthetics and Criticism," insist that Schiller is not a precursor of aestheticism, since his aim was not to divorce beauty from life but to explain its significance to man, he nevertheless idealizes it and privileges its function in society. Schiller had a vision of a better society, but one based on aesthetics. By conferring on beauty such a lofty mission and by identifying the aesthetic experience with the essence of humanness, Schiller helped to perpetuate the valorization of form over idea. The next step taken by the aesthetes was to forget about society and life and to rally around pure, autonomous form. Schiller's ideas proved extremely influential. His aesthetic philosophy, along with those of other German idealists, was taken up by such popularizers of German thought in France as Mme. de Staël and Victor Cousin. These ideas were also seized by Poe, Carlyle, and Coleridge and diffused in their respective countries. Eventually there arose an aesthetic discourse that celebrated an art oriented not toward life or society, but toward itself. As William Wimsatt and Cleanth Brooks put it: "On a tide of vaguely simplified Kantian thinking such terms as 'German Aesthetics,' 'Kant's aesthetics,' 'freedom,' 'disinterestedness,' 'pure art,' 'pure poetry,' 'form,' and 'genius' were floated into currency, and along with them the term of 'art for art's sake' " (1957: 477). The phrase 'art for art's sake,' first used by Benjamin Constant, soon became a popular slogan and polemical tool against the demands made by other theorists for a didactic and socially aware art. In February 1804 Constant recorded in his journal the following note concerning his acquaintance Henry Robinson, which included the idea of art for art's sake: "His work on the aesthetics of Kant. Very ingenious ideas. *L'art pour l'art* but without purpose; all purpose distorts art. But art aspires towards a purpose which it does not have" (Constant 1957: 266). Art has no aim other than to be art; it has no other cause than the aesthetic. Ideas such as these circulated in the salons and coffeehouses of the nineteenth century and found expression in both the art and the aesthetic writings of the period.

Théophile Gautier, in the preface to his *Mademoiselle de Maupin* (1835), fought relentlessly against the subservience of art to practical ends. "Everything that is useful is ugly," he contended, adding playfully that one cannot use an antithesis as an umbrella, or make a cap out of a metonymy (Gautier 1981: 34, 36). Similarly, Poe, in the "Poetic Principle" (1850), condemned didactic poetry, since in his view truth and poetry were incompatible. In order to free poetry from the constraints of morality and, indeed, representation, he called for a poem that bore no relationship to reality and that withdrew into its own self-referential terrain: "There neither exists nor can exist any work more thoroughly dignified, more supremely noble than this very poem, this poem per se, this poem which is a poem and nothing more, this poem written for the poem's sake" (Poe 1899: 202). Poe's poem, like the Kantian notion of beauty, consists of internally oriented properties; distanced and isolated, it suggests no end, has no purpose, and offers nothing more than itself. Poe's call was taken up by Baudelaire, who insisted that under no circumstances could poetry be assimilated into science or morality. It did not have truth as its subject; "It only has itself" (1925: 158).

Kant's conception of the aesthetic idea was transformed into the narcissistic artwork that gazes into the mirror, delighting in its own beauty. Mallarmé highlighted art's obsessive preoccupation with itself in this way: "There is only Beauty—and it has only one perfect expression, Poetry. . . . For me Poetry takes the place of love since it is in love with itself" (1959: 243). This notion of beauty supplants all other human values to become the poet's ultimate object of desire and absolute form of salvation. Following Mallarmé's substitution of love with beauty, the narrator of Moore's *Confessions of a Young Man* discloses that what saved him during his stay in Paris was not love and friendship—"What saved me was the intensity of my passion for Art" (1972: 57). Poetry replaces love as the poet's most supreme ideal and only source of redemption. In England other authors joined Moore in celebrating the aesthetic experience. A. C. Swinburne, for instance, vigorously defended the separation of art from morality in his poetic and critical writings. He championed freedom in art and the primacy of the work's formal components. In an essay on Baudelaire (1861), he reminded those critics expecting philanthropy of the poet that his business is to write good verses and not to redeem the age and remold society (Swinburne 1925: VIII, 417). The art of poetry, he added, has nothing to do with didactic matter. Art is not a good servant, like fire and water, and hence nothing practical can be expected from it. "Art for art's sake first of all," Swinburne announced emphatically (VI, 137–38).

Walter Pater, in *The Renaissance* (1873), echoed the call to honor beauty by advocating the pursuit of wisdom in "the poetic passions, the desire for beauty, the love for art's sake" (1910: 239). Pater's valorization of the beautiful was based on his more fundamental belief that it is not the fruit of experience, but experience itself that matters. He too brought form to the fore at the expense

Poetry

of content or context. Art, then, freed from the task of copying reality and pleasing or teaching the audience, seeks nothing but the promotion of its own sensuous patterns. As Wilde put it in "The Decay of Lying" (1891): "Art finds her own perfection within and not outside of herself. She is not to be judged by any external standards of resemblance. Art never expresses anything but itself" (1945: 29). Art is beautiful, therefore it is useless; or because of its uselessness, it is beautiful. Such is the gist of another of Wilde's provocative comments: "As long as a thing is useful or necessary to us, or affects us in any way . . . it is outside the proper sphere of art" (p. 20).

Cavafy's poetics may to a certain extent be understood through the perspective of aestheticism, since it shares two of aestheticism's principal precepts, the autonomy of art and its uselessness. We have seen that one of the common portraits of the artist in Cavafy is that of the aesthete, the sensitive individual who isolates himself from the commonplace to create beautiful forms. But the objects that the artist produces do not enter general circulation, since they contain no exchange value, they are deliberately useless. Cavafy underscores the anti-utilitarian nature of art when commenting on Ruskin's entreaty: "Remember that the most beautiful things in life are useless" (1893: 420). While recognizing that this statement is incompatible both with Ruskin's philosophy and with the moralizing arguments of the paragraph from which it is taken, Cavafy characterizes this remark as the "dogma of art." Similarly, in the "Ars Poetica" Cavafy states that "there are works of immediate utility and works of beauty. The poet does the latter" (1963c: 46). The idea of art's uselessness and its independence from nature appears in many of Cavafy's poems. The posthumous "Artificial Flowers" (1903) is the most noteworthy example (for further discussion, see Chapter 6). The most striking aspect of "Artificial Flowers," as of "Morning Sea" and "For the Shop," is the uncompromising rejection of nature for a world fashioned by the imagination:

> I do not want the real narcissus—nor do lilies
> please me nor real roses.
> They adorn the trite, pedestrian gardens. . . .

Poetry

> I love flowers fashioned of glass or gold,
> genuine gifts of a genuine Art;
> dyed in hues lovelier than natural colors,
> wrought with mother-of-pearl and enamel
> with ideal leaves and stalks. . . .

Implied in this separation of natural and artificial flowers is the existence of two conceptions of beauty: the one of nature, imperfect and perishable; and the other of art, perfect and timeless. This polarity between transcendental and natural beauty informs Cavafy's conception of art dividing the world, on the one hand, into the ugly, old, and commonplace; and on the other, into the beautiful, young, and idealized.

ART AND THE ABSOLUTE

The poet of the second half of the nineteenth century tended to dismiss the real as a subject of art. He denied any practical function to beauty; he idealized it and exalted it as the object of his desire and the sign of his redemption. Yet he still resided in the natural world and therefore suffered on account of its imperfect and ephemeral nature. Cavafy's artist is aware of the disjunction between what he sees as an unsatisfying and faulty world and that transcendental realm of forms that is impervious to change. Despising this hostile reality, he aspires to enter the haven of aesthetic form. But unable, except on a few occasions, to unite himself with the absolute, he remains unfulfilled, perpetually yearning for salvation. Art yields meaning for the poet in an essentially dispossessing time and in this way acts as a substitute religion. Art, then, that autotelic, autogenic, and autonomous form, took upon itself the properties of the departed deity. As romantics such as Hölderlin were announcing the flight of the gods and bewailing the consequences for man of this portentous event, art emerged and began to assume the function of a theology.

Earlier I outlined briefly the appearance of aesthetics with Kant and other German philosophers. Our modern concept of art, which incorporates under its aegis all the fine arts and demarcates them from all other spheres of human practice, and which the observer contemplates disinterestedly, is a product of this period.

Poetry

This notion has theological origins. Abrams has demonstrated in his "Kant and the Theology of Art" that the German thinkers of this time secularized such terms as "contemplation," "disinterestedness," and "beauty" by removing them from their theological context and employing them to differentiate the aesthetic experience from the moral, practical, and religious. They transferred into the realm of sensible beauty the Platonic idea of a perfect form and the religious doctrine of *autarkeia*, which until then had been the property of the divine (Abrams 1981: 91–93). Martha Woodmansee examines this development in the work of the philosopher Karl Moritz, who, she argues, salvaged elements of the religious creed of disinterested love and transferred them into the secular theory of autonomous art. Moritz translated the essential features of the deity to the work of art and indeed defined his model of art with recourse to a theological analogue (Woodmansee 1984: 15).[9]

These ideas in the latter part of the nineteenth century, with the emergence of the doctrine of art for art's sake, evolved into a substitute religion. The hope for the reconciliation with the departed gods was secularized into the pursuit of an aesthetic ideal. The gods for the postromantic poet were essentially dead, and because he lived in such a godless world, he erected a temple to beauty and worshiped it as a god. As art became more autonomous, Max Weber observed in his essay "Religious Rejections of the World and Their Directions" [1915], it began to assume the function of religion. "Art," he stated, "provides a *salvation* from the routines of everyday life. . . . With this claim to a redemptory function, art begins to compete directly with salvation religion" (Weber 1946: 342). Writing from the perspective of criticism, Arthur Symons similarly noted that symbolist literature attained a certain degree of liberty, but accepted a heavy burden for this insofar as it became "a kind of religion, with all the duties and responsibilities of a sacred ritual" (1923: 9). Wallace Stevens, the

---

[9] Regarding religion and criticism, see Eagleton's *Literary Theory* (1983), in which he illustrates how English studies emerged, in part, due to the "failure of religion." Eagleton argues that English "literature" grew as a response to the ideological empty space left by the disappearance of theology as an informing and shaping factor in society. See also Chris Baldick's *The Social Mission of English Criticism, 1848–1932* (Oxford: Oxford University Press, 1983). On the general relationship of art and religion, see Weber (1946).

Poetry

modernist poet, also emphasized the sacralization of art. "After one has abandoned a belief in god," Stevens stated, "poetry is that essence which takes its place as life's redemption" (1957: 58).

The notion of art as redemption is very prominent in Cavafy's work. Art saves the poet by providing him with a formalist sanctuary where he can escape from the sorrow, vulgarity, and ugliness of the world. The poet, as illustrated in "I've Brought to Art," submits to art because it knows how to fashion that ideal form to which he aspires:

> I sit in a mood of reverie.
> I've brought to Art desires and sensations:
> things half-glimpsed
> faces or lines, certain indistinct memories
> of unfulfilled love affairs.
> Let me submit to Art:
> Art knows how to shape forms of Beauty,
> almost imperceptibly completing life,
> blending impressions, blending day with day.

The artist of the poem regards reality as a disorganized mass of half-seen faces or lines and of indistinct memories of unfulfilled loves. Before the mediation of art, these base substances are twice removed from beauty, for they are not only imperfect, but also only half seen and hence only half remembered. The artist calls upon art to intervene by filling in the spaces and organizing the disparate images into unities: "blending impressions, blending days." Art, then, like Cavafy's conception of the imagination, acts as a synthesizing agent.[10] As in the case of the imagination, the

---

[10] This notion of the imagination, as pointed out in Chapter 1, has its roots in aesthetic discourse of the early nineteenth century. Schiller, for instance, stresses the role of art as a reconciling agent in a world of fragments, as a unifying impulse resisting the forces toward entropy. Beauty, for Schiller, resides in the attainment of that ideal that is the inclusion of all realities (1967: XVIII, 4). Coleridge also regarded art as a synthesizing organism incorporating all elements of life into itself. "Art is a reconciler of nature and man, it combines colors, forms, motion, and sound into unities" (1975: 253). For a modern restatement of these ideas that may be compared to Cavafy's poem, note the following passage from T. S. Eliot's "The Metaphysical Poets": "When a poet's mind is perfectly equipped for its work, it is constantly amalgamating disparate experience; the ordinary man's experience is

82

Poetry

unities created by art do not resemble exactly anything existing in nature, since art does not imitate nature, but works according to its own criteria. What Wilde said about aesthetic creation is appropriate to Cavafy: "[Art] takes life as part of her rough material, re-creates it, refashions it in fresh forms (Wilde 1945: 23)."[11] In Cavafy's poem art transmutes material substances into transcendental aesthetic form. In this respect, Cavafy's conception of beauty corresponds to the Platonic notion of the idea: it is otherworldly, self-contained, and perfect, existing in its own right within Cavafy's republic of ideas.

Art for Cavafy is a way of reaching this metaphysical realm, the instrument that mediates between an imperfect reality and desire. Art re-creates the artist's experience and compensates for the fleeting and faulty nature of life. We saw how in "Half an Hour" the poet through the imagination overcomes the absence of physical pleasure—relying partly on the presence of a real individual—and induces in himself a pleasure that seems wholly erotic. For the speaker of "On Hearing of Love," too, the pleasures created by fantasy are superior to those that are real and palpable. By its intervention, art can help the artist transcend momentarily the limitations of his existence and achieve a sensuous experience or vision that is almost completely fulfilling. Such privileged episodes are ephemeral, however; the artist is condemned for most of his life to a pitiless and vulgar reality. For this reason, then, art becomes even more indispensable as it is his only form of redemption, his only way of fleeing the pain inherent in the world. In the ideal temple of beauty fashioned by art the poet finds reprieve from toil, disease, depression, old age, and death. For Walter Pater, the high priest of aestheticism in England, this constitutes the quintessential function of art. All disinterested lovers of books, he asserts, will look to literature and to the other fine arts as a "refuge, a sort of cloistral refuge from a certain vulgarity in the actual world." According to Pater, a poem for "men of a finer thread," for

---

chaotic, irregular, fragmentary . . . in the mind of the poet these experiences are always forming new wholes" (1951: 287).

[11] This is exactly Kant's understanding of the function of the imagination: "This faculty is a powerful agent for creating, as it were, a second nature out of the material supplied to it by actual nature" (1928: §314).

Poetry

those who maintain the literary ideal, has "uses of a religious retreat" (1901: 17, 18).

Literature serves as a monastic sanctuary; the aesthetic experience is sacralized, and art in general assumes the function of a theology. The basis of this new worship was the notion of absolute, incorruptible, perfect form, which manifested itself in different ways for various authors. In Cavafy, as we saw, it appeared as an idealized conception of Beauty, in Flaubert as a book about Nothingness, and in Mallarmé as the *Grand Oeuvre*, which was supposed to subsume everything. As Flaubert wrote in a letter in 1852, what seemed to him beautiful and what he wanted to achieve was a book about Nothing: "a book without an external link, which would sustain itself by the internal force of its style, as the earth retains itself in the air without being supported, a book which would hardly have a subject, or where at least the subject would almost be invisible, if that were possible" (1974: XIII, 158). Flaubert's book is devoid of concepts; it is composed of imperceptible signifiers held together by their own density. The book is impersonal, since the author has almost disappeared. From another perspective, Mallarmé aspired to the same ideal with his notion of the *Grand Oeuvre*, an "architectural and premeditated" book that would exist autonomously without an author or reader and would beget itself like language, inexhaustibly producing different versions of itself (1945: 663, 373, 500).[12] This type of work would transmute everyday reality into a system of ideas, but would signify nothing itself. This text "véridique" would emerge as the law in the world, its only book, to which all other texts would refer. The *Grand Oeuvre* was destined to be the new Bible, the absolute

---

[12] Another example of the quest for the pure, self-referential, and ideal work of art is provided by Huysmans's novel *À Rebours* (Against Nature, 1884), which perhaps exemplifies, at their most ironic, fin-de-siècle aesthetic aspirations. Des Esseintes, the novel's protagonist, ponders the problem of writing a novel concentrated in a few sentences, but containing the material of hundreds of pages. The words of such a novel would be so unalterable that they would take the place of all other words. This literary enterprise is also supported by theological presuppositions: the novel "thus condensed in a page or two, would become an intellectual communion between a *hieratic* writer and an ideal reader, a *spiritual* collaboration between a dozen persons of superior intelligence" [my emphasis] (1959: 199). The author, as priest, communicates the sacred meaning to the select initiates of art.

Poetry

book, which would incorporate the world in its pages and textualize reality with its words (p. 367).

Radical formalism characterizes these three examples. In Cavafy's concept of Ideal Beauty, in Flaubert's Book, and in Mallarmé's *Grand Oeuvre*, content abdicates and form remains as the supreme value. All three authors aimed at creating an aesthetic realm of pure, dense, and self-mirroring signs that would hover in space beyond contingency, corruption, and connotation. Yet by definition this absolute lay beyond man's realization; it remained infinite, elusive, and remote. Mallarmé's and Flaubert's notion of the Book was theoretically inaccessible and imperceptible (apart from the fact that neither was ever written), since it represented simultaneously everything and nothing yet never revealed itself or its law completely. In Cavafy's case the Form of Beauty is rarely attained, and its integrative force is seldom felt; it exists as if on the horizon, inducing the poet's longing with promises of plenitude.[13] If distant, it is nevertheless still present, for even in the otherwise godless and meaningless world, art provides the only deliverance. It is for this reason that art is indispensable for the aesthete and that Cavafy, who subjects almost every notion and social value to relentless scrutiny, does not criticize the function of Beauty. Although religion, morality, responsibility, duty, integrity, and so on are treated ironically and are often repudiated in Cavafy's poetry, aesthetics is never questioned and is venerated with religious

---

[13] As stated earlier, the pursuit for an undifferentiated whole and the impossibility of ever reaching it is a romantic commonplace. Prominent in romantic thought is the elevation of the boundless over the bounded. Man strives for that absolute, but is thwarted by what Abrams calls the discrepancy between his infinite reach and finite grasp (1971: 216). One can argue, however, that this idea is already inscribed in the autonomous and autotelic concept of beauty. Schiller observed that the highest ideal of beauty, which exists as a perfect union of reality and form, can never be realized fully, since there is always a preponderance of one element over the other (1967: XVI, 1). For the romantics Schiller's equilibrium is shattered; the striving for the Ideal leads back to the earthly fragment. "We search everywhere for the Infinite," Novalis wrote, "and we find only things" (1945: 10). This notion of the impossibility of ever attaining the absolute manifests itself persistently in the poetics of the nineteenth century. Albert, the protagonist of Gautier's *Mademoiselle de Maupin*, seeks only beauty, but as he confesses, it must be so perfect that he will probably never encounter it (1981: 137). We see it in remarks such as the following, made by Basil in Wilde's *The Picture of Dorian Gray*: "And it had all been what art should be, unconscious, ideal, remote" (1974: 114).

conviction. The poet approaches Beauty as a suppliant begging for salvation from ugliness and the imminence of death. Although almost inaccessible, Beauty affords the poet, as the following poems reveal, rare moments of pleasure and temporary relief from the misery of existence.

ART AS REDEMPTION

One of the well-known poems that deal with the redemptive character of art is "Melancholy of Jason Kleander, Poet in Kommagini, A.D. 595" (1921):

> The aging of my body and my beauty
> is a wound from a merciless knife.
> I'm not resigned to it at all.
> I turn to you, Art of Poetry,
> because you have a kind of knowledge about drugs:
> certain sedatives, in Language and Imagination.
>
> It's a wound from a merciless knife.
> Bring your drugs, Art of Poetry—
> they do relieve the pain at least for a while.

The speaker, a poet, as is obvious from the title, bewails the onset of old age and the miseries accompanying it. The aging of his body and the disfigurement of his beauty are seen metaphorically as wounds from a merciless knife. Unable to withstand the pain of time any longer, the poet invokes the "Art of Poetry" to apply its sedatives, "Language and Imagination," in order to relieve his sufferings. Poetry can heal life's sicknesses by administering its drugs, it can remedy temporarily the diseases afflicting the artist.

In a poem with a similar theme, "Following the Recipe of Ancient Greco-Syrian Magicians" (1931), an aesthete pleads for magic herbs that will enable him to regain the beauty and vigor of his youth, if only for a short while:

> Said an aesthete: "What distillation from magic herbs
> can I find—what distillation, following the recipe
> of ancient Greco-Syrian magicians—that will bring back to me
> for one day (if its power doesn't last longer),
> or even for a few hours,

Poetry

> my twenty-third year,
> bring back to me my friend of twenty-two,
> his beauty, his love.
>
> What distillation, following the recipe
> of ancient Greco-Syrian magicians, can be found
> to bring back—as part of this return to the past—
> the little room we shared."

Like the poet in the previous poem, the aesthete cannot cope with the miseries of old age, so he longs to escape by returning to a time of former happiness. But the drugs he demands, coming from "Greco-Syrian magicians," will be of no avail and one is left with the impression that only the imagination and language of the previous poem can help the aesthete find again the "little room," his friend, and their love.

In the first poem and quite likely in the second, art serves as a therapeutic agent. Its prescriptions, however, are effective only for a short time, after which the poet or aesthete is condemned again to the very misery from which he sought relief. Qualifying statements in each poem stress the fact that art delivers, but only temporarily: "and surely only for a short while" ("Half an Hour"), "for a while" ("Melancholy of Jason Kleander, Poet in Kommagini, A.D. 595"), and "for one day . . . or even for a few hours" ("Following the Recipe of Ancient Greco-Syrian Magicians"). The art of poetry may enable the poet to experience total erotic pleasure or escape the realities of old age, but one brutal fact always intervenes to frustrate his desires, namely, the ephemerality of earthly beauty. The poet longs for permanent relief, for the reunification with the absolute, but manages only to capture a transitory fragment of this promised plenitude. In this sense art mediates in the space between the beatitude of the ideal and the wretchedness of existence.[14]

---

[14] This notion of therapy should be differentiated from the belief common in romanticism that poetry provides a cathartic effect on the poet. This function of poetry is described by Keats in one of his letters: "I live under an everlasting restraint—Never relieved except when I am composing—so I will write away" (1970: 67). For Cavafy, poetry promises the poet not so much a release of internal passions—since he does not conceive poetry as an overflow of powerful feelings—as it assists him to overcome deprivation. The poet writes not to lighten his soul, but

Poetry

Ideas on the therapeutic properties of art circulated widely during the late nineteenth century, especially under the influence of Schopenhauer's philosophy. This was true in fin-de-siècle France, where Schopenhauer's aesthetics received broad dissemination among the symbolists, decadents, and aesthetes (Lehman 1950: 55; Pierrot 1981: 57). Schopenhauer assigned to art a preeminent place in his philosophic system, since he did not regard it as pure ornament, but as a means of achieving knowledge of the Idea. It is through aesthetic contemplation, he argued in *The World as Will and Representation* (1818), that man can apprehend these eternal ideas and escape his temporality (1958: A, §36). Expanding on the principle of disinterestedness and self-sufficiency, he added that when perceiving the beautiful, the individual forgets his individuality and will and is delivered from endless longing, and in this state finds true happiness.

In the phenomenal world, Schopenhauer believed, no rest or satisfaction is possible for the individual, since he is condemned to suffer want and deprivation and to endure sickness, despair, and old age. The nature of man consists in the fact that his will strives, is satisfied, and strives again. Happiness is the transition from desire to satisfaction (A, §52). But this happiness is of a negative order, since it is not enduring; it delivers us from pain, but is followed by new pain, longing, or boredom (A, §58). A prolonged happiness is impossible, since it would require oblivion of the self and the denial of the will. Art, however, does afford fleeting but genuine experience of satisfaction. In the perception of beauty we enter a state of pure contemplation and are raised for a few moments above our willing selves, our desires, and cares. We are rid of ourselves, since by filling our consciousness with the object under contemplation our awareness of ourselves vanishes, we lose our individuality and exist only as pure subjects of knowing (A, §48). In this state, we forget our suffering and gain an insight into a reality of a higher order—the eternal, immutable Ideas. These moments are the most blissful in our experience and from them "we can infer how blessed life must be of man whose will is silenced not for a few moments but for ever" (A, §68). As this pas-

---

because only through aesthetic creation and contemplation can his desires somehow be satisfied.

Poetry

sage pessimistically reiterates, the deliverance of the individual from misery is transient for, after these seconds of felicity, art abandons him to the worldly condition of despair and desire.

Ideas such as these concerning the wretchedness of existence and the redemptive capacity of art manifest themselves in Cavafy, as in "Half an Hour," "Melancholy of Jason Kleander, Poet in Kommagini, A.D. 595)," "Following the Recipe of Ancient Greco-Syrian Magicians." In all three poems, life is portrayed as inescapably deficient and art as the drug by which the artist experiences erotic fulfillment, witnesses authentic beauty, or regains the vigor of youth; it aids him to overcome some deprivation, to forget his misery, and to transcend himself. To the extent that Cavafy's poetics can be situated in the context of aestheticism—where beauty, youth, and eroticism are cherished—the redemptive power of art is essential. In the godless, ugly, and odious environment of the aesthete, art represents the only potion, the sole instrument by the which the pain of existence can be soothed and the sensuous experience enjoyed. The poet who transfers these privileged moments into verse, however, faces another hurdle—that of preserving them. The poet's earthly objects of desire are impermanent. As the speaker in "Of the Jews (A.D. 50)" reminds us, the perfectly shaped white limbs will perish; to so save them from the corruption of time, the poet enlists the support of memory.

MEMORY

In Cavafy a vast disproportion exists between the past and present, between what took place and what can be retrieved. The fact that most episodes of erotic pleasure and visions of beauty belong to youth and are ephemeral intimidates the poet who tries to redeem those experiences from decay. The artisan in "Craftsman of Wine Bowls," who is about to depict his dead friend on an amphora, realizes that time frustrates the task of the artist:

This [the depiction of his friend] proved very difficult
    because
some fifteen years have gone by since the day
he died as a soldier in the defeat of Magnesia

Poetry

The loss of many details in the gap between the event and its recollection hinders the artist's attempt to reconstruct personal experience from the past. The possibility of forgetfulness is a source of concern:

> I'd like to speak of this memory,
> but it's so faded now—as though nothing's left—
> because it was so long ago, in my adolescent years.
> "Long Ago" (1914)

> Those gray eyes will have lost their charm—if he's still alive;
> that lovely face will have spoiled.
> "Gray" (1917)

It is to prevent this decay that the artist devotes himself to art and conveys to it his "desires and sensations," those "half-glimpsed faces or lines"; he relies on it to fashion the "forms of Beauty" ("I've Brought to Art"). Memory is inseparable from the artistic process. It is the preliminary step in saving worldly beauty, and is a prerequisite to composition. Often the poet addresses memory in a manner reminiscent of the epic's invocation of the muse:

> O memory, I begged
> for you to help me most in making
> the young face I loved appear the way it was.
> "Craftsman of Wine Bowls"

> Memory, keep them the way they were.
> And, memory, whatever you can bring back of that love,
> whatever you can, bring back tonight.
> "Gray"

Memory promises the poet that everything that eluded him can rightfully be restored, that he will be able to recapture those treasured episodes kept at a distance by time, and that he will be reunited with that former plenitude.

The poet in Cavafy is a remembering being whose memory can be triggered by any object or incident. A half-gray opal reminds the narrator in "Gray" of his friend's eyes and the circumstances surrounding their affair. An old building in "Outside the House" (1918) triggers the speaker's memory of pleasures once experienced inside:

Poetry

> And as I stood staring at the door,
> stood lingering outside the house,
> my whole being radiated
> the sensual passion stored up inside me.

The reading of a letter brings to the speaker's mind the "short beautiful life" of youth that fate had terminated:

> An echo from my days of indulgence,
> an echo from those days came back to me,
> something of the fire of the young life we shared:
> I picked up a letter again,
> read if over and over till the light faded.
>   "In the Evening" (1917)

Finally the photograph of the posthumous "From the Drawer" (1923), which has symbolically faded over the years, helps the speaker to recall the face it once faultlessly portrayed, a face now presumably blemished by old age. But for the photograph's owner, the face survives in his memory as it once existed. This is the way he will remember it, and remember it he will, as he will write of his remembering.

"What seems to be needed," Alexander Nehamas observes in his discussion of memory in Cavafy, "is not simply remembering but also the realization that what is remembered is to be written about, that it must be the source and content of poetry" (1983: 310). "I'd like to speak of this memory," the speaker of "Long Ago" reminds us. Edmund Keeley has observed that the governing theme of "Long Ago" is recollection itself rather than the specifics being recollected, as indeed is emphasized by the use of such typographical devices as dots and dashes (1976: 60):

> A skin as though of jasmine . . .
> that August evening—was it August?—
> I can still just recall the eyes: blue, I think they were . . .
> Ah yes, blue: a sapphire blue.

Punctuation and repetition convey the impression of an individual who is trying to restore details from the past. Recollection constitutes the subject in other poems. In "Gray" similar typographical techniques visually articulate memory at work. Likewise, the row

Poetry

of periods following the title of "Body Remember . . ." (1918) indicates the process by which the actual pleasures of youth are remembered. Memory in Cavafy serves as a defense against the decay of time. But memory is always a memory of an absence, it is a supplement to a lack, and its effects are only temporary. For although the individual may be reunited briefly with a former wholeness, these felicitous moments are liable to be forgotten in time, and with the poet's death, they may be obliterated. In order for experience to be irrevocably salvaged it must be elevated to the absolute realm of aesthetic form, it must be transformed into art. For Cavafy ultimate redemption, the answer to death, can only be provided by writing.

ART PRESERVES ESSENCE

One of the prime functions ascribed to art in Cavafy's poetics is the rescuing of human experience from decay. But art is very selective in this, since it does not save all the details from the past, but concentrates on those with aesthetic value. Art preserves corruptible earthly beauty, which, without its intervention, would be permanently lost. In the aestheticist context this is a calamitous event and one the artist mourns bitterly. Such is the case of the handsome young prince Aristovoulos, who dies prematurely. The whole house bewails his passing, but significantly poets and sculptors are also touched by his death, since they have lost an exquisite subject for their art:

> Poets and sculptors will mourn—
> they've heard of Aristovoulos
> yet their imagination could never conceive
> a young man with the beauty of this boy:
> Antioch hasn't been given a god's statue
> to compare with this child of Israel.
> "Aristovoulos" (1918)

Aristovoulos will probably be forgotten, since no statue was erected in his honor, his beauty was not extolled in poetry. Art neglected him. His fate is similar to that of his counterpart in modern Alexandria, a very handsome young man, "exquisite" and "perfect," but who is also lost to posterity since "no statue or painting was made of him" ("Days of 1909, '10, and '11" [1928]). Art has failed to record his beauty. This for this aesthete is tragic, since no other human quality is so cherished.[15] Like Aristovoulos, the young Evrion of the "Tomb of Evrion" (1914) is extremely beautiful and dies prematurely. The speaker of the poem enumerates the young man's personal attributes:

> He studied philosophy with Aristokleitos,
> rhetoric with Paros, and at Thebes
> the sacred scriptures. He wrote a history
> of the province of Arsinoites. That at least will survive.
> But we've lost what was really precious: his form—
> like a vision of Apollo.

Although Evrion's texts will outlive him, his most praiseworthy possession—his beauty—will irretrievably be lost because, as in the previous poems, it did not become a theme of art.[16]

Art saves corruptible beauty by inscribing it upon its own unperishable surface. This is the task assigned to the poet Raphael, who is commissioned to compose a poem extolling the virtues of the dead poet Ammonis. There is no doubt as to what Raphael should include in his eulogy:

> Of course you'll speak about his poems—
> but say something too about his beauty,
> about that subtle beauty we loved.
>   "For Ammonis, Who Died at 29, in 610" (1917)

The verses composed by Ammonis will survive, but other poems must be written about his beauty to salvage it from imminent oblivion. The artist in Cavafy takes it upon himself almost as a duty to erect statues, paint portraits, or write poetry in order to honor exquisite beauty. As such, the poem "When They Come Alive" (1916) may be taken as the poet's motto:

---

[15] Ironically, as Kelley (1976: 84) shows, the young man's beauty has been saved by Cavafy's poem. A discussion of modernism's preoccupation with marginalized figures follows later in this chapter.

[16] The complete opposite occurs in "Tomb of Lanis" (1918). In this poem Markos, friend of the dead Lanis, is told to leave his friend's gravesite and return home to the portrait where Lanis is still to be found: "The portrait that still keeps something of what was valuable in him; / something of what you used to love."

Poetry

> Try to keep them, poet,
> those erotic visions of yours,
> however few of them there are that can be stilled.
> Put them, half-hidden, in your lines.
> Try to hold them, poet,
> when they come alive in your mind
> at night or in the noonday brightness.

Poetry is inextricably involved in the salvaging of past experience; it remembers, searches, and resurrects those moments of blessedness. In this endeavor even nonhuman forces are enlisted. For instance, in "Before Time Altered Them" (1924), fate, personified as an artist, benignly intervenes to separate two young men whose beauty was at its peak:

> Fate appeared as an artist and decided to part them now,
> before their feeling died out completely, before Time altered
>   them:
> the one seeming to remain for the other always what he was,
> the good-looking young man of twenty-four.

Similarly, in "Days of 1908" (1932) the days assume human characteristics to witness and preserve the beauty of a young man by the sea. The speaker rejoices at the sight of the naked form previously concealed by the unseemly clothes:

> O summer days of nineteen hundred and eight,
> from your view
> the cinnamon-brown suit was aesthetically excluded.
>
> Your view has preserved him
> as he was when he took off those unworthy clothes,
> that mended underwear, threw it all aside,
> and stood stark naked, impeccably handsome, a miracle—
> his hair uncombed, swept back,
> his limbs a little tanned
> from his morning nakedness at the baths and on the beach.[17]

---

[17] I have translated the adjective *kalesthtika* as "aesthetically," since it fits my interpretation of the poem better than Keeley and Sherrard's rendition of it as "tastefully."

Poetry

Aesthetically, or perhaps for art's sake, the unbecoming clothes are cast off so as to reveal the young man's body. The days of summer in this poem, like fate in the example above, become artists in their own right actively engaged in the preservation of beauty.

Aesthetic experiences, whether of the past or present, are significant in that they serve as starting points for art. Such is the case in "Their Beginning" (1921), which dramatizes an "illicit" sexual episode between two anonymous individuals. This transient affair may seem trivial to most people and not worth noting, but as the speaker emphasizes, for the artist it holds special meaning:

> But what profit for the life of the artist:
> tomorrow, the day after, or years later, he'll give voice
> to the strong lines that had their beginning here.

The poet regards this event neither as sordid nor insignificant, but as fitting for poetry's recognition. The episode becomes important less as a sensuous experience than as a subject for art. It is as if it were experienced for the sake of art. Pleasure, it seems, acquires significance if it is mediated by the imagination. This is also true of the thematically related poem "Comes to Rest" (1919), which deals with an anonymous sexual encounter in a tavern. But here again the act is seen from the perspective of poetry:

> Delight of flesh between
> half-opened clothes;
> quick baring of flesh—a vision
> that has crossed twenty-six years
> and now comes to rest in this poetry.

This affair, like the one in "Their Beginning," gains its significance retrospectively and aesthetically in that it serves as a source for art, it acts as a pretext around which to write a poem. The image of this incident crosses the expanse of time to be recorded in verse. And inevitably the poetic vision in Cavafy is one of eroticism, a subject that, being bound with aesthetic creation, occupies a prominent place in his poetics.

EROTICISM

This eroticism seems to have a perceptible imaginative component. The subjects of Cavafy's poems acquire greater pleasure

Poetry

from reflecting retrospectively on a sexual episode, or from imagining a possible erotic encounter, than from the real act itself. The subject, as Nehamas observes, "is concerned with the 'visions' of its eroticism rather than with that eroticism, with the 'recollection of those hours' when it had its own pleasure rather than with that pleasure, with the image of a love-affair that crosses twenty-six years to 'come to rest' in a poem being written about it" (1983: 314–15). In "Half an Hour," the speaker induces an experience that is "totally erotic" without ever touching the person next to him: "I never had you, nor I suppose / will I ever have you." The truth is perhaps that he does not really want or need to possess him. Significantly, he does not say that he wants to hold him, but rather wants to look at his body and gaze at his lips, to imagine him the way he wants. More often than not, pleasure in Cavafy is derived through fantasy. Such is the import of "I Went":

> I gave in completely and went,
> went to those pleasures that were half real
> half wrought in my own mind.

In this poem erotic experience is still divided into the real and half real, but in "On Hearing of Love" there is no doubt as to which type of pleasure is superior:

> On hearing about great love, respond, be moved
> like an aesthete. Only, fortunate as you've been,
> remember how much your imagination created for you.
> The first, and then the rest
> that you experienced and enjoyed in your life:
> the less great, the more real and tangible.
> Of loves like these; you were not deprived.

True erotic satisfaction, according to these poems, is attained through the "intensity of the mind." For the aesthete, pleasure is experienced largely through reflection, either through the recollection of past events or the imagination of new ones. Eroticism in Cavafy is a matter of art.[18]

---

[18] This is perhaps another aspect of the homosexual nature of this pleasure. Fantasy, Foucault argues in an interview, is a key aspect of sexuality, but in homosexuals, due to social prohibitions, this is expressed largely through recollection rather

Poetry

Cavafy's writing provides an almost inexhaustible discourse on eroticism by virtue of the many poems and notes for which pleasure is a dominant concern. These texts are almost obsessively preoccupied with eros, in particular "deviant" love, as if through their hyperbole they aimed to overcome moral laws, to violate prohibitions, and to celebrate transgression. A case in point is the posthumous "Growing in Spirit," which, though not referring directly to poetry, advocates dissent from social norms and thus may serve as an introduction to this theme. (The text is found in Chapter 1, "The Poet and Society.") The poem contends that in order to strengthen one's character, it is necessary to go beyond public respectability and infringe on the socially acceptable; in this act of disobedience one can learn much from both pleasure and subversion: "Sensual pleasures will have much to teach him. / He won't be afraid of the destructive act." Knowledge, then, as the last line provocatively suggests, may be acquired through physical love, and even through violence, since both imply contravention of social limits. Wisdom can be gained in that very art of rule breaking, in the infringement of society's sanctions on discourse and behavior. It is by speaking of sin and living in it that a person may "grow virtuously into knowledge."

It is in such a context of transgression that the prose poem "The Regiment of Pleasure" functions most powerfully.[19] The poem is playfully phrased as a public anouncement attracting new recruits to the pleasure corps. The text overflows with excess, from the central hyperbolic metaphor of the regiment of pleasure to the many admonitions exhorting the reader to enlist in the service of physical love:

---

than anticipation. In contrast to Cassanova, who claimed that the "best moment of love is when one is climbing the stairs," the homosexual, according to Foucault, says that "the best moment of love is when the lover leaves in the taxi. . . . It is when the act is over and the boy is gone that one begins to dream about the warmth of his body, the quality of his smile, the tone of his voice. It is the recollection rather than the anticipation of the act that assumes a primary importance in homosexual relations. This is why the great homosexual writers of our culture (Cocteau, Genet, Burroughs) can write so elegantly about the sexual act itself, because the homosexual imagination is for the most part concerned with reminiscing about the act rather than anticipating it" (Foucault 1982–83: 19).

[19] This poem was published posthumously in the journal *Lexi* (March–April 1983) and is dated by Savidis 1894–97.

Poetry

> Don't speak about guilt, don't speak about responsibility. When the Regiment of Pleasure passes by with music and flags, when feelings shiver and tremble, foolish and disrespectful is the one who stays away, who does not rush into the beautiful campaign which aims to conquer the pleasures and desires.

As in "Growing in Spirit," those drafted into the contingent of pleasure fight against the notions of guilt and respectability; they step over moral laws that are "poorly formulated" and "poorly applied." They fight on, surrendering only to desire, so that upon their death they will be considered worthy of burial "in the Cemetery of the Ideal where the mausolea of Poetry glitter." To infringe upon these moral norms is not "dangerous," as the "blasphemous" insist, but a noble task through which one ultimately gains passage into the absolute realm of poetry. In this text pleasure and writing exist as two points on a common axis of transgression; they are inseparably linked insofar as both entail the violation of the law.

This relationship between pleasure and writing is forcefully articulated in the following posthumous note:

> Who knows what ideas of lasciviousness reign over the composition of most literary works! Ideas of lasciviousness *solitaires*, which corrupt (or transform) the perception. And how often in various novels (especially in English novels)—those which critics condemn—certain parts indeed where they are at a loss because the author seems to do deliberate harm—result from the compulsory service the writer paid, while he was composing, to an impression of a state of lasciviousness. That feeling is so powerful—and sometimes how poetic, how beautiful!—that is tied to the words the birth of which it accompanied. (Cavafy 1983b: 28)

There is no doubt that in this text writing yields pleasure and vice versa. The inception of a literary work is accompanied by a "beautiful" and "poetic" feeling of pleasure; lust presides over the composition of literature; sensuality is inseparably interconnected with writing.

Poetry

The poem "Understanding" (1918) highlights this subtle relationship between pleasure and the word:

> In the loose living of my early years
> the impulses of my poetry were shaped,
> the boundaries of my art were plotted.

Through debauchery poetry is born; eroticism and writing go hand in hand. But as noted earlier, pleasure in Cavafy is in most cases associated with anomaly. In "Understanding" the speaker's life is characterized as "dissolute"; in "Passing Through" the sensuality to be experienced by the ephebe is called "unlawful":

> The things he timidly imagined as a schoolboy
> are openly revealed to him now. And he walks the streets,
> stays out all night, gets involved. And as is right (for our
>   kind of art)
> his blood—fresh and hot—
> offers itself to pleasure. His body is overcome
> by forbidden erotic ecstasy; and his young limbs
> give in to it completely.
>   In this way a simply boy
> becomes something worth our looking at, for a moment
> he too passes through the exalted World of Poetry,
> the young sensualist with blood fresh and hot.

Access to the "exalted World of Poetry"—reminiscent of the "Cemetery of the Ideal" and "the mausolea of Poetry" in "The Regiment of Pleasure"—can be gained only through certain rites of erotic initiation. The young boy must first surrender to illicit pleasure before he can be worthy of being admired and desired, and above all, before he can progress through the aesthetic realm. To climb Theocritos's sublime ladder of poetry, the novice must violate the laws prohibiting certain modes of love. Another parallel is drawn here between lust and writing, underscored of course by the theme of transgression—the pleasure to which the young boy submits must be forbidden, if not perverse.

The Cavafian artist, as demonstrated in Chapter 1, wishes to portray himself as deviant and abnormal. He sees himself proudly as a transgressor. In "And I Lounged and Lay on Their Beds," the

Poetry

speaker boasts of how he shunned the rooms of celebrated pleasures and entered the secret and shameful chambers of lust:

> But not shameful to me—because if they were,
> what kind of poet, what kind of artist would I be?
> I'd rather be an ascetic. That would be more in keeping,
> much more in keeping with my poetry,
> than for me to find pleasure in the commonplace rooms.

For the speaker-poet the accepted sexual behavior is incompatible with his craft, since art entails neither identification with, nor support for, social norms, but their violent renunciation. Knowledge, as argued in "Growing in Spirit," is gained through disobedience and revolt; pleasure and writing, as shown in "The Regiment of Pleasure," share a mutual relationship. Strength, as suggested by the following posthumous note, is found in perversion: "I don't know if perversion yields strength. Sometimes I believe so. Certainly, however, it is the source of greatness" (Cavafy 1983a: 29). Art speaks of corruption and the transgression of social limits; it exceeds the decorous and permissible and urges one toward the condemned.

In this context the term "art" assumes a broad significance not limited to verse composition or the creation of beautiful forms. It expands its meaning to become a *Weltanschauung*, a way of understanding the world and life. To the extent that Cavafy's poetics may be situated in the aestheticist discourse of the late nineteenth century, his notion of art does not connote only imaginative skill, but implies as well an attitude in which aesthetic experience predominates. In this sense, art signifies a way of life, as illustrated by the poem "Of the Jews (A.D. 50):"

> Painter and poet, runner, discus-thrower,
> beautiful as Endymion: Ianthis, son of Antony.
> From a family on close terms with the Synagogue.
>
> "My most valuable days are those
> when I give up the pursuit of sensuous beauty,
> when I desert the elegant and severe cult of Hellenism,
> with its over-riding devotion
> to perfectly shaped, corruptible white limbs,

Poetry

>and become the man I would want to remain forever:
>son of the Jews, the holy Jews."
>
>A most fervent declaration on his part: ". . . to remain
>   forever
>a son of the Jews, the holy Jews."
>
>But he didn't remain anything of the kind.
>The Hedonism and Art of Alexandria
>kept him as their dedicated son.

The speaker, an artist and athlete, declares his will to abandon his decadent life-style and return to the pious Jewish tradition. His plans are never realized, however, and he remains faithful to the "Hedonism and Art of Alexandria." The concept of "art," as used here, does not mean simply a craft or skill, but signifies a world view, an aesthetic way of life. This meaning is found also in "Julian and the Antiochians" (1926), which concerns the Antiochians' dismissal of Julian's religious and puritanical reforms:

>How could they ever give up
>their beautiful way of life, the range
>of their daily pleasures, their brilliant theatre
>which consummated a union between Art
>and the erotic proclivities of the flesh?

Significantly, the phrase "Way of Life" (*diaviosi*) appearing in the second line is characterized elsewhere in the poem as "delectable and absolutely aesthetic." Art in Cavafy is embodied in a hedonistic way of life. It unites with pleasure to form a distinctive outlook on the world—one recognized by its privileging of the aesthetic experience, its devotion to beauty, its celebration of youth, its valorization of hedonism, its predilection for elegance, and its emphasis on sensitive sensibilities. All of these qualities, in some form or another, circulated in the discourse of aetheticism of the late nineteenth century.

CAVAFY AND RUSKIN

As mentioned in the previous chapter, some theorists vigorously protested a categorization of art that isolated it from other

Poetry

human activities. John Ruskin, among others, attacked the detachment of art from its social environment, believing that art reflected society's moral fabric. According to Ruskin, art neither creates itself autogenetically nor exists autonomously, but stems from a social source to which it has a duty, namely, the edification of man and the enforcement of his ethical state. Ruskin's writings circulated widely and were extremely influential. Cavafy knew of his work and, indeed, wrote a commentary (posthumously published) on certain passages from Ruskin that dealt with aesthetics. (The text Cavafy used was *Selections from the Writings of John Ruskin* [1893].) These scholia, when set against the relevant texts of Ruskin, constitute not only an interesting dialogue between formalism and moralism/utilitarianism, but also elucidate Cavafy's position on matters relating to aesthetics and poetics.

Contrary to the school of *L'art pour l'art*, Ruskin believed that art did have a social function and an ulterior aim beyond that of reflecting its own beauty. Art, he argued, had a didactic purpose, it had to be sincere to the author and had to render reality faithfully. Art and morality were inseparable, and indeed, he defined poetry as "the suggestion by the imagination of noble grounds for noble emotions" (Ruskin 1893: 123 [*Modern Painters III*, IV, 1, §14]). In his comment on this passage Cavafy noted that such a definition is both restrictive and untrue. "The confinement of poetry," he observed, "within the prison of the 'noble grounds' is false" (in Tsirkas 1971: 229). Further on in his text Cavafy questioned the possibility (and desirability) of any definition of poetry, particularly one set in the framework of moral judgments. Ruskin, on the other hand, insisted on the necessity of linking art with morality and on the primacy of having appropriate subject matter for art. The "noble emotions" to which he refers above are not poetical in themselves since their poetical quality is determined by the object that is depicted and that inspires them. Whether a work is artistic or not depends on the suitability of the object it portrays: "energetic admiration may be excited in certain minds by a display of fireworks, or a street of handsome shops; but their feeling is not poetical because the grounds of it are false, therefore ignoble" (Ruskin 1893: 123 [*Modern Painters III*, IV, 1, §14]). Obviously,

Poetry

Ruskin does not consider fireworks or shop exteriors appropriate subject matter for art.

Cavafy, however, does not concern himself with the nobleness of the subject, or even with the subject at all, since for him the feeling that subject matter evokes is paramount: "Good and great works can be created within the context 'of the street of handsome shops' not with regard to the nobleness or not—trite words—of 'the street etc.,' but to the emotion or feeling which will be associated with the 'street' and will enclose it completely with the others" (Tsirkas 1971: 230). In his comment Cavafy shifts from content to form, from subject to style, from message to response which has the effect of expanding the thematic range of art and of emancipating it from the constraints of mimetic representation. Crucial to the aesthetic function is not the subject, but the feeling that it evokes; therefore anything can be used as suitable thematic material. Art need no longer abide with Ruskin's restrictive hierarchy of noble emotions and lofty subject matter.

Cavafy's argument is clear enough, but less obvious perhaps is the break it attests from traditional nineteenth-century thinking about art's subject matter. During this time artists began to incorporate previously unsanctioned topics, such as madness, sin, disease, perversion, and vice, within art's thematic corpus. This was particularly true of symbolist poets, such as Baudelaire, who readily celebrated the inadmissible and the condemned and who offered his readers an exotic vision of anomaly and the artificial flowers of evil. Baudelaire referred to this shift in art's thematic preoccupation in one of his essays, "Salon de 1846," in which he complained that traditional artists restricted themselves to public and recognized subjects such as victories, achievements, and heroism while they ignored the quotidian. There is a range of subject matter, he argued, that is equally heroic: the spectacle of an elegant city, the thousands of stray individuals, the criminals and prostitutes who circulate in the subterranean spaces of a big city (Baudelaire 1923: 199). The modern poet, such as Baudelaire and Cavafy, brings to the center of attention those aspects of life deemed unworthy of art and which, as a result, are relegated to its margins.

Ruskin, as noted earlier, regards such *sujets privés* as inappro-

Poetry

priate material in the artists's civilizing mission. He expresses contempt for a painting by Murillo, finding the representation of barefooted, dirty peasant children degrading. He wonders whether the painting was worth the trouble: "But is there anything else than roguery there, or was it well for the painter to give his time to the painting of those repulsive and wicked children? Do you feel moved with any charity towards those children as you look at them?" (Ruskin 1893: 319 [*The Stones of Venice II*, VI, §60]). To Ruskin's indignant questions Cavafy responds with his own: "What is the meaning of these questions? How do they relate to Art? Should a work of Art answer such questions?" (Tsirkas 1971: 229). Clearly, for Cavafy, Ruskin's objections have little to do with art, since they introduce moral, that is, nonaesthetic criteria that are ultimately invalid in the judgment of art. Yet these questions highlight the incompatible positions of Ruskin and Cavafy.

Their divergences become even clearer when superimposed on Foucault's instructive differentiation between traditional and effective history. In his essay "Nietzsche, Genealogy and History," Foucault designates as the main characteristic of traditional history its tendency to establish a close relationship between proximity and distance, taking into its field of interest the heights, noblest periods, purest forms, most abstract ideas, and greatest individuals; effective history, on the other hand, shortens its vision to things nearest it, concentrating not on distant, transcendental phenomena or ideas, but on the reality at hand (1977: 155). If one substitutes for traditional history the aesthetics of Ruskin, with its insistence on noble emotions and sublime themes, and for effective history Cavafy's radical view of art, with its emphasis on this world and its sordidness and banality, it is possible to schematize the two positions and the assumptions informing them. Ruskin represents the traditionalist school, which held the view that art reflects the moral fabric of society and contributes to its edification; Cavafy stands for an aesthetic trend, which rejected moralistic theories of the aesthetic and incorporated those subjects that had hitherto been excluded from the concerns of high art.

MODERNISM

One such area is art or poetry itself. Art may often have made self-reflexive references, but the work itself did not become a dominant artistic preoccupation until the end of the nineteenth and especially the beginning of the twentieth century with the advent of modernism. The roots of this development no doubt lie in the Kantian isolation of the aesthetic judgment, and in the subsequent detachment of beauty from its social context. A shift took place in the priorities of art, away from content to form, from representing to the mode of representation. This departure from tradition manifested itself in both the theoretical and poetic texts of the nineteenth century: for instance, Gautier's attack on the utilitarian notion of art; Poe's laudation of the poem itself as "thoroughly dignified" and "supremely noble"; Mallarmé's autotelic aesthetic structure, which falls in love with itself; Wilde's artwork, which revels in introspective admiration; Pater's advocacy of art for art's sake; and finally Cavafy's own celebration of formalism and his affirmation of both the artificiality and function of art.

Fascinated with its internal construction and obsessed with its perfectibility, art essentially withdrew within its own borders and proposed itself as subject. Like its prototype, the romantic notion of the organism, it was essentially self-mirroring, self-sustaining, and self-sufficient. The work thematized its narcissistic obsession. It projected a portrait of itself as a self-conscious, autonomous structure, one that was aware of its aesthetic existence and that spoke about the process of its creation. To return to Abrams's grid, with the growing emphasis placed on the work as a legitimate object of concern, art came to be understood less from the perspective of the world, the audience, or the artist, and more from itself.[20] With modernism the self-conscious work reached its ultimate apotheosis and became one of that movement's most recognizable features. As Malcolm Bradbury explains in his introduction to *Modernism*: "A modernist work tends to be technically introverted and analytic, incorporating its own critique to a point at

---

[20] In criticism a comparable change occured with the emergence of Russian formalism, and its heirs Czech and French structuralism. All three schools examined the text from the perspective of its formalist qualities and intrinsic devices and strove to differentiate literature from nonliterature. In the Anglo-American world, new criticism was equally text-oriented, seeking empirically to analyze a work apart from its social environment. Anglo-American deconstruction also belongs to this tradition of aesthetic and exegetic isolationism in that, in attempting to determine the text's internal paradoxes and fissures, it ignores its social and historical aspect.

Poetry

which this critique may form the true subject—the work is about its own making, questioning its own practices and presuppositions" (Bradbury and McFarlane 1976: 370).

Indeed, as art became more autonomous, as it shed all that was alien to itself, it became problematic to itself, crisis set in, and this self-criticism was incorporated as one of its themes (Bürger 1984: 27).[21] This criticism, according to Clement Greenberg, was not necessarily negative or subversive, but resulted in each art gaining a better understanding of itself; it acquired specialization and a delineation of its own field of control. Every art set out to prove that it could provide something missing in other arts; it had to determine "through the operations peculiar to itself, the effects peculiar to itself (Greenberg 1973: 68). The work became aware of itself as art; it grew conscious of the problems involved in producing art and spoke about them. The modernist work calls attention to itself as a man-made product; it presents itself, not as a window to the world, but as an opaque structure that undermines the reader's attempts to grasp reality by constantly reminding him or her, through its allusions to itself, of its artistic and artificial nature. The illusions of a traditional text, which facilitate self-forgetfulness and an identification with the world, are suppressed, and conversely, those properties that define the work's "artisticality" are foregrounded. Such a work demands to be understood not as a reflection of reality, nor as an expression of the artist's soul, but as an autonomous subject existing in its own right. The work is acutely aware of the problematics of art, of its genesis, and its aesthetic status.[22]

---

[21] Peter Bürger argues further that the historical avant-garde (dadaism, surrealism, futurism) reacted against this notion of autonomy and attempted to eliminate the concept of art as an institution—which had come into existence with German idealism and the emergence of the bourgeois class—by first calling attention to art's institutional nature and by then deconstructing the idea of aesthetic individuality through the introduction of mass-produced art, such as Duchamp's "readymades." The avant-garde tried to subvert art's separation from life, which modernism promoted through its exaltation of high, pure art. Cavafy, of course, being a member of high modernism, cannot be classified in this extremely radicalized and iconoclastic manifestation of modernity. Cavafy's writing never carries the idea of universal negation so characteristic of the avant-garde, and his aesthetic assumptions tend to support the autonomy of art rather than destroy it. For a useful distinction between the historical avant-garde and modernism, see Calinescu (1977).
[22] Walter Ong, in his *Orality and Literacy* (1982), provides another account of the appearance of self-sufficiency and autonomy in art. He sees it as a product of our

Poetry

This aspect of modernism represents an important dimension of Cavafy's poetic writing as many of the poems deal directly or indirectly with poetry and art in general. Cavafy's poetry is to a large extent preoccupied with itself; it is self-conscious. This examination of his poetics is itself facilitated by the fact that the poems either "speak" of themselves as poems or are concerned with questions such as the position of the poet, the role of imagination, the nature of beauty, the function of memory, the mechanisms of tradition. "Kaisarion," a poem dramatizing its own coming into existence, vividly demonstrates this modernist feature of self-referentiality. (See Chapter 1 for the text.) "Kaisarion" opens with a reference to the text out of which it emerged. The speaker-poet explains that in order to pass some time and also to get acquainted with a historical period, he consults a collection of Ptolemaic inscriptions. He browses indifferently through the register of famous names and their eulogies, but does not stop until he discovers a minor reference to an insignificant king.

> When I'd found the facts I wanted
> I would have put the book away, but a brief
> insignificant mention of King Kaisarion
> suddenly caught my eye . . .

The poet's eye passes over the hackneyed epithets of glorious kings and pauses at the contrastingly unbombastic reference to the barely known Kaisarion, whom he then chooses as subject of the poem. He selects Kaisarion precisely because of the king's lack of historical stature and notability. This seemingly unorthodox strategy is quite typical of postromantic, and especially modernist, poetics and reveals its penchant for marginalized figures. In so doing, the modernist poet sets out his priorities and also implicitly criticizes his precursors for valorizing in their verse the "brilliant, glorious, mighty, and benevolent." Cavafy's disagreement with Rus-

---

typographic culture. According to Ong, print encourages the sense of closure and finality and gives rise to self-enclosed and privately consumed texts (which are legally protected by copyright) (p. 131). The notion of an autonomous utterance created by writing and fostered by print is foreign to oral culture, which did not divorce poetry from its context (p. 161). Indeed, such recent innovations as the concept of intertextuality, which undermines aesthetic autonomy and originality, was taken for granted by manuscript culture, since it deliberately and unashamedly created texts out of other texts (p. 133).

Poetry

kin is clear here as the poet in "Kaisarion" descends from the sublime heights occupied by traditional poets and chooses instead material deemed by them unworthy of poetry. He defamiliarizes the accepted notion of the poetic theme, but more important, by selecting the forgotten Kaisarion, he, as a belated poet, makes his own original contribution to tradition. Though much has been written about the illustrious heroes and heroines of history, the Caesars and Cleopatras, little has been said of Kaisarion; thus as a subject he offers much more scope for creativity:

> Because so little
> is known about you from history,
> I could fashion you more freely in my mind.

These lines give testimony to the direction taken by modern art in making central the margins of society and the displaced elements of history, and in enabling its repressed voices to speak.

It is important to note that the emphasis in the poem falls not so much on the historical figure of Kaisarion, as on his rescue from oblivion and transformation into a subject of poetry.

> I made you good-looking and sensitive.
> My art gives your face
> a dreamy, appealing beauty.

Tehni (art making) is foregrounded throughout the poem by references to poetry and its composition. From the initial allusion to the poem's textual source, to the discussion of relevant topics of imagination and tradition, the poem is engaged in self-reflection, its own coming into existence, the techniques of poetic composition and their effect. In this respect "Kaisarion" is a poem conscious of itself as art.

Another poem operating in a similar manner is "Orophernis" (1915). The principal figure, Orophernis, is so obscure that history books have devoted only a few lines to him. That thesaurus of classical learning, the *Real-Encyclopädie der klassischen Altertumswissenschaft*, has a very short listing for him, and the *Oxford Classical Dictionary* mentions him indirectly in the entry dealing with his father. The modernist poem, however, rescues him from historical indifference by converting the scanty information into a poem. As

Poetry

in "Kaisarion," the first stanza refers to the poem's source of inspiration, which in this case is a drachma coin bearing the portrait of Orophernis. This and the last stanza both differ from the rest of the poem in that they concern the coin, which the narrator is holding before him, and significantly, in that they are typographically separated from it, enclosing it in a ring composition. They are situated in the narrator's present, during the time of the poem's composition, whereas the inner six stanzas recount Orophernis's life. The inner stanzas serve as the poem that has been inspired by the face on the coin, while the outer stanzas act as a reminder that what has taken place is the making of a poem. The temporal space separating the two acts suggests the composition of the poem within the poem.

While this inner text traces the life history of Orophernis, the outer frame emphasizes that this is done through the medium of poetry, which has resurrected the forgotten footnotes or failures of history. The story of Orophernis as dramatized in the poem runs as follows: as a child, he was exiled from his ancestral palace in Cappadocia and raised in Ionia as a Greek; when the Syrians invaded Cappadocia, he was installed on the throne only to be overthrown by the Cappadocians, so he returned to Syria and gave himself to dissolute living. One day, recalling his royal heritage, he began scheming an unspecified plot:

> he tried to start an intrigue
> to do something, come up with a plan;
> but he failed pitifully and that was that.

The account ends on an uncertain note, as if information were lacking on this particular point. In any case, Orophernis did not succeed and almost disappeared from the annals of history.

> His end must have been recorded somewhere only to be lost;
> or maybe history passed over it
> and rightly didn't bother to notice
> a thing so trivial.

This penultimate stanza, with its somewhat brutal conclusion, brings sharply to the fore the difference between history and the modernist poem: history chose not to commit to writing the end of

Poetry

Orophernis (or many other details of his life); it ignored him and allowed him nearly to disappear. By contrast, art preserved his beauty by inscribing it on the coin, and then devoted an entire poem to this obscure figure. Whereas traditional historiography primarily records sensational events, golden ages, and great men, the modernist poem undermines this lofty approach by designating as subjects the failures and the forgotten. This is one of the functions of modernist art; it seeks the mediocrities of the world—the Kaisarions, Orophernises, Wozzeks, Leopold Blooms, Willy Lomans, Salieris—and absolves them.

This preservation of a marginalized entity serves as one of the poem's main concerns, for the poem does not so much re-create the life of Orophernis as transform the disparate historical data into a work of art. The conspicuous positioning of the two outer stanzas, with their implicit criticism of traditional historiography, and the consequent valorization of the powers of poetry highlight the dual function of the poem as art and as a site of art making. The self-consciousness of the text obstructs the reader's identification with the story of Orophernis by interrupting the illusion of mimesis, that is, that the poem is "about" him; it heightens the immediate artistic experience by calling attention to its own techniques and to its creative capacities. "Orophernis" reflects on itself as an object to be read, studied, and aesthetically appreciated. As mentioned earlier, many of Cavafy's poems can be termed self-referential inasmuch as they are interested in various aspects of poetry and art—its creation, reception, and place in the world—and they present themselves essentially as autonomous, autotelic, and autogenous entitites. Not all poems, however, see themselves as self-enclosed and self-consuming artifacts; some strive to shatter the self-sufficiency of modernism and, in so doing, to explore other factors in the production and dissemination of art.

TOWARD A POSTMODERNISM?

"Of the few things one can affirm with certainty," Cavafy writes in a comment about Ruskin, "is that no one is competent to say where art begins and especially where it ends" (Tsirkas 1971: 241). In this passage, Cavafy discards the notions of *arché* and *telos* and the idea of aesthetic perfection, since without any definable

Poetry

beginnings or ends, art cannot exist as a self-sufficient object, an immutable *Ding an sich*. Art is an open not a closed system, its boundaries are variable, and its meaning is subject to revision. The problem of the relativity of meaning is raised in many of Cavafy's posthumously published texts. For instance, in the "Ars Poetica" Cavafy observes: "Things cannot and should not be lasting, for man would then be 'all of a piece' and stagnate in sentimental inactivity" (1963c: 54). Cavafy makes allowances for change and renewal, which he sees as two desirable qualities. (Yet, as we remember, Cavafy saw beauty primarily as an absolute and indelible ideal, which hovered above contingency.) In the same text Cavafy argues that art may be inconsistent as feelings themselves are contradictory: "a state of feeling is true and false, possible and impossible at the same time, or rather by turns. And the poet . . . gives one side which does not mean that he denies the obverse, or even . . . that he wishes to imply that the side he treats is the truest, or the oftener true" (1963c: 42). This passage diverges from previous theoretical observations, which regarded art as a source of coherence, unifying the disparate elements of life into meaningful wholes. Here contrariness and paradox disturb the transcendental order of art; disorder and discontinuity emerge through totalization and static unities. Poetry therefore is denied access to the Idea, since in a world where contradiction is embraced, where things can be both true and false, possible and impossible, such absolute values are no longer necessary or beneficial.

Under these conditions, Cavafy argues, a poet presents one side at a time; he "merely describes a possible and occurring state of feeling" instead of aspiring toward the absolute and the eventual initiation to truth. It follows that truth itself is not an immutable concept but variable and also ephemeral: "If a thought has been really true for a day, its becoming false the next day does not deprive it of its claim to verity. It may have been only a passing or short-lived truth, but if intense and serious it is worthy to be received" (Cavafy 1963c: 54). In this context of instability and inconstancy poetry simply records these local or private truths, without privileging any one of them as the "truest or the oftener true." This of course contrasts with the position held in some of the early poems, such as "The Poet and the Muse," which affirmed poetry's exclusive right to truth: "Only the chords of the harp / know the truth." In many of the posthumous notes, as in the one examined, the existence of truth is disputed and no fixed answer emerges for poetry to know and preach. "Do Truth and Falsehood really exist?" Cavafy asks. "Or is there only the Old and the New—and Falsehood is simply the aging of Truth?" (1983a: 24). With this very Nietzschean aphorism Cavafy posits truth in a relational framework; refusing to oppose truth to falsehood, he denies it the privilege that this dichotomy necessarily grants it.

It is from this perspective that Cavafy attacks Ruskin's idealist aesthetic theory. Ruskin, alluding to the relationship between painting and reality, proposes that the noblest pictures "are true or inspired ideals seen in a moment to be ideal, that is to say, the result of the highest powers of the imagination engaged in the discovery and appreciation of the purest truths" (1893: 118–19 [*Modern Painters III*, IV, 10, §19]). Picking up Ruskin's reference to the "purest truths," Cavafy asks: "But what are these truths? By truth does he mean Beauty? But Beauty is sometimes contradictory (truth they want positive and affirmative) and is often the product of opinions and habits and very often the product of a sickened and deceiving soul" (Tsirkas 1971: 236). This passage introduces two issues. The first concerns the mutable nature of beauty, which, like truth, changes from day to day and from person to person. It does not exist as an absolute in the idealist context described by Ruskin (or sometimes by Cavafy). Furthermore, it is not a pre-given idea, but a human construct, a result of "opinions" and "habits," not hovering in a transcendental realm, but produced by specific social and cultural forces. It is subject to concrete and material factors, which, along with the opinions and habits, change from time to time. These two elements, the opinions and habits, recall the word "fashions," which was also used in connection with art in "The Reflections of an Old Artist." From his examination of tradition the old poet concluded that "literature is a vain thing with its fashions [*sirmus*] that change often." In both passages it is argued that art, or beauty, is directly affected by changes in public taste, hence its value is relative, varying with the social context and historical periods in which it is judged.

Such arguments suggest that another notion of art exists in

Poetry

Cavafy's work, which contrasts with the dominant concept of art outlined in this chapter. In this view, art exists not as an autotelic structure, which all men and women recognize and value, but is rather constructed and used by them. Art flees its idealist realm and settles in history. The work of art, the poem, repudiates the notion of perfection and no longer aspires to timelessness. It cannot be described as self-enclosed or self-sufficient, since it reaches out to culture and history in which it is implicated.

A poem that exemplifies these attributes is "The Enemies" (mentioned in Chapter 2 and to be discussed further in Chapter 5). This poem, unlike much of Cavafy's poetry, cannot be designated as simply self-reflexive, since it lacks that concern with the autonomous and hermetic inner self so characteristic of modernism. This text exists less as a self-consuming artifact and more as an embodiment of *energeia*, which it exercises on previous texts and which will in turn be forced on it. In contrast to the modernist poem, it is not preoccupied with its own internal structure and aesthetic properties; rather, it deals with its position in the broad system of intertextuality and the power of interpretation it wields. By focusing on a text's possible fate at the hands of its future interpreters—a reception presented in terms of power and conflict—instead of on its inherently timeless qualities, "The Enemies" replaces the notion of artistic perfection with that of violence, the hermeneutic violence brought to bear on each text by its "enemies." The poem sees itself and other texts as participants in this power struggle to interpret and be interpreted; in this sense it does not reside, like its modernist counterparts, in its own niche, distanced from the world and divorced from life, but involves itself in history's struggles for the appropriation of notions and concepts. It draws attention not to its aesthetic wholeness, but rather to the conditions that make it what it is. It brings to the fore its very worldliness and its position in the public sphere. "The Enemies" occupies a prominent place in Cavafy's poetics inasmuch as it rejects the aesthetic isolationism characteristic of most of his poetry, and in so doing points to new directions for the analysis and understanding of art.

4. LANGUAGE AND WRITING

In Chapter 3 I mentioned that the appearance of the autonomous and autotrophic artwork was related to a similar development in the latter part of the nineteenth century, when language emerged as an opaque and independent object of study. A crisis in the way language was understood and used led to a questioning of its expressive and referential function. This linguistic skepticism manifested itself in the preoccupation with artistic form and in the search for an autonomous poetic discourse, a pure yet absolute type of poetry that would subsume all reality yet allude only to itself. My aim in this chapter is to determine how Cavafy's poetics relates to this general crisis in language. I examine Cavafy's conception of language in order to see whether language appears in his work as a problematical notion, or whether he regards it as a transparent medium for the expression of feeling. It is important to clarify two issues related to this subject. First, as outlined above, my intention is to study Cavafy's *conception* of language as a theoretical construct and not his understanding of the Greek language itself, nor his use of the Greek linguistic tradition. The latter is a valid approach, yet it does not concern itself with poetics but with a stylistic examination of his work.

The second difficulty is related to this and has to do with the virtual absence in Cavafy of any prose texts dealing with language theoretically. Cavafy did, however, write a series of articles and essays that deal, sometimes indirectly, with matters concerning the Greek language. In the essay "Professor Blackie on the Modern Greek Language" (1892), Cavafy examines an article published by the English scholar John Blackie on both Polilas's translation of *Hamlet* (1889) and the Greek linguistic tradition. Cavafy's review essentially addresses the historical development of the Greek language. He writes: "According to Blackie, Hellenism was never the recipient of those strong influences which shape new languages. The four centuries which the Greek nation passed under a foreign yoke was a short period for the formation of a language" (Cavafy 1963b: 37). Cavafy's perspective in the essay is empirical. He ana-

Language and Writing

lyzes the state of the Greek language under the Turkish and Venetian occupations and explores the points of divergence between ancient and modern Greek. While much of the review quotes directly from Blackie's article, Cavafy often clarifies certain linguistic points, offering lexical and syntactical variations.

In other essays, such as "The Poetry of Stratiyis" (1893), "Hristos and not Hrestos" (1901), the review of Politis's *Selections from the Songs of the Greek People* (1914), and of Hubert Pernot's *Grammaire du Grec Moderne* (1917), Cavafy takes a similarly diachronic approach to various aspects of Greek grammar—syntax and morphology—as well as to the literary uses of the Greek language. The central linguistic theme in most of these texts remains the Greek language. The majority of Cavafy's observations are of a practical nature, relating to either a historical or a grammatical approach to Greek. They indicate the range of his linguistic knowledge, his attention to details and matters of orthographical propriety, and his strong interest in the development of the Greek language. They also demonstrate Cavafy's real concern for the literary application of Greek. In these texts Cavafy seems to want to know the Greek language in all its aspects. Language itself, however, is never discussed theoretically; it does not appear as an object of knowledge or as a center of the poetic concern. In these articles language is seen as a medium facilitating the communication of meaning.

An analysis of the poems, however, reveals that another conception of language informed their composition. Examined from an intertextual perspective, their language is shown to be opaque and dense, an object existing in its own right much like the modernist autonomous poem. It signifies not so much an outer reality as it foregrounds itself as an amalgamation of words. Attention focuses on the word, which does not transport readers to the thing, but compels them to observe the properties and mysteries of language. Such a view of language began to appear in the poetic and theoretical discourses of Europe during the late nineteenth century. By situating Cavafy's ideas in the intellectual history of this period, it would be possible to explore his relation to these paradigms and to determine if and how his understanding of language was affected by them.

Language and Writing

LANGUAGE AS OBJECT

The shift in the view of language is investigated by Michel Foucault in *The Order of Things*, in which he explains that in the nineteenth century language became theoretically isolated as a result of the analysis of grammatical structures; it turned into an object of study in its own right (1973: 296). In the seventeenth and eighteenth centuries, Foucault shows, language functioned in the domain of knowledge itself. It was a way of knowing things, since only through the medium of language could the world be understood: "Not because it was part of the world, ontologically interwoven with it (as in the Renaissance), but because it was the first sketch of an order in representations of the world; because it was the initial inevitable way of representing representations" (p. 296). The word stood for the thing, not being a thing in itself; it was transparent. With the independent analysis of grammar, however, as practiced in the nineteenth century, language came to be treated as an organic structure; it acquired a separate mass containing the laws that govern it. Having lost its transparency, it became one object of analysis among others, such as living beings, wealth, value, and history (p. 296). In this respect, the study of language did not result in a more meaningful knowledge of the world but in a better understanding of a particular domain of objectivity—language itself. The emergence of the modern notion of literature, that is, the isolation of particular aspects of language as literary, is the direct consequence of the change in the conception of language. "From the Romantic revolt against a discourse frozen in its own ritual pomp, to the Mallarméan discovery of the word in its impotent power, it becomes clear what the function of literature was, in the nineteenth century, in relation to the modern mode of being of language" (p. 300). Literature withdrew within itself and became a manifestation of language; it gained an independent form, repudiated mimesis, and detached itself from its former values of taste, pleasure, naturalness, and truth. By differentiating itself from the discourse of ideas, literature emerged as an opaque subjectivity, a structure with its own rules and regulations, which expressed nothing but itself. Literature began to address itself to itself as writing.

Language and Writing

In *Writing Degree Zero*, Roland Barthes delineates a similar course in the development of the understanding of language. He draws attention to the period around 1850, when the writer ceased to be a witness to universal truths, the traditional notion of writing began to disintegrate, "and the whole of Literature from Flaubert to the present day, became the problematic of writing" (1968: 3). This was when the notion of Literature came into being, when it entered the system of the fine arts, when literary language lost its transparency and assumed the status of an object that was the result of literary labor.[1] Literature was seen to be produced by a craftsman's labor rather than bursting spontaneously from his imagination. Writing was to be saved, Barthes says, "not by virtue of what it exists for, but thanks to the work it had cost" (p. 63).

The rise of this notion of literature led to the questioning of traditional writing and to the eventual dissolution of its uniformity and unity. The word became isolated, opaque, and dense; language no longer postulated the possibility of communication with others, but was reduced to words as static entities. The word itself was converted into an absolute quantity, bereft of purpose, context, and content. Freed from social overtones, it assumed its existence as an autonomous entity. Literary discourse turned into a vehicle for these "isolated" and "dense" words, which seemed lifeless and unintentioned. Writing became impersonal, as if it no longer emanated from an author. "Literature," declared Mallarmé, "consists in abolishing the man who remains while writing" (1945: 657). The disintegration of language resulted in the silence of writing, as evidenced by Mallarmé's insurmountably difficult textuality. (Paradigmatic of this type of writing is Mallarmé's own untranslatable and almost unreadable poem "Un coup de dés.") Having disassociated itself from its former communicative and mimetic function, the word declared its independence and its exile.

Many nineteenth-century poetic developments occurred in such a theoretical context. Two noteworthy examples already discussed are Flaubert's designs for a book without any external reference, which would be held together by the internal force of its

---

[1] On the question of the emergence of the concept and institution of literature, see Williams (1960, 1977), Wellek (1978), Eagleton (1983), and Bürger (1984).

signs, and Mallarmé's proposal for the ultimate Book, the *Grand Oeuvre*, containing all other texts yet expressing Nothingness.[2] In both, linguistic form comes to the fore; the work exists as unadulterated language, as a series of signifiers without the ponderousness of the signified. In this respect, Mallarmé more than any other poet pushed these ideas to their outer and frightening limits through his attempt to separate literary and nonliterary discourse. For Mallarmé the "literary" and "fictional" were distinct from the "real" and the "worldly"; indeed, he strove to break any connection that might tie the "outside" to the "inside" by isolating the poetic word in empty space so that it would reflect only its own solitary being. He noted in a letter written in 1866 that once we defined poetic form, our task should be to make "the words of a poem self-mirroring—since they are sufficiently autonomous to begin with and need no outside impression—to such a degree that it will seem they do not have a color of their own but are like modulations in a scale" (1959: 234). The Mallarméan word becomes—as Joyce's would later—a floating signifier fully liberated from signification. Mallarmé was one of the first to conceive of literature as a matter of written language, thick and dense, autonomous and anonymous. This conception of language emerged in the dominant current of modernist literature, turning inwardly on itself, its principal aim not to enable signification, but to promote its own palpable being.

    Such literary texts present themselves primarily as written language, insofar as they highlight the strata of textuality cutting through their borders. They are conscious of their position in this network of books. The art of the late nineteenth century, as Foucault explains, is transformed in the phenomenon of the library (1977: 90). Foucault points to two prototypes of such art: Flaubert's *The Temptation of Saint Antony* (written on three separate occasions, 1840, 1856, and 1872) and *Bouvard and Pécuchet* (unfinished but published in 1881). These two novels, Foucault argues, are explicitly situated in a field of books and are produced from other books. *Bouvard and Pécuchet* is profoundly permeated by tis-

---

[2] Here one may add symbolism's envy of and aspirations toward such a nonrepresentational art form as music, which was considered to be pure, autonomous, and free from the substantiality of matter.

Language and Writing

sues of other texts; it incorporates within itself elements of other books and thus presupposes the library as its genesis and grid of reference. *The Temptation of Saint Antony* seems to envelop within its pages the entire spectrum of the world's erudition and take on the grandiose scope of the encyclopedia. The texts of Flaubert, Cavafy, Joyce, Valéry, Rilke, Pound, Borges, and so many authors of the last 150 years are aware of their intertextual relationship with other textures; they are ineluctably implicated in a network of references and allusions to other writings.

LITERATURE AND THE LIBRARY

Cavafy's work is to a certain extent a manifestation of the library from which it stems and about which it speaks. The poems are not only aware of themselves as autotelic and autotrophic entities, but also acknowledge the boundaries they share with other books. When reading a Cavafian poem one is conscious of the other documents assimilated by the poem. In some cases even the narrator or speaker of the poem is involved in this reading. In "Kaisarion" the speaker-poet declares that in order to verify a certain historical period he has consulted a collection of Ptolemaic inscriptions. In the posthumous "Coins" (1920) the speaker examines a book dealing with coins and their inscriptions:

> This is how the wise book renders the Indian
> inscriptions for us on one side of the coins.
> But the book also shows us the other side. . . .

The posthumous "The Rest I Will Tell to Those Down in Hades" (1911) begins with a reference to a book:

> "Indeed" said the proconsul closing the book.
> "This line is beautiful and very true.
> Sophocles wrote it in a deeply philosophic mood."

The "book" in this case is Sophocles' "Ajax," a line of which (865) serves as the title of the poem. In all three examples the idea of the book or the notion of reading are emphatic themes. But the books to which the poems allude do not necessarily act as the source of the poem as much as they highlight the poem's textual nature. The

Language and Writing

poem "Tomb of the Grammarian Lysias" (1914), which concerns a grammarian and a library, strongly underscores this aspect of Cavafy's poetry. The grammarian Lysias has appropriately been buried next to the library of Beirut, near his most cherished possessions:

> The spot is beautifully chosen.
> We put him near those things of his
> that he remembers maybe even there:
> notes, texts, commentaries, variants,
> voluminous studies of Greek idioms.
> Also, this way, as we go to the books,
> we'll see, we'll honor his tomb.

Lysias and the other scholars in the library worked with texts; they analyzed manuscripts and wrote commentaries. By dramatizing the theater of textuality, this poem sets the scene for so many other texts of Cavafy's that share this preoccupation with writing, knowledge, and books. Cavafy's poems are populated with Bouvards and Pécuchets, with scholars, students, sophists, philosophers, and rhetoricians who wander through the domain of textual reference. In this labyrinth of books the concept of written language prevails as a literary language, which having repudiated its communicative function, partakes in the drama of its own being.

LITERATURE AS WRITTEN LANGUAGE

In Cavafy this preoccupation with written language manifests itself in three distinct paradigms of textual reference that are enacted by the poems. Cavafy's poetry illustrates its "writerly" aspect by absorbing within itself other texts so as to remind the reader that it is inescapably infiltrated by written documents. Many of the poems conspicuously cite other poems or books and display them either within or without the poem, indicating in this way their very textual composition and their existence in a grid of writing. As mentioned above, the poems may be grouped in three categories, the first of which is characterized by the inclusion of passages of other authors, usually between the title and the verses.

Language and Writing

Here is a list of these poems, followed by the source of the quotation:[3]

CATEGORY A

Rejected Poems
1. "Speech and Silence" (1892)—Arabic proverb

Posthumous Poems
2. "To the Ladies" (1884?)—Shakespeare, "Much Ado about Nothing" (II, iii)
3. "Nous n'osons plus chanter les roses" (1892)
4. "In the House of the Soul" (1894)—Rodenbach
5. ["La Jeunesse Blanche"] 1895—Rodenbach
6. "Distinguishing Marks" (1895)—Imerius
7. "The Intervention of the Gods" (1899)—Emerson; Dumas, "L'Etrangère"
8. "Poseidonians" (1906)—Atheneus, *Deipnosophistai* (XIV, 31A)
9. "The Rest I Will Tell to Those Down in Hades" (1913)—Sophocles, "Ajax" (865)

Published Poems
10. "Che fece . . . il gran rifiuto" (1901)—Dante *Inferno* (III, 60)
11. "Unfaithfulness" (1904)—Plato, *Republic* (II, 383)
12. "King Dimitrios" (1906)—Plutarch, *The Life of Dimitrios*
13. "That's the Man" (1909)—Lucian, *The Dream* (II)
14. "The Wise Perceive Things about to Happen" (1915)—Philostratos, *Life of Apollonios of Tyana* (VIII, 7)
15. "Julian and the Antiochians" (1926)—Julian, *The Beard-Hater*

With the exception of "Che fece . . . il gran rifiuto" and "The Rest I Will Tell to Those Down in Hades"—where the foreign passages actually serve as the title—the quoted material provides either a motto or an introduction to the poem. These poems themselves can be divided into two subcategories: the ones borrowing

---

[3] The author and/or work of each quotation is supplied, if available. In some cases neither has yet been determined.

Language and Writing

passages from literary works and those from nonliterary sources. In the first case, by referring to other works of literature, the quotations set the poems in a literary context and provide another perspective to the poem. They offer the reader another tool in the deciphering of the often cryptic meaning. Examples 1–5, 9, and 10 fit this classification. In the second subcategory, the passages originate largely from discursive writing, such as history, biography, and philosophy, and situate the arguments of each poem in their respective historical or cultural background. Again such information becomes useful to the reader in the interpretation of the poem. This is true of "Julian and the Antiochians," in which the passage from Julian contributes actual historical data to the poem. In some cases, as in 12 and 13, the poem elaborates on the original quotation; indeed "Poseidonians" may be seen as an extended paraphrase. The quoted material in both subcategories is acknowledged, the source often identified; outside the poem proper, it comments upon it.

In the second category of intertextuality quotations are incorporated within the poem most often as fragments, occasionally in their entirety:

CATEGORY B

Posthumous Poems
1. "Correspondence according to Baudelaire" (1891)—Baudelaire, "Correspondances"
2. "Parthen [It Was Seized]" (1921)—verses from modern Greek folk songs

Published Poems
3. "If Actually Dead" (1920)—Philostratos, *Life of Apollonios of Tyana*
4. "Young Men of Sidon (A.D. 400)" (1920)—Aeschylus (his alleged epitaph)
5. "Anna Komnina" (1920)—Anna Komnina, *Alexiad*
6. "Julian Seeing Contempt" (1923)—letter of Julian the Apostate
7. "Apollonios of Tyana in Rhodes" (1925)—Philostratos, *Life of Apollonios* (V, 22)
8. "Anna Dalassini" (1927)—royal decree

Language and Writing

9. "You Didn't Understand" (1928)—speech given by Julian, in Sozomenos, *Ecclesiastical History* (V, 18)
10. "Come, O King of the Lacedaimonians" (1928)—Plutarch, *Life of Kleomenes* (28)
11. "In the Year 200 B.C." (1931)—document

In these poems the non-Cavafian texts provide more than an additional commentary, since in most cases they are integrated within the body of the poem and sometimes, as in "Parthen," within its syntactical structure. Embedded in the poem, they cannot be removed from it or ignored. Yet despite this intricate relationship, they are marked out conspicuously as foreign material by the use of either the original language or quotation marks. Often the source is actually cited.

The tension between the poem proper and the foreign textual matter may be seen clearly in "Parthen," which concerns Greek folk songs. It begins with the following verses:

> These days I have been reading demotic songs
> about the exploits and the wars of the klephts . . .
> I have also been reading mournful songs about the loss of
>   Constantinople.

In the subsequent stanzas the poem incorporates verses from these demotic songs, but keeps the actual Pontic dialect of the original, setting it off with quotation marks:[4]

> But alas, a fateful bird "comes from Constantinople,"
> on its "little wing it had a written paper
> and it did not even perch on the vine or in the orchard,
> but went and perched on the root of the cypress."

The poem has conspicuously absorbed another text within its boundaries. The reader, confronted with two linguistic registers, notices the two modes of writing and the two different types of composition. Similarly, the original language of the supposed epitaph of Aeschylus is retained in the excerpt quoted in "Young

---

[4] Obviously the effects of this tension here and in the following poems are lost in translation.

Language and Writing

Men of Sidon (A.D. 400)," but the border between the words of the narrator and the cited passage remains deliberately perceptible:

> They were readings from Meleager, Krinagoras, Rhianos.
> But when the actor recited
> "Here lies Aeschylus, the Athenian, son of Euphorion"
> (stressing maybe more than he should have
> "his renowned valor" and "sacred Marathonian grove")
> a vivacious young man, mad about literature,
> suddenly jumped up and said.

The fragments from the tragedian's epitaph, the text within the quotation marks, are interwoven within the poem, yet epitaph fragments and poem are linguistically incompatible; the editor provides in the notes a modern Greek translation of the original for the benefit of the contemporary Greek reader, who must cope with two distinct usages of the language. In "Anna Komnina" the speaker quotes from the prologue of Komnina's *Alexiad*, juxtaposing them with his own remarks:

> Her soul is all vertigo.
> "And I bathe my eyes," she tells us,
> "in rivers of tears. . . . Alas for the waves" of her eyes,
> "alas for the revolutions." Sorrow burns her
> "to the bones and the marrow and the splitting" of her soul.

The anonymous narrator here in a sense provides a running and ironic commentary to Komnina's text, which is written in Byzantine Greek. The phrase "she tells us" indicates that he is engaged in textual analysis, explicating the prologue for his readers.

Similar devices are employed in other texts to inform the reader that the particular passage is a citation. In "Come, O King of the Lacedaimonians" the clause "says Plutarch" is inserted between the eleventh and twelfth lines to identify the source of the quoted fragment and, moreover, to emphasize that it has infiltrated the poem. We see the same thing in "Anna Dalassini," in which the very process of textual borrowing is highlighted. The encomia, the narrator says, appearing on the royal decree that was issued by Alexios Komninos in honor of his mother are many: "here *let us transfer* one phrase only / a phrase that is beautiful, sub-

Language and Writing

lime: / She never uttered those cold words 'mine' or 'yours' " [my emphasis].[5] What is interesting here is that this phrase actually calls attention to the transference of sentences from one written document to another, the transcription of signs from one discursive level to another. As such, the last line (again in Byzantine Greek) is significant not as a reference to Anna Dalassini, but as a quoted text; the sentence does not so much describe a historical figure or situation as reflect upon itself as a document and on the process of its composition and repetition.

Readers of this type of poetry are relentlessly made aware of "foreign" passages in the texts at hand and of their reproduction, paraphrase, and parody. They are also compelled to maneuver through the labyrinth of writing and translate these texts into modern Greek, since (with the obvious exception of Baudelaire's "Correspondances") the fragments are extracted from classical, Hellenistic, or Byzantine sources. As readers work through the layers of reference, exegesis, and annotation, they become conscious of the writing in which they are enmeshed. This grafting represents an extensive variety of texts, including literature, philosophy, and history. The passage in "Julian Seeing Contempt," for instance, is taken from a letter written by Julian the Apostate (A.D. 361–63) to Theodoros, high priest of Asia. The thematically related poem "You Didn't Understand" contains extracts of a speech delivered by Julian to the Christians. In "Anna Dalassini" the last line comes from a seal, whereas the first verse of "In the Year 200 B.C." quotes part of an inscription sent to Athens by Alexander the Great. The emphasis consistently falls on the broad grid of the written word—epic, history, biography, epistle, official decrees, inscriptions, and epitaphs. It is in this sense that Cavafy's poetry may be said to contain the archive within itself; it incorporates written documents and openly boasts of its intertextuality. The poem calls attention to the texts it has absorbed, which in turn refer to other documents, creating an effect of infinite bibliographical allusion.

One poem that embodies several layers of text, and in so

---

[5] I translate *metaferume* literally as "transfer," whereas Keeley and Sherrard render it as "offer." The literal translation is much more helpful to my argument.

Language and Writing

doing dramatizes its intertextuality, is "If Actually Dead." This poem succeeds in "reading" a number of texts simultaneously and in grafting one on the other:

> "Where did the Sage withdraw to, where did he disappear?
> After his many miracles,
> the renown of his teaching
> which spread to so many countries,
> he suddenly hid himself and nobody knew for certain
> what became of him
> (nor did anybody ever see his grave).
> Some spread it around that he died at Ephesus.
> But Damis doesn't say so in his memoir.
> Damis says nothing about the death of Apollonios.
> Others reported that he disappeared at Lindos.
> Or maybe the story is true
> about his assumption in Crete,
> at the ancient sanctuary of Diktynna.
> But then again we have that miraculous,
> that supernatural apparition of his
> before a young student at Tyana.
> Maybe the time hasn't yet come for him to return
> and show himself to the world again;
> or maybe, transfigured, he moves among us
> unrecognized—. But he will come again
> as he was, teaching the ways of truth; and then of course
> he'll bring back the worship of our gods
> and our elegant Hellenic rites."
>
> These were the musings of one of the few pagans,
> one of the very few left,
> as he sat in his shabby room just after reading
> Philostratos' *On Apollonios of Tyana*.
> But even he—a trivial and cowardly man—
> played the Christian in public and went to church.
> It was the time when Justin the Elder
> reigned in total piety,
> and Alexandria, a godly city,
> detested pitiful idolators.

Language and Writing

The poem's title, in archaisizing Greek, at once alerts the reader to the foreign documents included in the poem, in this case an excerpt quoted from Philostratos's *Life of Apollonios of Tyana* (A.D. 200). There follows the first stanza in quotation marks, which, as the reader discovers in the second one, contains the reflections of an imaginary sophist that have been inspired by his reading of Philostratos. The reader of the poem is thus lodged in the context of reading. But there occurs an allusion to another text, that of Damis, a student of Apollonios, on whose reminiscences Philostratos allegedly based his work. So there emerges out of the poem a series of successive texts extending from the first to the twentieth century, each one framing its predecessor:

1. memoirs of Damis (latter half of first century A.D.);
2. *Life of Apollonios of Tyana* by Philostratos (A.D. 200);
3. reflections of the sophist (first stanza; mid-sixth century A.D.);
4. original draft of poem (1897);
5. final draft (1920).[6]

The memoirs of Damis, which are incorporated in the biography composed by Philostratos, serve as a foundation; this evokes the sophist's own interpretation, the first stanza, which is followed by the poem as a whole. In these overlapping layers of textuality, however, there plays the shadow of still another text—the first version of the poem, written in 1897 and entitled "Apusia."

The Greek draft of this poem is still missing, but a translation of it, "Absence," survives (Cavafy 1963b: 241). This original poem, which roughly corresponds to the first stanza of "If Actually Dead," refers to no other authors or texts. In the revision of the poem (1910) and in the final version, Cavafy changed the title and included the allusions to Damis and Apollonios. More important, he enclosed this first stanza in quotation marks and composed another stanza, informing the reader that the first constitutes a dif-

---

[6] As deconstructionists would argue, this increasing proliferation of texts does not terminate with the final draft of 1920, but continues with each new reading and/or translation of the poem. The issue of where the sage withdrew, the fact with which all texts are concerned, is left unresolved. What seems to be important is not the life of the sage, but the various textual accounts it has prompted.

Language and Writing

ferent level of discourse, the reflections of a sophist inspired by Philostratos's *Life of Apollonios of Tyana*. The original poem had been drastically transformed, for while "Absence" has as its subject an unspecified sage, "If Actually Dead" addresses itself to his biography as it was transcribed by various modes of narrative. It deals with the readings and interpretations to which Apollonios's life was subjected and suggests that we know of this life only through textual intervention; thus, we will never come to understand Apollonios's "real" life, but only its representation in various documents. "If Actually Dead" differs appreciably from "Absence" in acknowledging its debt to previous narration, and in so doing it highlights the intertextual relationship between itself and its precursors. "If Actually Dead" sees itself as one element in a signifying chain that addresses the life of Apollonios. In this way it understands itself as writing, as a language that does not so much inform or give access to thought as bring to the fore its own linguistic form. It is a literary language that, in the words of Mallarmé, gives the initiative to words (1945: 336).

This foregrounding of the opaque word becomes more apparent in the third category of intertextuality in Cavafy, characterized by the absorption into the poem of fictitious texts, that is, passages actually composed by Cavafy but presented as authentic historical documents. Whereas in previous examples the original texts were recovered from the archive of history, these are invented and filed in a fabricated literary library. As in the previous groups, different modes of writing are represented:

CATEGORY C

Published Poems
1. "In the Month of Athyr" (1917)—inscription
2. "Imenos" (1919)—epistle
3. "Dimaratos" (1921)—epideictic essay
4. "Those Who Fought for the Achaian League" (1922)—epigram
5. "Epitaph of Antiochos, King of Kommagini" (1923)—epitaph
6. "In a Township of Asia Minor" (1926)—proclamation

Language and Writing

7. "Kimon, Son of Learchos, 22, Student of Greek Literature (in Kyrini)" (1928)—epitaph

As in the former Category B, similar strategies are employed to identify and highlight the supposed quotation. The difference here is that these "pretexts" far outweigh the rest of the poem in importance and in fact develop into its most dynamic part. The nonquoted material is relegated to the function of introducing or commenting on the fictitious document.

The earliest of these poems, "In the Month of Athyr," contains excerpts of an imaginary inscription interwoven within its syntactical structure, which a modern reader (the speaker of the poem) attempts to decipher. Even the first line of the poem sets us in the context of reading: "I can just read the inscription on this ancient stone." The difficulties inherent in the extraction of meaning from the stone's fragmented state are visually conveyed through punctuation and typography. For instance, rather than being arranged in stanzas, the poem is divided vertically, so that in the very act of reading it one encounters a caesura in the flow of the sentences. The wear and tear of the stone is illustrated by dots and lacunae, whose threatening gaps the reader-speaker attempts to complete by supplying missing parts within square brackets. The emphasis falls on the process of reading, on the speaker's undaunted endeavor to uncover meaning from an almost arbitrary dispersion of signs.[7]

> I can just read the inscription   on this ancient stone.
> "Lo[r]d Jesus Christ."   I make out a "So[u]l."
> "In the mon[th] of Athyr"   "Lefkio[s] went to sleep."
> Where his age is mentioned   "lived to the age of"—
> the Kappa Zeta shows   that he went to sleep a young man.
> In the corroded part I see   "Hi[m] . . . Alexandrian."
> Then there are three   badly mutilated lines—
> though I can pick out   a few words, like "our tea[r]s,"
>   "grief,"

---

[7] For the notion of reading in Cavafy, see Dimiroulis (1983) and Lambropoulos (1983a). With regard to "In the Month of Athyr," although I am working with Keeley and Sherrard's translation, I have decided to divide the poem vertically as in the original Greek, since this is more useful for my purposes.

Language and Writing

>   then "tears" again,   and "sorrow to [us] his [f]riends."
>   I think Lefkios must   have been greatly loved.
>   In the month of Athyr   Lefkios went to sleep.

The many verbs of reading and deciphering highlight the speaker's effort to discover the message in the corroded stone. He tries to extract its meaning, to decode the private truth inscribed in the signs. Yet the reader's longing for such an unmediated experience remains unfulfilled, for his attempts to resurrect the dead letter, to transcend the corruption of the epigraph, and of time, end in failure. The written word intervenes to make its presence felt in all its opacity; it suspends its representational function, refusing to reveal the cryptic message of the inscription. Despite the reader's exhaustive efforts, he is able to determine with some certainty only the name Lefkios, his age, date of death, and that he was greatly loved. The words do not disclose any additional information, nor do they lead to the world or to the private experience that the reader wishes to discover. In this way the poem affirms itself as written language that, as Vassilis Lambropoulos points out, must be read visually and not heard (1983a: 663). Literary language here foregrounded, unlike the standard language, is not expressive but self-referential, and is aware of its own aesthetic techniques and devices.

This literary language is powerfully emphasized in "Dimaratos," a poem comprising two thematic units, the introductory verses and the following five stanzas, enclosed within quotation marks, which enact the life of Dimaratos, King of Sparta (510–491 B.C.). Like "If Actually Dead," the framed section could stand on its own as another historical poem, since it is set apart from (and thematically does not need) the first stanza. These initial four lines do not so much introduce the main topic as set it in the context of textuality and rhetoric:

>   His subject, "The character of Dimaratos,"
>   which Porphyry proposed in conversation
>   was outlined by the young sophist as follows
>   (he planned to develop it rhetorically later):

The philosopher Porphyry (A.D. 263–305) assigned the character of Dimaratos as a topic for the young sophist's epideictic essay, on

Language and Writing

which he would apply his rhetorical and linguistic skills. The five stanzas following the one above represent the sophist's provisional formulation of his theme, which he planned "to develop rhetorically later." It would seem that this initial version lacked the stylistic sophistication mandatory in an essay celebrating the powers and effects of language. In this poem to write means to select any subject arbitrarily as a pretext for the composition of an elaborate exercise in discourse. The theme itself is inconsequential; on the following day the *logographer* will receive another topic to "develop rhetorically;" he will display his skill with the sole aim of executing a text that revels in its own sophistry.

The textual strategies this sophist applies are emphasized in "In a Township of Asia Minor." By underscoring the relativity of a text, this poem, like "Dimaratos," interrupts the referential function of language and demonstrates literary language at work. Historically the poem is set in an insignificant town of Asia Minor at the time of the battle between Antony and Caesar at Actium (31 B.C.). In anticipation of Antony's imminent victory, the citizens of this town prepare a declaration to honor his character and eulogize his achievements. When the unexpected news of his defeat arrives, no major changes are envisioned for the text apart from the substitution of names:

> But there's no need for us to draw up a new proclamation.
> The name's the only thing that has to be changed.
> There, in the concluding lines, instead of: "Having freed the Romans
> from Octavius, that disaster,
> that parody of a Caesar,"
> we'll substitute: "Having freed the Romans
> from Antony, that disaster, . . ."
> The whole text fits very nicely.
>
> "To the most glorious victor,
> matchless in his military ventures,
> prodigious in his political operations,
> on whose behalf the township ardently wished
> for Antony's triumph, . . ."
> here, as we said, the substitution: "for Octavius' triumph,
> regarding it Zeus' finest gift—

Language and Writing

>   to this mighty protector of the Greeks,
>   who graciously honors Greek customs,
>   who is beloved in every Greek domain,
>   who clearly deserves exalted praise,
>   and whose exploits should be recorded at length
>   in the Greek language, in both verse and prose,
>   in the *Greek language*, the vehicle of fame,"
>   et cetera, et cetera. It all fits brilliantly.

The unrestrained adulation of the victor is achieved through the Greek language. But as the poem devastatingly stresses, this language is so preposterously nonspecific that it can apply to either of the Roman generals. This is illustrated by the effortless transformation of the document's message brought about simply by the substitution of Caesar's name for Antony's. The language of the proclamation is literary; it uses eccentric wording and intricate syntactical formations to execute a sycophantic and ostentatious text of bathetic grandiloquence; it sets out to glorify Antony/Caesar, to immortalize his victory for all ages, to proclaim him through the known world, but stumbles (quite consciously) over too many commas. The text, sophisticated yet empty, signifies the power of language and amuses itself with that power. Although the declaration was originally intended for Antony, it is equally appropriate to Caesar, or potentially anyone else. The subject recedes in importance; with some ingenuity and only minor alterations the text can serve many purposes. The relativity of textuality is emphasized by the statements denoting change and variability: "The name's the only thing that has to be changed. / There, in the concluding lines, instead of . . . / we'll substitute . . ."; or "The whole text fits nicely"; or "here as we said, the substitution." In this underlying context of conventionality and arbitrariness the mighty Antony and glorious Caesar are capriciously turned into names, interchangeable signs with no substantial content or meaning.[8] The text and literary language matter most.

---

[8] Perhaps the poem "Epitaph of Antiochos, King of Kommagini" functions in a similar manner. Upon the death of King Antiochos, his sister commissions the sophist Kallistratos of Ephesus to compose an epitaph for him. Although the language of this text is not as exaggerated as that of "In a Township of Asia Minor," it still lavishes pretentious praise on the king and is equally sophisticated in its de-

Language and Writing

The prime feature of these texts is this literary language placed in the framework of other writing. The poems direct attention to their "writerly" dimension by acknowledging, through quotation marks, rows of dots, brackets, the "foreign" texts that infiltrate them. The poem "Imenos" employs most of these strategies, as well as another device, the separation of the two stanzas by not double but quadruple spacing.[9] This conspicuous gap visually emphasizes the thematic autonomy of each stanza. While the first concerns pleasure and perversion, the second identifies the preceding one as a fragment of a letter written by Imenos, supposedly living in Syracuse during the reign of Michael III (842–57).

> ". . . to be cherished even more
> is a sensual pleasure achieved morbidly, corruptingly—
> it rarely finds the body able to feel what it requires—
> that morbidly, corruptingly, creates
> an erotic intensity which health cannot know. . . ."
>
> Extract from a letter
> written by young Imenos (from a patrician family)
> notorious in Syracuse for his debauchery
> in the debauched times of Michael the Third.

To appreciate the effect of this second stanza on the first and on the whole poem it is necessary to examine the original version of "Imenos," the poem "Love It More" (1915), which is an early draft of the first stanza:

> Love it more if you acquire it with anguish.
> Imagine how loose and how inferior
> the easily acquired pleasure is.

---

ployment and display of rhetorical strategies. The text of the epitaph, which constitutes the second stanza of the poem, runs as follows: " 'People of Kommagini, let the glory of Antiochos, / the noble king, be celebrated as it deserves. / He was a provident ruler of the country. / He was just, wise, courageous. / In addition he was that best of all things, Hellenic— / mankind has no quality more precious: / everything beyond that belongs to the gods.' "

[9] Such use of spacing occurs in "Orophernis" (for a discussion of the poem see Chapter 3) and in "Those Who Fought for the Achaian League," where the second stanza identifies the first as a text written in Alexandria during the reign of Ptolemy Lathyros (116–80 B.C.).

Language and Writing

> Your pleasure which you attain
> sometimes with lies, always in secret,
> seeking it with uneasiness and insistence,
> rarely finding the body which feels as you want,
> which through fantasy you supplement,
> —do not compare it with the easy delights of others.[10]

Thematically this poem and the first stanza of "Imenos" are very similar. Both deal with a type of sensual love that is unique, rarely experienced, and superior to normal forms of pleasure. The obvious difference between them is that the stanza from "Imenos" is condensed, framed by a row of dots and quotation marks. Thus, although the content of this stanza may basically be the same, its form has been converted into a written text, an epistolary excerpt. This is achieved by the dots and quotation marks and, above all, by the addition of the second stanza, which identifies the first as a text and situates it in a historical period. In the process of its revision the poem has been given a historical position and an intertextual status. The poem is now aware of the text that has infiltrated it. The appendage of the second stanza acts to fabricate a drama of textuality out of which emerges a self-conscious literary language.

While the poems examined in the previous chapter highlighted their existence as aesthetic objects, those analyzed here bring to the fore another aspect of their form—literary language. By incorporating other textual material and by ceaselessly drawing attention to this, these poems stress the relationship of language to other texts and hence to its position in the network of writing. In this context of cross-references literary language is emphasized, a language neither transparent nor a vehicle for communication, but an opaque and dense materiality that, by postponing representation, promotes its own being. These poems are preoccupied with this self-reflective and self-consuming literary language. It is possible to conclude that, although there exist no essays in Cavafy devoted exclusively to literary language, this

---

[10] My translation. The text of this poem is found in Cavafy (1968: 1). For an analysis of this poem from the perspective of the clash of discourses for the appropriation of meaning, see my "The Modes of Reading or Why Interpret: A Search for the Meaning of 'Imenos,'" *Journal of the Hellenic Diaspora*, 1/2: 137–48.

Language and Writing

topic did not remain unproblematical. Literary language is in fact a major concern of the poems examined here. A poem in Cavafy often becomes a fusion of texts, sources, quotations, all grafted upon one another and framed within the limits of language; it occupies that dimension of language that has recognized its literary potential, the space devoted to aesthetics. Questions of reality here are temporarily suspended and the world becomes textualized; an art arises almost for language's sake. It seems, as Mallarmé noted, everything in the world exists to end up in a book (1945: 378).

This does not imply that all detail is reduced to language or that Cavafy's poetry is a matter of self-reflecting words, for no single approach or outlook dominates his poetics. It means simply that a linguistic apprehension of reality characterizes this aspect of his poetics. In the poems examined here Cavafy seems to restore in modern Alexandria a library resembling the renowned house of knowledge erected in that city during the Hellenistic period. In this total, absorptive system of citations, references, words, ideas, and catalogues, Cavafy poses the question of language. He weaves bookish fragments into his work to remind the reader of the textual nature of the material at hand. By incorporating into his verse "notes, texts, commentaries, variants," to cite "Tomb of the Grammarian Lysias," Cavafy outlines the space for us inhabited by perpetual writing, a writing that repeats what was said before and expands its network into the library of vast, unlimited possibilities. With the idea of the library Cavafy reflects on language. He interlaces his poems with other textual fabrics not to declare that everything is words, but rather to make language palpable, to bring the notion of language to the surface, to incorporate this dimension of poetry into his poetics. Although Cavafy did not write specific theoretical texts on this topic, it is obvious that the concept of language concerned him profoundly. As is so often true of Cavafy, he did not discuss issues directly in prose, but rather let his poetry talk about them.

5. TRADITION

As was shown in Chapter 4, many of Cavafy's poems call attention to the texts they have absorbed and in this way emphasize not only their fictionality, but also their nonreferential language. By visibly exhibiting the layers of textuality they have incorporated, such poems reaffirm the intertextual nature of literature. A text undoubtedly belongs to a reticulation of citations and allusions. But these poems do not touch upon the process by which a poem is constructed out of these tissues of texts. They do not discuss the relationship between the poem and its past, between the text and its literary tradition. Whenever we read a work of literature we are aware of traces of other works—many of which are unacknowledged—as well as of features we have not seen before. We recognize the presence of the past as manifested either by the work's identification with or rebellion against it. An author may choose to rearrange the old material or to remain faithful to it. In this choice lies one of the most enduring oppositions in literary history: imitation and invention, being influenced and being original.

In this chapter I investigate the theoretical notion of tradition in Cavafy, his sense of the literary past (not his understanding of his own Greek literary tradition, nor his exploitation of it in his poetry).[1] Several questions lead my exploration. How does Cavafy conceive the dynamics of the literary tradition; is it a source of inspiration or anxiety? How does he see the relationship between newcomer and precursor; is this based on imitation or violation or both? And how does tradition develop for Cavafy; does it evolve uniformly toward a *telos* or change arbitrarily without an improvement or end? Cavafy, it should be noted, did not write any essays

---

[1] This constitutes a separate study in itself, since its presuppositions are incompatible with this examination, which attempts to determine Cavafy's poetics. There have been to date no comprehensive examinations of Cavafy's use of the Greek (and non-Greek) literary tradition in his poetry. It would be interesting, however, to discover the extent to which Cavafy's work represents a continuation or a violation of his literary past.

exclusively devoted to the subject, such as, for instance, Eliot's "Tradition and the Individual Talent." But this topic is an object of concern in many of his articles and poems.

TRADITION AS A SOURCE
OF KNOWLEDGE

We can get an idea of Cavafy's conception of the Greek tradition in his essay "The Byzantine Poets" (1892), in which he seeks to evaluate the significance and position of those poets in Greek literary history. Cavafy claims that although they did not achieve the heights of the classical Greek authors, or those writing in the late nineteenth century, they do not deserve the contempt and neglect of European scholars. They are important in that they demonstrate that the "Greek lyre . . . never ceases sending forth its sweet sounds" (1963b: 43). For Cavafy, the Byzantine poets constitute "the bond between the glory of our ancient poets and the grace and golden hopes of our contemporaries" (pp. 43–44). These observations suggest that Cavafy views Greek literary history as an unbroken continuity ranging from the classical to contemporary authors. The Byzantine period is an affirmation not an interruption of this development; it is a bond connecting the two ages. Noteworthy is the metaphor of the lyre to describe the Greek literary tradition and the reference to the poets as "bards," features reminiscent of the rejected poems. Cavafy's perspective in this article is that of the literary historian as he analyzes, in an almost scholarly fashion, one historical period of Greek culture. He does not state, however, how he or any other poet conceives it, or how (and if) he would use it.

Cavafy adopts this point of view in his article "Lamia" (1893), in which he examines the relationship between a European poet, Keats, and a late Greek antique author, Philostratos, particularly the capacity of the latter to inspire the modern poet. He considers Philostratos an influential author insofar as his *Life of Apollonios of Tyana* has countless episodes that transform it into a "treasury of poetic material" (p. 51). This work of Philostratos is a repository of potential poetic subject matter for the modern writer. Cavafy proceeds to illustrate how one such poet, Keats, adapted this late antique work in his composition of "Lamia." After summarizing

Tradition

Keat's poem, Cavafy compares the two texts thematically: "Undoubtedly, the beauty of the verses, the inimitable grace of the narration belong exclusively to Keats, but to the intelligent Greek belong the idea, the imagination of the work. However, one should not forget that Keats found two to three lines in the *Life of Apollonios* which contained the allusions of a plot and out of which he created a long and perfect poem" (p. 60). Although he acknowledges the mastery and genius of Keats, Cavafy reserves more praise for Philostratos, whose work served as the later poet's source. Cavafy seems to prefer the origins and author of an idea. Latecomers such as Keats, who must borrow their material, take a secondary place. Yet, Cavafy emphasizes that the modern poet is not condemned to imitate, since in his return to the texts of the past, he is not completely constrained by them, but has a certain degree of creative freedom. Cavafy makes allowances for the revision of tradition: "Keats distanced himself somehow from the mythological tradition of the ogress (lamia). He was justified in doing so. Poets form their own ideas and build upon them: they deserve total freedom in the elaboration of their work" (p. 65). Although priority may be given to the original inception of an idea, the modern poet is free to deviate, within limits, from his borrowed topic, to expand and develop it. The past is indispensable to the modern poet since it acts for him as a treasury and as a source of inspiration. Tradition is here seen as a valuable quarry to which the artist returns in search of raw material for his own work.

A similar conception of literary tradition emerges in Cavafy's examination of the poetry of the modern Greek poet Stratiyis. In his article "The Poetry of K. Stratiyis," Cavafy draws attention to Stratiyis's utilization of themes from ancient Greek literature and emphasizes the usefulness of the past to the modern artist. The poet finds in his classical ancestry a rich variety of ideas for possible poetic development, and now he can profit from the research of scholars on ancient culture (pp. 69–70). He encourages Stratiyis to compose poetry that deals with ancient Egypt, where he could find "many noble themes for poetry and plentiful virginal ground" (p. 73). In this respect, the scholars of the Museum of Giza are unwitting benefactors as their excavations and translations of papyri

Tradition

"bring into light not a few poetical themes" (p. 73).[2] The ancient Greek and Egyptian traditions are seen here as sources of knowledge for the poet; they serve literally as a museum, storing valuable treasure that may inspire a poem. Tradition is benign; it enriches the poet, acting almost like an encyclopedia that the poet consults. No doubt, many poets in Cavafy's poetry do just that. The poet in "Kaisarion" browses through a book of Ptolemaic inscriptions in order to investigate a certain historical period, out of which, incidentally, emerges the poem. Poems such as "The Rest I Will Tell to Those Down in Hades" and "Tomb of the Grammarian Lysias" draw attention to the significance of books to poetic composition.

There are other poems, however, such as the posthumous "The Saving of Julian," which highlight the potential of the text as source.

> When the outraged soldiers killed
> the relatives of the dead Constantine
> and when even the small six-year-old child
> of the Emperor Constantine was threatened by their wrath,
> the compassionate Christian priests
> found him and took him into the sanctuary
> of the church. There they saved the six-year-old Julian.
>
> However it should be added
> that this information comes from a Christian source.
> Yet it is probably true.
> Historically it presents nothing unusual:
> Christian priests
> saving innocent Christian children.
>
> Yet if this is true, perhaps the very wise
> Augustus would have said this about even this matter:
> "Let this dark episode be forgotten."[3]

[2] Cavafy's own posthumously published "The Mimiambi of Herodas" (1892) has an archaeological perspective. The first two stanzas concern the discovery of a papyrus of Herodas, and the subsequent six portray scenes that can be deduced from the information contained in the fragmented papyrus.
[3] This, along with five other poems on the Julian theme, was first published by Renata Lavagnini in *Byzantine and Modern Greek Studies* (See Cavafy 1981.)

Tradition

This poem's theme is the priests' salvation of the infant Julian from imminent death at the hands of the soldiers, following the death of his father Constantine (A.D. 337). This episode from the life of Julian the Apostate is recorded, as Renata Lavagnini reveals, in Allard's *Julien l'Apostat*, and indeed Allard's name is cited by Cavafy in a margin of one of the poem's drafts.[4] A passage from Allard quoted by Lavagnini indicates that the original textual reference to the salvation of Julian by the priests is attributed to Gregory of Nazianzus, who is alluded to in the second stanza as "information from a Christian source." This second stanza is particularly relevant to my discussion, since it emphasizes both the notion of the source and doubts about its validity and significance. The second stanza is not directly related to the first in that it is not concerned with the salvation of Julian, but with the historical document that allegedly refers to that event—not with the historical fact, but with the interpretation of this fact, with its textualization. This stanza draws attention to the source of the poem and then scrutinizes its veracity. It recognizes its biased nature; being a Christian, Gregory of Nazianzus would naturally portray the priests favorably. In time, the narrator concludes that the information provided by Gregory of Nazianzus presents nothing extraordinary. The second and third stanzas address the problems in the evaluation and analysis of texts, stressing the textual character of tradition and foregrounding its place as poetic wellspring.

The significance of the historical source is further emphasized in Cavafy's personal note about the posthumous "Athanasios":[5] "In Migne 67 (Sozomenos and Socrates) and 82 (Theodoritos) the tradition of Butcher does not exist. If it is not found elsewhere, in some Life of St. Athanasios the poem cannot stand" (Cavafy 1981: 60). This passage, as Lavagnini points out, refers to an episode in the life of Athanasios cited by E. L. Butcher in *The Story of the Church of Egypt* (1897) (Cavafy 1981: 60). As G. Bowersock points out, the passage relates the story of two monks traveling with Athanasios on the Nile, who ascertained, through supernatural means, Julian's death (Bowersock 1981: 94). Cavafy could not find

---

[4] P. Allard, *Julien l'Apostat*, I (Paris: V. Lecoffre, 1902), pp. 263–64; cited by Lavagnini (Cavafy 1981: 76).
[5] For the poem, see Cavafy (1981: 62).

Tradition

an older source for this incident, apart from Butcher's reference, but without such verification the poem could not be considered viable, and indeed was not published. This note demonstrates the concerns expressed by Cavafy in the prose texts examined at the beginning of this chapter. Historical documents, however marginal or obscure, may yield material for poetic exploitation. Literary tradition, as it emerges from these texts, takes the form of the library of almost unlimited resources. It assumes authority and demands respect. Yet the poet is not constrained by his sources, but is free to improvise on the subjects he borrowed. The poet returns to the past as if consulting an encyclopedia or entering a museum. This benign conception of tradition is limited to Cavafy's discussion of discursive writing, such as that of Philostratos, Gregory of Nazianzus, and other authors found in inscriptions, papyri, and scholarly texts. It informs, enlightens, and teaches, but never threatens the poet. When Cavafy examines the work of other poets, though, and more specifically when he addresses the relationship between poets, a contrasting picture of tradition arises: one that is not necessarily a benevolent treasurehouse of inspiration, but a source of intimidation.

TRADITION AS A SOURCE OF ANXIETY

Cavafy's posthumous essay "The End of Odysseus" (1895) introduces this different conception of tradition. In this text Cavafy explores the various ways in which Homer in the *Odyssey*, Dante in the *Inferno*, and Tennyson in "Ulysses" bring to a conclusion their individual interpretations of the Odyssean theme. It begins with the *Odyssey* and, in particular, Odysseus's encounter with Teiresias in Book XI (90–149), where the seer prophesies that after his arrival in Ithaka Odysseus would undertake a final voyage to a mysterious land whose inhabitants have no knowledge of the sea; after making sacrifices there to Poseidon he would return to his native island to pass his final days in peace. Cavafy then summarizes briefly variations on Homer's account by unspecified ancient authors. This leads to the first modern treatment of the Odyssean theme in Dante's *Inferno*, where Odysseus does not end his days in Ithaka, but rather meets his death at sea in the pursuit of new dis-

Tradition

coveries. Tennyson, while largely following Dante's interpretation, concludes not with the hero's death, but with his departure on a new voyage.

A large portion of the essay is devoted to a comparison of Dante's and Tennyson's rendering of Odysseus's end, leading eventually to an exploration of the nature of tradition and the relationship between precursor and latecomer. Dante, with his major reinterpretation of the Odyssean theme, occupies a dominant position in this tradition, which must be taken into account by subsequent poets writing on the same subject. According to Cavafy, Dante becomes the origin of this reading and the source of future readings. Tennyson, Cavafy states, followed the tradition established by Dante in taking certain ideas from the Italian poet, such as the introduction of the companions (Cavafy 1974: 9, 13).[6] As with Keats and Philostratos, Cavafy here again privileges the initial inception of an idea, thereby giving Dante more credit for originality. "The English poet deserves less praise," Cavafy notes, "because he found the idea ready-made. But he elaborated on it as an experienced artist" (p. 15). Although Cavafy recognizes Tennyson's achievement in deviating somewhat from the original, he nevertheless places him a rank below Dante, who, Cavafy adds, "created a picture not unworthy of the 'sovrano poeta' " (p. 16). Despite Tennyson's revision of Dante—ending the poem not with the hero's death, but with a new voyage—he seems overshadowed by the sovereign poet.

In his juxtaposition of Dante and Tennyson Cavafy recognizes a tension affecting poetic creation, the conflict resulting from the expanding disjunction between the latecomer and the work preceding him. Cavafy calls attention to this anxiety-ridden relationship between old and new in the essay's concluding paragraph, noting that it "is difficult and dangerous for one to wish to continue the sentence which Homer decided to end" (p. 16). Cavafy points to a central problem vexing the poet as he confronts his literary tradition, namely the difficulty of contributing something original to it. Cavafy raises the question of whether or not modern

---

[6] It will be recalled that none of Odysseus's companions survived to return to Ithaka.

Tradition

poets can still be inventive when they face what Harold Bloom has called a tradition that "has grown too wealthy to need anything more" (Bloom 1973: 21). Can poets create novelty when they are relentlessly made aware of an intolerable accumulation of literary works? The existence and unceasing celebration of poetic giants such as Homer disturbs the latecomer, who must assume this threatening burden. The task before the modern poet, Cavafy insists, is "difficult" and "dangerous;" a space in tradition has to be fought for; it cannot be inherited gratuitously. Yet the poet does not withdraw in defeat, and so Cavafy adds the following to his original observation: "But it is in difficult and dangerous works that great artists distinguish themselves" (1974: 16). This crucial sentence refers to Dante, who successfully met Homer's challenge and therefore deserved to be hailed as "sovrano poeta." The question remains open as to whether Tennyson and other modern poets are capable of any significant inventions in the face of not only Homer's conclusion, but Dante's and other celebrated artists' as well. Cavafy implicitly asks if originality is possible for a belated poet, coming at the end of a long tradition of masters and masterpieces.

Although not directly concerned with poetics, it is nevertheless relevant to point out here that Cavafy, by his own practice, did believe modern poets were capable of invention. He himself composed a collection of poems that have won a prominent place in Greek literature. With the composition of "Ithaka" (1911) he also chose to add his name to the distinguished list of poets writing on the Odyssean theme. In this poem he takes up not only Homer's concluding sentence, but Dante's and Tennyson's as well—a challenging and frightening venture no doubt. In "The End of Odysseus" Cavafy comments on the originality of Dante's and Tennyson's contributions to this theme, the fact that they portray the hero as bored in his native land and launch him on new voyages and adventures. By writing on this very popular *topos*, especially after Dante and Tennyson, Cavafy of course was faced with the difficulty of adding something new. His own supplement to the Odyssean story is to address the hero before his *nostos*, that is, before he begins to amass the experiences of his ten-year journey home. This exhortation aims to instill in Odysseus the real mes-

Tradition

sage of the voyage, so that on his return he will not be disappointed by Ithaka:

> Keep Ithaka always in your mind.
> Arriving there is what you're destined for.
> But don't hurry the journey at all.
> Better if it lasts for years,
> so you're old; by the time you reach the island,
> wealthy with all you've gained on the way,
> not expecting Ithaka to make you rich.
>
> Ithaka gave you the marvelous journey.
> Without her you wouldn't have set out.
> She has nothing to give you now.
>
> And if you find her poor, Ithaka won't have fooled you.
> Wise as you will have become, so full of experience,
> you'll have understood by then what these Ithakas mean.

Future travels are not precluded, but here the significance of the journey itself is made clear.[7]

It is interesting that after "Ithaka" Cavafy largely abandoned Homeric and indeed classical themes, opting instead for the relatively marginalized—from the perspective of Greek poetry—Hellenistic, Roman, and Byzantine eras (and of course his own contemporary period). Did he feel that with this novel strategy he could defamiliarize Greek poetry and capture a much more prominent and secure place in its tradition? Perhaps one of Cavafy's successes was that, as a modernist, he chose to write about the Kaisarions of history, those obscure "heroes" (and periods) about which few lines exist in traditional poems and whom the poet can freely fashion in his mind, as "Kaisarion" demonstrates. (See Chapter 3 for a discussion of this poem.) It is undoubtedly true that there is greater room for originality if a poet writes about Kaisarion and Orophernis rather than about Odysseus and Achilles. This indeed may be how Cavafy met the challenge of tradition: by simply refusing to complete Homer's sentence and

---

[7] For an interesting study of the permutations of Odysseus as literary *topos*, see W. B. Stanford's *The Quest for Ulysses* (New York: Praeger, 1974).

choosing instead obscure, half-forgotten lines to explore and amplify. The question of tradition, nevertheless, posed many serious problems to him.

This in no way was a personal battle, but rather represents the general predicament of the modern poet who, casting an eye to his literary past, discovers an unendurable amassing of precedent poems. The anxiety arises from what is seen as the disconnection between the vigor of the past and debility of the present. The poet must differentiate himself from this amplitude of texts in order to secure his poetic identity. In this respect, as Walter Bate argues, the dominant question vexing the poet of the last three centuries, in the face of the rich but intimidating legacy of the past, is what is left for him to do (Bate 1971: 3–4).[8] Bate cites a passage from Samuel Johnson that attests to the existence in the late eighteenth century of a discourse on belatedness and originality. Johnson writes: "It is indeed always dangerous to be placed in a state of unavoidable comparison with excellence, and the danger is still greater when that excellence is celebrated by death. . . . He that succeeds a celebrated writer, has the same difficulties to conquer" (in Bate 1971: 3). These words, which may be compared to Cavafy's remarks on Homer quoted earlier, highlight the modern artist's dilemma, and also stress his anxiety and embarrassment before two thousand years of achievement in art. Although this anxiety, Bate writes, may be common to societies that perceive

---

[8] Indeed, this call for originality is peculiar to our modern aesthetic. As Walter Ong has argued, manuscript culture had few if any anxieties of influence and deliberately created texts from other texts. Poets, sculptors, and painters of previous ages worked within the guidelines prescribed not only by their traditions, but also by the wishes and plans of their patrons. Contracts survive from the Renaissance indicating that the painter agreed to detailed stipulations concerning subject matter, materials, and location. (See Michael Baxandall, *Painting and Experience in Fifteenth Century Italy* [Oxford. Oxford University Press, 1972].) As E. H. Gombrich states in *The Story of Art*, an Egyptian, Chinese, or Byzantine master would have been puzzled by our demand to be original. "Nor would a medieval artist of western Europe have understood why he should invent new ways of planning a church, of designing a chalice, or of representing the sacred story where the old ones served their purposes so well. The pious donor who wanted to dedicate a new shrine for a holy relic of his patron saint, not only tried to procure the most serious materials he could afford, he would also seek to provide the master with an old and venerable example of how the legend of the saint should be correctly represented. Nor would the artist feel hampered by this type of commission" (1950: 113–14).

Tradition

themselves in decline, such as Alexandria and Rome, it has become even more pressing in modern times, to the point where the concept of originality has become an essential feature of art. Bate points to a spate of critical writings in England around the middle of the eighteenth century that are informed by one overwhelming fact—"the obviously superior originality, and . . . the greater immediacy and universality of subject and appeal, of the poetry of earlier times" (104–106).[9]

This concomitant relationship between belatedness and anxiety forms the central theme of Harold Bloom's entire tetralogy, in which he explores the problems relating to originality and influence. The main thesis of the first and perhaps most influential book in this series is that the covert subject of most poetry in the last three centuries has been the anxiety of influence, which Bloom defines as "each poet's fear that no proper work remains for him to perform" (1973: 148). This anxiety stems from a feeling that the poet has simply arrived too late and finds the ground before him already worked. Although Bloom acknowledges that this sense of belatedness is a malaise of Western civilization, he agrees with Bate that this concept underwent a change in the latter half of the eighteenth century (1975: 76). At this time, Bloom adds, the old anxiety of style (the need to write differently from others) merged with the recent anxiety of influence (the fear that nothing remains to be done), reaching proportions unbearable to the poets. As a result, originality became the dominant poetic value, and poetry was judged not simply on its truthfulness, but on its individuality and distinctiveness from other poems.

The anxiety over the vitality of the past relates to the emergence of the poet as the factor primarily responsible for poetic creation. (See Chapter 1.) Since inspiration was thought to flow from the poet himself and since his sensibility distinguished him from other people, it followed that his personal compositions would re-

---

[9] See the following essays by Samuel Johnson and Edward Young, which discuss originality, invention, imitation, and belatedness: "The Dangers of Imitation—the Impropriety of Imitating Spencer," "The Criterions of Plagiarism," "The Difficulty of Defining Comedy—Tragic and Comic Sentiments Confounded" (Johnson 1827); "Apology for Apparent Plagiarism: Sources of Literary Variety" (Johnson 1817); and *Conjectures on Original Composition* (Young [1759] 1961).

Tradition

flect his own individuality and would differ from the work of other poets. Romanticism apotheosized this difference and distinctiveness. "Only the individual interests us," declared Novalis (1945: 59). Whereas orally oriented cultures placed a premium on standardization, repetition, and the commonplace as structural poetic principles, romanticism vehemently rejected the formula and castigated repetition as a fatal flaw in art. A poem had to be personal, local, and temporal; the poet was compelled to bring something completely novel into existence.[10] "Every poet," Shelley wrote in "The Defense of Poetry," "must inevitably innovate upon the example of his predecessors in the exact manner of his versification" (1977: 84). For romantic and postromantic art the most damning aesthetic error was the creation of a work of art that imitated its precursors. The great commandment of romanticism was, as Arthur Lovejoy puts it: "Be yourself, which is to say, be unique" (1936: 307). A heavy onus fell on the poet to invent, originate, and initiate. But with the expansion of tradition and with the ceaseless accumulation of masterpieces this task became progressively more formidable. To start at Homer's concluding sentence is, as Cavafy noted, a dangerous and difficult venture.

Such an observation reveals a different conception of literary tradition from the one formulated at the beginning of this chapter. In "The End of Odysseus" there is a sense of this anxiety, of the fear that there might be little room for further invention. In this essay tradition comes to be regarded more as a burden against which the poet must distinguish himself and less as a depository of knowledge containing useful poetic subjects. The authority emanating from tradition does not necessarily inspire as much as it threatens the future poet. However, the modern poet does not submit passively to this exercise of power, but reacts against it. As Cavafy observed in his essay, it is in dangerous and difficult works that poets become great. Revision of past rules and deviation from preceding models are both possible. The poet's critical attitude vis-à-vis his precursor, which Cavafy hints at in "The End of

---

[10] In the eighteenth century, originality became legally enforced through the introduction of copyright laws guaranteeing that each text remain the sole property of its creator. See "What Is an Author?" in Foucault (1977); also Ong (1971, 1982).

Tradition

Odysseus," is explored in depth in a note Cavafy wrote concerning Saint Simeon Stylites after reading a passage on him in Gibbon.[11]

The first part of the note deals with a reappraisal of Saint Simeon in the light of Gibbon's harsh criticism of the monk. Gibbon uncomplimentarily compares Saint Simeon to the fanatics of every age who, inflamed by stern indifference and religious hatred, lacerate themselves both physically and emotionally. For Cavafy, however, this monk is a wonderful saint and an object of admiration and study. And it is to this that Cavafy devotes his attention, for, after listing the authors who have written about Saint Simeon (Ferdinand Gregorovius, Evagrius, Theodoret), he moves to a discussion of the first modern and poetic treatment of the theme, in Tennyson's "St Simeon Stylites" (1842):

> The poem of Tennyson, though it contains some well-made verses, fails in tone. Its great defect lies in its form of a monologue. The complaints of Simeon, his eagerness for the "meed of saints, the white robe and the palm," his dubious humility and latent vanity, are not objectionable in themselves and may be [*sic*] were necessary to the poem, but they have been handled in a common, almost vulgar manner. It was a very difficult task—a task reserved, perhaps for some mighty king of art—to find fitting language for so great a saint, for so wonderful a man. (Cavafy 1963c: 72–74)

The reasons for such an uncompromising rejection of Tennyson's poem are vague. Cavafy does not demonstrate why the poem "is not worthy of the subject," nor how it fails in tone, nor why he considers the monologue a defect. Yet the poem in Cavafy's eyes constitutes a complete failure, since it lacks a "fitting language for so great a saint, so wonderful a man."

This repudiation of Tennyson's "St Simeon Stylites" is not an isolated instance, for Cavafy elsewhere attacked Tennyson's

---

[11] Gibbon, *Decline and Fall of the Roman Empire* (Philadelphia: William Birch and Abraham Small, 1804), vol. 4, chap. 37, pp. 389–90. Cavafy's note first appeared in *Anekdota Peza* (Cavafy 1963c: 70–75). Subsequently this and the other notes on Gibbon have been published by Diana Haas "Cavafy's Reading Notes on Gibbon's 'Decline and Fall,' " *Folia Neohellenica* 4:25–96.

Tradition

work.¹² Savidis suggests that, taken collectively, these incidents indicate an antagonistic attitude on Cavafy's part toward Tennyson. Indeed, one wonders whether this attitude is not a manifestation of the anxiety of influence, the fear that Tennyson, having composed poems both on the Odyssean theme and on Saint Simeon, had effectively denied Cavafy the opportunity to write on these subjects. Is Tennyson another of the multitude of poets that Cavafy, or any other writer, had to face? Do Cavafy's attacks on one of his predecessors represent an attempt to overcome the intimidation of the past and its debilitating authority?¹³ Perhaps these questions cannot be answered with any measure of certainty, but what is clear in this note, as well as in "The End of Odysseus," is the feeling of anxiety that accompanies the modern poet's perception of his literary legacy. The relationship between newcomer and predecessor is seen as one of conflict.

THE STRUGGLE IN TRADITION

The metaphor of the struggle implied in Cavafy's note on Tennyson and in "The End of Odysseus" emerges as one of the major concerns in two texts discussed in Chapter 2: "The Reflections of an Old Artist" and "The Enemies." Running through both works is a distrust of the authority of the past and, specifically, of the precursor's imposing influence. In both texts revision rather than servile imitation is emphasized. In each case, the new authors wrote against the established system of rules and conventions and opposed the norms set up by their predecessors. The artist of "The Reflections of an Old Artist" is, as will be recalled, despondently aware of the revisionary nature of poetic success. He observes the appearance of a group of young poets who neither recognize him as a great literary figure nor consider his work exemplary. These poets do not follow his lead; they do not imitate the poems he has so successfully canonized; they form another poetic school with a distinct style: "They think, and above all, they write differently." The old poet's work represents the poetic orthodoxy, the standard

---

¹² See Savidis's commentary to "The End of Odysseus" (Cavafy 1974: 20); also Savidis (1966: 111, 115).
¹³ These and similar questions are explored in my article "Cavafy, Tennyson and the Overcoming of Influence" (Jusdanis 1982–83).

Tradition

against which all other works are measured. And it is precisely for this reason that the young poets refuse to conform to this conception of "poeticity," since in order to win a position in tradition they must first reject the old and replace it with something uniquely their own. Their attitude toward his work is hostile; since the patron deity of tradition—"originality"—demands this, it requires that the newcomer subvert the assumptions of his precursor. Only after he has accomplished this deed will he be revered and his work canonized. The old poet understands the dynamics of this rejection, since, as he admits, he too strove to overcome the authority of his predecessors. As he recalls: "He was one of some fifty young men who established a new school, wrote in a different style, and *changed* the minds of the millions who honored a few old artists and their predecessors. The former made the young men's *victory* easier when they died" [my emphasis] (Cavafy 1971: 102). In the essay as a whole, but particularly in this passage, the relationship between predecessor and successor is presented as a conflict of interest, as a struggle whose outcome is the defeat of the latter at the hands of the former. The words "victory," "changed," "condemned," and "replaced" point to the force used by the young poets in their attempt to supplant the celebrated poets, and by the latter in their battle to maintain their privileged position. Each generation, it seems, attacks the work of the established masters so as to discredit it and have its own recognized as true literature.

Literary tradition, as portrayed in this essay, does not provide the future poet with an aesthetic heritage, nor is it for him a beneficial source of inspiration. Indeed, it is because tradition is an accumulation of past excellence that the modern poet contests its authority. He struggles against his predecessors in order to define a space for himself, his ultimate aim being to promote a favorable reception of his own work, a task that entails writing not in the manner of his own precursors—since by adhering to their principles he will remain in their shadow—but against them. It is only then that his work will be recognized as unique especially by an aesthetic community that values originality. The poet will acquire his own identity and gain a place in tradition only if he sucessfully deviates from the past and forges a distinctive mode of expression. He and poets like him will then constitute the norm, the new or-

Tradition

thodoxy, and their creative work will be celebrated as the embodiment of literature, a model to be emulated. But at this crucial point, as soon as they reach their zenith of success, resistance to their work will materialize, new poets will emerge to whom the accepted poetic practice will seem "strange and ridiculous." These new poets will introduce a poetic medium that will defamiliarize the old; the battle will begin anew.

Struggle as the perennial and ineluctable force in tradition becomes a central theme in "The Enemies." (See Chapter 2 for the text.) As was pointed out in the second chapter, the arguments of this poem are in many ways like those in Cavafy's essay, but with one major difference. The principle figure of "The Enemies" is a sophist, as opposed to a poet, who addresses all modes of writing and communication, thereby expanding the perspective of the poem. He understands the power of the word, its ubiquitous nature, and its recalcitrant resistance to all attempts to possess it permanently. While the consul warns the three sophists to guard themselves against their enemies' written word, the sophist responds with solemn words, reversing the consul's proposition: not their present but their future enemies pose the greater threat. In their lifetime the sophists can answer the criticism of their adversaries; they can compete in their discursive field simply by writing. (The sophist demonstrates that the consul's argument, by concentrating on the present, is superficial and unconvincing.) But from the perspective of history—where the sophist situates the dialogue—the author's previously defensible position is made precarious; after the writer's death there is no protection from revision. As the old poet of "The Reflections of an Old Artist" admits, his victory was facilitated by his precursors' death. The sophist also recognizes this tragic situation, that in the anonymity of the future the writing of the present will be read irreverently and unsympathetically: "Later will our enemies the new sophists come. / When we in our old age will lie wretchedly / and some of us will have gone to Hades." The coming generation will challenge the sophists' authority over their own texts by transforming their writing: "Our present words and works will appear strange (and ridiculous / perhaps) since the enemies will change sophistics, / style and tendencies." The real enemies, like the young poets of

Tradition

the essay, will think in antithetical terms; they will write antagonistically. They will transform the texts of the sophists by subjecting them to countless contradictory readings, they will put them to uses never imagined by their original authors, and they will analyze them in contexts so foreign they will be almost unrecognizable. The sophist anxiously senses that an author cannot influence the reception of his work, since enemies will always appear who will either ignore his texts or, perhaps, treat them disrespectfully and employ them for their own politically motivated ends. The sophist fears not so much the future's capacity for "creative treason" as the capricious appropriation that ominously awaits all texts:[14]

> Like me and them who so much
> transformed the past things.
> What we portrayed as beautiful and proper
> the enemies will reveal to be foolish and useless,
> repeating the same things differently (without much effort).
> Just as we spoke the old words in another manner.

No text and no author can escape the arbitrariness of future readings, the aim of which is not necessarily to be faithful to the "original," or to discover the "truths" embedded within it, but simply to say something different. Thus, what was—or rather, because it was—portrayed as beautiful or correct will be inverted. The emphasis falls on the phrase "saying the same things differently," on reiteration, on the repetition of past statements in another manner, and in their abuse. Revision is not rationalized; it simply exists as the main agent that brings about change in tradition.

Innovation is the vital principle in the conception of tradition that emerges from the analysis of "The Reflections of an Old Artist" and "The Enemies." Both texts stress that change is possible. Perhaps masterpieces can no longer be created—neither the poem

---

[14] Robert Escarpit (1961) calls the reinterpretation of a work of art "creative treason," inasmuch as it brings about a transformation of the original. Yet, despite this treason factor, Escarpit still imagines an arcadian tradition. Although there is a shift in poetic values and a rearrangement of poetic patterns, no radical break occurs in an otherwise continuous process of creation. Missing in this notion of interpretation, but quite perceptible in that of "The Enemies," is the element of power and the idea of contingency it introduces.

Tradition

nor the essay refers to great art or great artists—but new things can emerge. In each text, the new generation tries to bring about a shift in values by seeking to overturn its inheritance, replace the established rules with its own, and disseminate its version of literary truth. The code of ethics is the politics of opposition. Tradition exists, but as the enemies remind us, constant resistance disrupts its seemingly stable development with strategic interventions. For the enemies tradition has no beginning and no end; it does not follow a path of perfectibility guided by a common edifying goal, such as the discovery of Knowledge. It is made of successes and failures. It consists of sophists and poets who struggle over literary and nonliterary values, and who, if victorious, manage momentarily to consolidate themselves and their work, and impose in the name of Literature their local truth upon the "millions" in the community. Inherent in this conception of tradition is the morality of dissent, since it is that which guarantees change and postpones inertia—the permanent appropriation of power by one group.

This theme of disagreement and opposition, central to the sophist's argument, is powerfully articulated in "Growing in Spirit." This poem was discussed previously (see Chapter 2), but a brief summary may be helpful at this point. The speaker argues that one should go beyond respect and admiration for tradition by revolting against it and revising it; some rules will be kept because it is impossible to construct from nothing, but most of the established practices must be transgressed. Success involves the violation of the dominant code. This is not nihilistic but creative, an act that leads to knowledge. The poem articulates a relationship between power and knowledge, and these words frame the entire text between them—the *dinamosis* of the title, implying the process of acquiring power, and the last word, *gnosi*, meaning knowledge. The use of power advocated in the poem is constructive rather destructive in the Foucauldian sense, as it leads to formation of new knowledge. For Foucault, "the exercise of power itself creates and causes to emerge new objects of knowledge and accumulates new bodies of information" (1980: 51). "Growing in Spirit" shows that power brings about the destruction of the given and the deficient, but gives rise to new knowledge, novel poetry, and untried read-

Tradition

ings. Half the old conventions are overthrown, but only to make room for new ones. This is the ethics informing the political practice of the young poets of "The Reflections of an Old Artist" and of the sophist in "The Enemies." Each generation strives to undermine the assumptions of its predecessors in order to prevent them from establishing themselves permanently and from forming a monopoly over literary discourse. In this way the aspirations of totalitarian politics, the final and perpetual seizure of the rules by one group, will never be realized. As all three texts relentlessly stress, an equilibrium is never reached, since in the future new enemies will fight to undermine their inherited order. In this sense tradition is disruptive; it contains the elements of violation and resistance that assure the possibility of innovation.

Yet I should emphasize that this conception of tradition is not the only one found in Cavafy. At the beginning of this chapter I demonstrated that in other texts tradition was portrayed as a treasury that inspired and informed poets. The poet strove not to violate its rules but to learn from it and, in a sense, to unify himself with it. As in the conception of art and of the audience, we see here that there is no uniformity of views and two or more (sometimes incompatible) notions coexist in Cavafy's poetics. Their contradiction cannot easily be resolved by the standard resort to the poet's evolutionary development, by which he repudiates one idea before he accepts another, since the majority of the texts examined here were written within one decade (the 1890s). We must accept that such traditional essays as "Lamia" were composed in 1893, while the more radical "The Reflections of an Old Artist" between 1894 and 1900, and "The Enemies" in 1900. If we cannot speak of uniformity and consistency of views, or of a stable, logical growth, perhaps it is possible to differentiate between dominant and secondary positions. If Cavafy's poetry can be seen as a revaluation of its particular Greek poetic tradition, then perhaps the conception of tradition, the one initiating deviation and conflict, may seem the more consequential of the two. Indeed, as I noted earlier in this chapter, Cavafy conceived of and wrote a poetry sufficiently revisionary of his own poetic tradition and perceptibly different from the work of his contemporaries that he is recognized as one of the most "original" modern Greek poets. As I discuss in the After-

Tradition

word, one of the reasons for the initially hostile reaction to Cavafy was that his work could not easily be accommodated within traditional paradigms of Greek poetry and criticism. Cavafy's poetry challenged both severely. It would be safe to assume that such an "original" oeuvre was informed by an equally innovative view of tradition.

This of course s tuates Cavafy squarely in the poetics of modernism. The ethos of opposition running through his work is characteristic of this entire movement, which promoted the idea of historical relativism and brought to culmination the attack on tradition inaugurated by the Enlightenment. In this respect Cavafy's oeuvre resembles more that of Eliot, Woolf, and Rilke than that of the historical avant-garde.[15] We see in it a questioning of poetic tradition rather than a radical undermining of the institution of art itself. Although we do not find in Cavafy the avant-garde's sense of militancy and negation, we recognize a critical attitude toward the past and a commitment to modernity. This view of poetic tradition, as expressed in such texts as "The Enemies" and "The Reflections of an Old Artist," allowed him to build a position at a slight angle to Greek poetry so as to defamiliarize it. Since my study of Cavafy deals primarily with poetics, I have not investigated his experimentation with form and critique of Greek poetry. It would be sufficient to add, however, that the dismay and indignation his poetry initially provoked, the poetic tradition it has inspired, and the dominance it has maintained in the canon of twentieth-century Greek verse seem to point unequivocally to the success and strength of Cavafy's questions.

[15] On the historical avant-garde, see Calinescu (1977) and Bürger (1984).

6. WORLD

Cavafy sees art principally as an autonomous and autotrophic entity relying on its intrinsic resources and making minimal reference to reality. This conception of art was analyzed in Chapter 3, where it was shown that it is of recent date, stemming from the philosophical speculation of the late eighteenth century. It represents one of several ways of understanding the aesthetic. The earliest and most familiar approach to art is the mimetic, according to which art is a reflection of the world: people, ideas, actions, events, places, and things in general. Art takes the world as its subject and accordingly is judged by the faithfulness and accuracy with which it renders this reality. Mimesis constitutes one of the most persistent concepts by which art is discussed; it was prominent from classical times to the eighteenth century and still reigns in contemporary, nonacademic approaches as the principal method by which the aesthetic experience is judged. In Cavafy, however, as in the dominant postromantic orientation toward literature and art, the notions of reality, world, and nature play a secondary role. Art is primarily concerned with itself. It constitutes its own microcosm and forms the center of critical reference. As such, questions of reflection and truthfulness are not as relevant as they would be in a mimetic theory of the aesthetic.

In this chapter I analyze Cavafy's view of the relationship between art and the world, with emphasis on the concept of world. To this end, I examine art's rejection of the phenomenal reality and the implications that this break poses on art itself. I should stress, however, that the aesthetic isolationism so dominant in Cavafy is contradicted by the view that art is a worldly institution, and the artist is enmeshed in its politics. As the discussion in the second half of Chapter 2 illustrates, art, far from being an atemporal and abstract idea, is produced in a historically defined space and time; it is subject to constant change and is affected by other social forces and institutions. I do not deal with art's location in this social reality, but rather with the world it supposedly refers to; I examine the relationship between art and the object it is

World

thought to represent. Hence by "world" I do not mean the social network of artists, readers, publishers, students, and teachers involved in the production and dissemination of art (as in Chapter 2), but more traditionally, the external phenomenal reality art is usually believed to signify. I concentrate on those texts that problematize this relationship with the aim of exploring the consequences this relationship imposes on art.

MIMESIS

A hallmark of our own modern aesthetic tradition is its successful suppression of mimesis and the accompanying valorization of art's autonomy. As will be recalled from Chapter 3, Kant distinguished the aesthetic experience (the disinterested contemplation of sensuous patterns) from the practical (that enabling the individual to adapt to his environment). Kant's theory, widely disseminated, eventually gave rise to a radical aesthetic isolationism. Théophile Gautier became one of the most vociferous writers repudiating mimesis and literalness. We witness his distaste for naturalistic art in the polemical preface of his *Mademoiselle de Maupin*, in which he argues forcefully against a utilitarian conception of art. In the following passage taken from his *Histoire du Romantisme* his position on representational art becomes even clearer: "The purpose of art, which we have much forgotten in our day, is not the exact reproduction of nature, but the creation of forms and colors which it delivers to us, of a microcosm where our dreams can live and produce themselves" (1877: 216). Art does not copy reality, but rather constitutes its own aesthetic realm equal in value to the outside world and a sanctuary to the artist from that hostile world.

In the nineteenth century the accepted idea of art's subordination to nature was reversed. Baudelaire, for instance, argued that nature was in fact deficient and meaningless before art intervened and began working on it. Nature simply provided material for the artist; it existed only as an incoherent mass organized by the imagination. There was no line or color in nature, Baudelaire insisted in his essay on Delacroix [1863]; it was man who created the lines and colors (1925: 15). Art in this case was superior to nature in that it conferred purpose and a sense of order on nature's inherent imperfection.

Toward the end of the nineteenth century, the arguments repudiating nature took on extraordinary and flamboyant proportions. Huysmans's novel *À Rebours* (1884) is a good example. Des Esseintes, its protagonist, is a dandyish, anemic, morbidly sensitive aristocrat who withdraws into a villa, surrounds himself with rare and unusual objects, reads late-antique literature, and substitutes his imaginary creation for reality. Des Esseintes prefers the dream, cherishes illusion, and considers artifice the distinctive mark of genius. He despises everyday varieties of plants so much that his "inborn taste for the artificial" leads him to throw out his real flowers and to start a collection of artificial plants, those fashioned by artists out of india rubber, wire, calico, taffeta, paper, and velvet (1959: 97). When he grows tired of this, his taste changes to uncommon and exotic real plants, though he insists in an argument underscoring his contempt of reality that "not one of them looked real, it was as if cloth, paper, porcelain, and metal had been lent by man to Nature to enable her to create these monstrosities" (p. 101). Here aestheticism has achieved its most radically ironic limits. The apotheosis of art reaches such a degree that nature begins to worship art and resorts to copying its absolute, imperishable forms in order to compensate for its own ephemerality. The tables have been turned.[1]

In England, writers such as Oscar Wilde were conducting their own revolt against nature with an equally polemical, if not mocking, force. In "The Decay of Lying" Wilde seeks to demon-

---

[1] One can cite more of Des Esseintes's eccentric (and humorous) attempts to replace reality with make-believe. For instance, he was terribly disappointed by Holland when, on his visit, it did not correspond to the image conveyed by Dutch paintings he had seen in the Louvre. In another episode, on his way to London, he terminated his trip in Paris and conjured up visual images of the English city, then drove back home so as not to spoil his fantasy with the real thing. This ultimate renunciation of, and abdication from, life is supremely captured in the provocative statement uttered by Axel, the protagonist of Villier's *Axel* (1890): "Live? Our servants will do that for us!" (Villiers 1925: 284). Life is so full of misery, so hideous, so marred by imperfection that the only solution is to forsake it and embrace death. "In death," says Axel, "a man takes nothing with him but what he has renounced in life" (p. 289). Thus Axel and his bride, Sara, drink poison and die with the faith that they would attain the absolute so pitifully absent from life.

World

strate nature's inadequacy and incompleteness. "What art reveals to us," he claims, "is Nature's lack of design . . . her absolutely unfinished condition" (1945: 9). Art, on the other hand, aspires to perfection, and in so doing "takes life as part of her rough material and recreates and refashions it"; yet it always "keeps between herself and reality the impenetrable barrier of beautiful style, of decorative or ideal treatment" (p. 23). For Wilde, the proper school in which to learn art is not life but art itself; life imitates art far more than art imitates life (pp. 26, 30). By this provocative statement, Wilde means that art ultimately influences man's perception of the world. As Wilde puts it: "There may have been fogs for centuries in London. . . . But no one saw them, and so we do not know anything about them. They did not exist till art invented them." These lines, reminiscent of remarks made by some twentieth-century theorists, to the effect that nothing exists until it has been textualized, represent the aestheticist position vis-à-vis art and nature at its most blunt and farcical.

Whistler, in the "Ten O'Clock Lecture," takes a similar position, stressing that art is preoccupied with its own perfection and hence does not confine itself to mere reproduction. It chooses certain elements from nature in order to fashion the beautiful and the perfect from the essentially imperfect. As such, Whistler insists, nature should never be taken in its original state before it has become transformed by art. "Nature is very rarely right, to such an extent even that it might also be said that Nature is always wrong: that is to say, the condition of things that shall bring about the perfection of harmony worthy of a picture is rare, and not common at all" (1979: 25). Whistler assigns to nature a secondary position; for him it is raw, unordered matter awaiting the intervention of man and art.

Parallels can be drawn between Huysmans's, Wilde's, and Whistler's aestheticism, explicated above, and Cavafy's conception of art and nature. Indeed, Cavafy's "Artificial Flowers" (1903) may be compared thematically to the passage in Huysmans. This poem, which more than any other in Cavafy embraces the doctrine of artificiality, may easily be situated within the direct mainstream of late nineteenth-century aestheticism and decadence:

World

    I do not want the real narcissus—nor do lilies
    please me, nor real roses.
    They adorn the trite, pedestrian gardens.
    Their flesh embitters, tires and pains me—
    I am weary of their perishable beauties.

    Give me artificial flowers—glories of glass and metal—
    with never-wilting, never-spoiling, never-aging forms.
    Flowers of superb gardens of another land
    where Theories and Rhythms and Knowledge dwell.

    I love flowers fashioned of glass or gold,
    genuine gifts of a genuine Art;
    dyed in hues lovelier than natural colors,
    wrought with mother-of-pearl and enamel,
    with ideal leaves and stalks.

    They draw their grace from wise and purest Taste;
    they did not sprout unclean in dirt and mire.
    If they have no aroma, we will pour fragrance,
    we will burn myrrh of sentiment before them.[2]

In a letter to his friend Anastasiadis, Cavafy describes this poem as a "flight to the lovely realm of pure Fantasy and Extravagance." Indeed, in "Artificial Flowers" there unfolds a fanciful and unnatural world from which the beauties of nature are deliberately banished. The natural narcissi, lilies, and roses are uprooted from art's garden as common and boring to those observing them. The artist (as was shown in Chapter 1) avoids the commonplace in every way, preferring the artificial flowers made out of nonperishable materials. Like the flowers in Huysmans, these plants are formed by the artist who applies "Theories" and "Knowledge" in his task. Herein lies the difference between the natural and the artificial; while the natural is thought to emerge spontaneously from nature, the artificial is produced by man's imagination and labor. Implicit in this opposition is that distinction in Cavafy between temporal and ideal beauty: the one is earthly and ephemeral, the other oth-

---

[2] I have modified Dalven's translation slightly, rendering the Greek *Theories* as "Theories" (instead of "Contemplations") and *Gnoseis* as "Knowledge" (instead of "Learning").

World

erworldly and timeless.³ The poem privileges the second element of this polarity; it prefers the artificial flower as representing victory over ugliness and mortality; having delivered itself from the mud and soil, it aspires to the eternal realm of "pure art." It uncompromisingly rejects nature both as source and model of art; the artist can fashion his own aesthetically superior flowers, and if they release no fragrance, man-made perfumes can be poured over them.

The opposition between art and nature so prominent in "Artificial Flowers" is also a central theme of "Morning Sea" in which an anonymous speaker reflects, by means of an interior monologue, upon his perception of nature. (See Chapter 1, "Alienation," for the text and another discussion of the poem.) In the first stanza the speaker ventures out into the open, to behold the view. The phrase "let me, too, look at nature awhile" suggests a sense of alienation, giving the impression that until this moment, he, unlike others, has not experienced this sight. It seems that he is opening his eyes to nature for the first time. The reader thus expects an overwhelming reaction of joy from the speaker as he witnesses the sea, sky, and shore; but what follows is a conventional description of the sight, related in reserved and unspectacular vocabulary, an account befitting the most familiar and automatized everyday scene. The language is as stereotypical as the view is commonplace. The speaker, as in "Artificial Flowers," fails to be excited or moved by nature. It does not draw his interest, and as he admits in the second stanza, he has been deceiving himself, since he has actually seen nature only "for a minute." The landscape outside becomes visible to him merely for an instant, or perhaps he lacks the necessary language to make it personally and aesthetically meaningful. In contrast, his internalized world—the fantasies, memories, and erotic visions—remain vivid and opaque. In this sense the poem embodies an opposition between the mimetic and expressive approaches to art, according to which the former is oriented toward the external world and the latter toward the individ-

---

³ Underlying this division is the much more fundamental dichotomy of culture and nature. The artist, as a member of culture, fashions his art through his knowledge and thought; he uses tools to construct forms of beauty out of nature's raw material. The aesthetic object is a produt of his conscious effort.

ual himself. "Morning Sea" stresses that nature is not a compelling artistic theme, since its portrayal has been reduced to a habitual and conventional exercise. Art turns toward the inner microcosm of the poet. With the change in subject matter, it follows that descriptive language, which realistically rendered the external universe, becomes incapable of expressing the inner conflicts, dreams, and reflections of the individual. Along with nature, this language is rejected from art's concerns and the emphasis shifts from the outside to the inside as art undertakes to make manifest this esoteric and private world.

In "Morning Sea" the conflict between mimetic and expressive discourse is superimposed on the inside/outside and man/nature dichotomies. The poem brings to the fore that barrier preventing the speaker from partaking in nature's wholeness. This exclusion from the natural differs markedly from the harmony and plenitude that overflow in the early poems. The rejected "The Poet and the Muse," for instance, affirms the solidarity between the poet and nature, which prepares for him garlands of roses and narcissi. This unity is also asserted in "Correspondence according to Baudelaire," which depicts nature as the poet's familiar garden. The thematic orientation of "Morning Sea" contrasts with the identification of poet and nature so forcefully expressed in the early poems. Nature in these verses inspires and illuminates; the poet's consciousness merges with his environment. In "Morning Sea," however, the relationship between artistic and natural being is put into serious doubt, as the poet fails to achieve an unmediated vision of the natural object. His private preoccupations, his daydreams, memories, and erotic fantasies intervene, rendering the space dividing him from nature opaque and impermeable.

It is these intermediating factors that come to the fore in aesthetics and art. The preoccupations of art change, and the natural object, once dominant in the artistic process, is superseded by another realm of experience. Nature no longer serves as the principle reference point for art, since art has become antinatural, nonmimetic, and self-referential. It no longer attempts to copy the world. Indeed, as "Morning Sea" demonstrates, art opens a window to the artist's soul and also reveals its own being. The artwork is not an extension of nature (although it obtains its raw materials

World

from her) but an artifact of culture; it is the product of the self-conscious use of tools and techniques and the application of theories and knowledge. In this way it differentiates itself from the natural world by foregrounding its artificiality and "artisticality."

ART AND GUILT

Art's self-proclaimed independence from the phenomenal world and its consequent rejection of the notion of moral duty and didactic purpose did not escape consequences. Having repudiated its place in society and refused to partake in its daily affairs, art withdrew inwardly, and in so doing deprived itself of any seriousness. It promised its practitioners entertainment only. Art did not want to and could not do anything else than be beautiful. Indeed, when the artist of the late nineteenth century was invited to abandon his solitary existence and involve himself in society's struggles, he responded with a peremptory no, saying that he did not want anything to do with history. He relinquished life and action and retreated into his aesthetic villa to amuse himself with forms. Art became play.

This idea of play is one of the legacies bequeathed to our modern conception of art by Kantian idealism. Kant's attempt to isolate a neglected sphere of human experience, the aesthetic, to render it as an object of knowledge, was historically necessary, since it liberated the judgment of taste from the previously narrow moralistic and utilitarian discursive framework. But ultimately this inquiry into the inherent features of the aesthetic experience gave rise to the separation of art from life. Art abandoned the world for an alternative reality created by the "free play" of the imagination. Indeed Kant defined poetry as "mere entertaining play of the imagination," which does not desire to ensnare the understanding (1928: §217). Poetry indulges in play; it has few other concerns.[4]

---

[4] In this respect, as Israel Knox argues, Kant and those following him succeeded in separating life into work and play, the working poor and the idle rich. Their aesthetic doctrines were, according to Knox, timely in that they flattered the vanity of the rising bourgeoisie and sanctioned its demand that art not deal harshly with reality (1958: 75). Knox cites a verse from the prologue of Schiller's "Wallenstein"— "Ernst ist das Leben, heiter ist die Kunst" [Life is serious, art is cheerful]—which for him exemplifies the divorce of art from life, and the identification of art with play.

World

This division between the phenomenal and the aesthetic world, which allows the latter only value as play, results in what Frank Lentricchia calls a dialectic of guilt and desire: " 'guilt' because we recognize our indulgence in art as mere play, a holiday from the real business of our cognitive and ethical life: 'desire' because the aesthetic idea is a representation of that for which we eternally yearn but can never have in human time—a way it will never be" (1980: 42).

If art spurns life, if it resists even the idea of responsibility, then how can it justify its self-indulgent existence in the face of the misery and toil that is the lot of so many men and women? This question has haunted art from its inception in the eighteenth century. How can it defend its idle pursuits when, as Schiller despairingly observed, in comparison to utility the insubstantial merits of art scarcely tip the balance? Art unavoidably and inevitably compares itself to utility. With the declaration of its independence, it fell victim to a series of enervating dichotomies (theory versus practice, thought versus action, beauty versus life, inside versus outside), which necessarily accompanied the notion of autonomy. As Derrida points out, the latter element of this opposition is privileged in Western culture. Art, belonging to the first part of the opposition, ultimately loses. Clearly the position of art has become precarious, a development agonizing the postromantic poet, who finds himself lodged within this dichotomous framework. This anxiety was perhaps first and most eloquently expressed by that famous question of Hölderlin in "Bread and Wine," namely, "What is the use of poets in such a destitute time?" This line, which was cited by George Seferis as an introduction to his collection of poems "Imeroloyia Katastromatos A" and the sentiment of which is reiterated at the end of James Purdy's novel *Cabot Wright Begins* ("I won't be a poet in a place and time like the present"), runs through postromantic literature, emphasizing poetry's guilt over its insubstantiality.[5]

---

[5] The questions raised in these passages are still relevant for us insofar as we still believe in aesthetic autonomy and the separation of life and art. Ours, however, is an age of disillusion with the saving powers of high culture. Consider Theodor Adorno's uncompromising condemnation of all "post-Auschwitz culture, including its urgent critique" as garbage and George Steiner's sense of loss at the failure

World

Art's fear of insignificance in the world has given rise to sometimes contradictory responses. There have been Schiller's and Shelley's attempts not only to defend, but also to demonstrate the indispensable role of the imagination in culture. On the other hand, there is the denial of art, best exemplified in literature by Rimbaud's uncompromising and total renouncement of poetry for the act and Kafka's never realized request that his manuscripts be destroyed. Other writers, such as Mayakovsky and Karyotakis, have sought in suicide complete abdication from art and life. In Cavafy guilt over the insubstantial merits of art permeates many prose and poetic texts, and this despite the pervasive belief in art's autonomy. It is because Cavafy relentlessly pursued the removal of the natural from his domain of ideal beauty that he ultimately had to acknowledge that within this retreat only play is possible. By following the other poets of the nineteenth century in segregating art from life, he necessarily lodged art in an oppositional structure. This foundation was not sound, since the enervating tension between outside and inside and between theory and practice threatened to undermine his entire poetics. The texts analyzed in the following section concern the poet's attempts to resolve the contradictions inherent in art's autonomy.

Cavafy first touches on this issue in the second half of the "Ars Poetica" (1902), where in the manner of Schiller and Shelley he formulates a defense of art, arguing for its essential role in society. The essay is based on Cavafy's examination of his posthumously published "The Pawn" (1894). According to Cavafy, this poem deals with the "domain of theory translated into action," and thus enacts in poetic form the opposition existing between these two poles. It is an allegory, taking a game of chess as its theme and drawing parallels between this game and life. In particular, the

---

of civilized values "to offer adequate resistance to political bestiality" (Adorno 1973: 367; Steiner 1969: 15). For Adorno and Steiner culture has failed because it does not prevent barbarism. Both express guilt or anguish over the shattering of their faith in the redemptive capacity of culture. But one may ask, what gives culture the power to save? We have conferred upon high culture a very lofty mission indeed, yet by elevating it above other practices of life we have undermined its very ability to perform this task. Our disenchantment in art has been predestined by our original segregation of art from the social praxis and our privileging of the aesthetic experiences over all others.

World

poem focuses on the fate of one pawn as it strives to reach the other side safely; its intention is to resurrect the queen, who could then save the other players. Once this goal is accomplished, it dies. For the purposes of the essay, Cavafy comments on only two verses of an earlier version of the poem: "Thus ends the sublime attempt. / Thus the great attempt is paid." These two lines elicit the discussion concerning, as Cavafy says, the relationship between theory and action.

Cavafy begins his analysis by calling attention to the noble sacrifice of the pawn, noting that, although an artist or philosopher does not undergo similar trials, he does perform his own sacrifices. Their discoveries lay the foundation for the hero's act. Yet unlike the hero's labors, the hardships of the theorist are underrated, misunderstood, or generally ignored. Cavafy wishes to shift the focus onto the theorist, to demonstrate that "the theoretical life, the life of the artist and the philosopher have also their sacrifice, bitter and unjust" (1963c: 20). Cavafy concludes that the theorist endures struggles that differ from those of the hero, but nevertheless make a practical contribution to the well-being of others. He then examines the nature of the theorist's sacrifice. The theorist's effort, he says, is made manifest in his plans and teachings, put into practice by the hero, and brought to fruition through his sacrifice. Cavafy insists that the possibility of this action is conceived by the theorist, without whose thought "the hero, brave but unable to think, would be useless, no asset of profit to the world" (p. 62).[6] The task of the pawn is to "put into practice the player's action because it can, it is fit for this. The theorist is fit for other work. He pays his pain in other fashions" (p. 64). He is the benefactor to whom millions owe their happiness, and it is for this reason that Cavafy considers his sacrifice more productive. In the final analysis, the hero's role becomes almost superfluous, since even without his deed, the planned good would eventually be realized; in con-

---

[6] Cavafy reiterates this point in a note on capital punishment written in 1902, which states that he opposes capital punishment not because his opposition will lead to its abolition, but rather because it can contribute to that end. His words will not be lost, since they will be repeated by others. "I recognize that I am a coward and that I cannot act. This is why I speak only. But I don't believe that my words are superfluous. Another person will act. But my many words—the words of me the coward—will facilitate his effort. They clean out the ground" (1983a: 25–26).

trast, the theorist is indispensable because he develops the theories upon which the hero acts. Cavafy confers priority on theory, and by implication on art, since it establishes the conceptual conditions in the context of which the act becomes possible and realizable.

In this text, through what often seems simplistic reasoning, Cavafy sets out to explore the relationship between theory (including art) and action, so as to defend the former against the latter, and ultimately to resolve the tension inherent in this dichotomy. In this respect, this section of the "Ars Poetica" may be seen as Cavafy's "Defense of Poetry." It takes up the challenge posed by the act concerning art's alleged superfluity and worthlessness. Cavafy exonerates art by affirming its indispensable role in the amelioration of the human lot. Yet although Cavafy seems to have dispelled the menace of the act, largely by repressing it and valorizing art, he never questions the conceptual soundness or validity of the dichotomy; he simply privileges one of its elements. Indeed, this duality, as stated earlier, is structurally embedded in the theoretical matrix of aesthetics. It is for this reason that, although Cavafy strove in this essay to confront and repel the threat of the act, he was not entirely successful. It returns to haunt and intimidate his poetry, weaving itself thematically through many of his poems, particularly the well-known "Young Men of Sidon (A.D. 400)," "Dareios," and the posthumously published "Simeon."

In "Young Men of Sidon (A.D. 400)" the problem is approached with strategies similar to those employed in "Ars Poetica." The poem goes perhaps even further than the essay in celebrating the value of art and simultaneously in attacking the conventional priority conferred upon action. The poem is set in an elegant villa in Sidon where five young men listen to an actor reciting some epigrams of the Hellenistic poets Mcleager, Krinagoras, and Rhianos. When the actor begins his declamation of the epigram that Aeschylus supposedly composed as his own epitaph, one of the youths rises abruptly and castigates the tragedian for composing such objectionable verses as his final testament to posterity. Aeschylus's epigram runs: "In this tomb lies Aeschylus, son of Euphorion, an Athenian, who died in wheat-bearing Gela. The Marathonian grove may proclaim his renowned valor, and

World

long-haired Medes, who knew it well."⁷ What seems to have incited the young man's vehement reaction is the text's laudation of Aeschylus as a warrior and its neglect of his accomplishments as a tragedian. From the young Sidonian's perspective, Aeschylus gives the impression that he prefers to be remembered primarily for his valor in war rather than his composition of great tragedies. It is the tragedian's implicit privileging of action over art that so provokes the young man, who, after all, is "mad about literature." His response takes up the entire last stanza of the poem:

> "I don't like that quatrain at all.
> Sentiments of that kind seem somehow weak.
> Give, I say, all your strength to your work,
> make it your total concern. And don't forget your work
> even in times of stress or when you begin to decline.
> This is what I expect, what I demand of you—
> and not that you completely dismiss from your mind
> the magnificent art of your tragedies—
> your *Agamemnon*, your marvelous *Prometheus*,
> your representations of Orestes and Cassandra,
> your *Seven Against Thebes*—merely to set down for your
>   memorial
> that as an ordinary soldier, one of the herd,
> you too fought against Datis and Artaphernis."

In these verses the fanatical young man exhorts Aeschylus never to forget this work even in suffering and near death, for to create art is the noblest aim. Aeschylus's failure to recognize this has aroused the young man to defend his tragedies. For the young man art must remain paramount; it should be commemorated and must exist as an object of total concern. He believes that Aeschylus's "marvelous tragedies" have a greater intrinsic value than his valorous acts in war.⁸ Art is more significant than action. Indeed, in

---

⁷ The Greek text appears in Cavafy (1963a: 11, 99), and the translation is found in Keeley and Sherrard (1975: 224).

⁸ Of course it never occurs to Cavafy that such exclusive privileging of art is a characteristic of our culture only. Although the poem is set in the period of late antiquity, the values it espouses are of the modern age. It is quite conceivable that Aeschylus, or whoever wrote this epitaph, considered the participation in a battle against an enemy to be worthy of more praise than the composition of tragedies. The young man's spirited response is informed by aestheticism.

World

the Sidonian's sweeping retort, art has nothing about which to feel guilty, since in his value system it occupies a foremost position. Culture should celebrate the work of art more than the act. Hence Aeschylus should be remembered for his tragedies and not for the courage he displayed in fighting the Greek foe. In "Young Men of Sidon (A.D. 400)" the status of art is defended once more, whereas action is given secondary value. Despite the glorification of art, however, its existence is still precarious, since it remains lodged within the theory/practice dichotomy. As in "Ars Poetica," the young man simply supports one side of this polarity by asserting the primacy of art. This same opposition reappears in "Simeon," in which the literary pursuits of a sophist are fundamentally challenged by the absolute act of Saint Simeon Stylites, the man who lived on top of a column for thirty-five years so as to make manifest his devotion to God.[9]

"Simeon" takes the form of a dramatic monologue that explores the consequences of poetry's confrontation with the absolute deed. The speaker, a sophist, and his implied listener, Mebis, are engaged in a casual discussion concerning the leading poetic figures of contemporary Syria. With the third line, the sophist abruptly terminates this conversation, unable at that moment to talk about literature:

> I'll study them some other day.
> I can't today because I'm upset.

He has been made uneasy, he tells Mebis, by his encounter with Simeon and the worshipers beneath his pillar, which has apparently shaken his faith in the study of poetry:

> But Mebis, why talk about Libanius
> and books and all these trivialities?
> Mebis, yesterday (it happened by chance)
> I found myself under Simeon's pillar.

In a state of despondency, the sophist is prepared almost to disavow literature, which in comparison with the immensity of Simeon's deed, appears trivial and banal. This act of complete self-sac-

---

[9] For Cavafy's personal remarks on Saint Simeon and his interpretation of Tennyson's "St Simeon Stylites," see the discussion in Chapter 5.

World

rifice, of absolute devotion and unyielding conviction, has caused him to "tremble" and "shudder." Simeon's achievement continues to torment him, since it brings to his attention the insubstantiality of his own pursuits. Unavoidably, the sophist juxtaposes the inaction and negation of the man of letters with the commitment and devotion of the saint, a debilitating comparison that anguishes the sophist and nurtures doubts of art's superiority:

> Please don't smile; for thirty-five years—think of it—
> winter and summer, night and day, for thirty-five years
> he's been living and suffering on top of a pillar.
> Before either of us was born (I'm twenty-nine,
> you must be younger than me),
> before we were born, just imagine it,
> Simeon climbed up his pillar
> and has stayed there ever since facing God.

In the sophist's account, Simeon symbolizes the man of heroic and absolute action (of the type described in the "Ars Poetica") and of ultimate self-sacrifice for a noble cause. His action exemplifies the "lofty attempt" that characterized the pawn's sacrifice in "The Pawn." In like manner, Simeon has willingly undertaken excruciating suffering so as to attain the absolute and bear witness to God. In contrast to this sublime achievement, the sophist's poetic preoccupations seem irrelevant and self-indulgent. This realization triggers the haunting line that, more than any other verse in Cavafy, expresses art's impoverishment, demoralization, and inadequacy: "But Mebis, why talk about Libanius / and books and all these trivialities?" What validity has a life of books and poetry in the light of Simeon's supreme achievement? When compared with the absolute act, art seems diminished, succumbing to the artist's guilt, since, as shown in Chapter 3, it also aspires to the absolute. In the poem, however, and as far as the sophist is concerned, art has failed to reach this lofty goal and is doomed to remain in the shadow of Simeon, humbled by his great art. For art, the absolute once more becomes both elusive goal and source of guilt. Unlike "Ars Poetica" or "Young Men of Sidon (A.D. 400)," where the conflict between art and action is temporarily resolved, the tension here is further intensified by the lack of any final reas-

World

surance of art's relevance. Many of the assumptions of postromantic poetry are shaken in "Simeon," particularly those concerning art's autonomous and autotrophic nature; claims that justification for art stems from its own intrinsic resources fail to convince the sophist. Aesthetic perfection cannot dispel the threat posed by the act, and so a sense of resignation permeates the entire poem. The very possibility of art and poetry is now subjected to grievous skepticism.[10] Only the last stanza, in which the sophist returns to the question of Syria's foremost poet, somehow redeems art and prevents the poem from turning into a repudiation of it:

> I'm in no mood for work today—
> but Mebis, I think it better that you tell them this:
> whatever the other sophists may say,
> I at least recognize Lamon
> as Syria's leading poet.

Yet, in the light of the previous questions raised by the sophist over art's relevance and value, these concluding lines do not so much defend art as willfully repress the threat facing it. The conflict between art and action is not resolved, only forgotten. In the final verses of "Simeon," art fails to reappropriate its glory and ac-

---

[10] The concern over the possibility and viability of art expressed in this and other poems may be compared to similar ideas recorded in a posthumous text written in 1902. The theory/action–art/action polarity is present in this note. Cavafy states that if he wanted he could become a great doctor, lawyer, economist, or engineer, provided he had time to study and, more important, the will to renounce literature. By this he implies that literature and a life of action are mutually exclusive. Cavafy plays with the idea of abandoning literature for the "practical life," though he realizes that without great effort—which would "break" his soul—he would be unable to uproot his "hankering" for literature. Cavafy writes: "My weakness—or strength, if one assumes that literary work has value—is not to be able to renounce literature, or to be precise, the pleasurable agitation of the imagination" (1983a: 23). This private note contains many of the issues found in the "Ars Poetica" and the poems examined in this chapter concerning the opposition of art and the "practical life." This polarity, as the note indicates, may lead to the repudiation of literature. But it should be pointed out that neither Cavafy nor the speakers in the three poems renounce poetry. They agonize over what they see as poetry's social ineffectiveness, but they continue writing. Each text expresses doubt about the very possibility of poetry/art, but each concludes with a justification of the poetic/artistic act. Although not all remain as fanatical about poetry as the young Sidonian of "Young Men of Sidon (A.D. 400)," none can say the unequivocal no to art.

cepts itself as an inconsequential exercise practiced by guilty and alienated individuals.

The poem "Dareios" tackles similar problems concerning art's position in the world. The central figure, the poet Phernazis, is compiling material for his epic poem on King Dareios (521–486 B.C.). When he is about to complete the most crucial part of the epic, a messenger rushes in with ominous tidings that leave Phernazis speechless—the Romans have crossed the Cappadocian frontier:

> The poet is dumbfounded. What a disaster!
> How can our glorious king,
> Mithridatis, Dionysos and Evpator,
> bother about Greek poems now?
> In the middle of a war—just think, Greek poems!

The war disrupts the poet's work and dashes his hopes of distinguishing himself as artist and of silencing his critics. As the previous discussion of the poem shows (see Chapter 2, "The Audience as Receiver and Interpreter of Texts"), during the invasion of Cappadocia the king will not show the slightest interest in Greek poetry. Phernazis hopes that the interruption may only be a minor setback to his grand designs. He admits, however, that the Romans will probably be victorious and establish themselves as the new rulers, replacing Mithridatis. Phernazis fears that the conquerors will not concern themselves with an epic about an ancestor of the vanquished king. Furthermore, the Romans will introduce other customs, procedures, novel literary discourses, and a new patronage system. Under such circumstances Phernazis's chances for success are very much reduced. He realizes from the beginning that his poetic endeavors have been rendered useless by the war.

In "Dareios," poetry is once again juxtaposed with action, which, in this case, eclipses it. The forces leading to and accompanying this momentous historic event overcome poetry and cast it aside. As in "Simeon," the writing of poetry becomes an almost worthless and ridiculous exercise, as indeed the perplexed cry of Phernazis suggests—"In the middle of a war—just think, Greek poems!" This anguished exclamation, reminiscent of the sophist's "Why talk about Libanius and books / and all these trivialities,"

World

voices poetry's fear that it has lost its significance and credibility. Amid death and destruction what meaning does verse composition have? Should the poet withdraw into his retreat to create beautiful verses while the world outside is ravaged by war? Can he ignore the violence and oppression outside his hermetic text? Such are the fundamental questions raised by the poem. Yet Phernazis himself refuses to concede defeat, for despite the acknowledged vanity of his efforts, he takes up the same idea that preoccupied him at the beginning: "But through all his nervousness, all the turmoil, / the poetic idea comes and goes insistently." Although on the historical level the very possibility of poetry is put into grave doubt, for the poet its existence is somehow affirmed. But does Phernazis redeem the poetic task, or does he, like the sophist of "Simeon," simply forget the implications of the questions he himself has posed? The historical condition will not change in his favor despite his lapse into amnesia. In other words, the conflict inherent in the art/action and theory/practice dichotomies is unresolved, as the poem still remains lodged in this oppositional taxonomy. The absolute act continues to haunt poetry.

These three poems call attention to the entire issue of aesthetic isolationism, which, as this study has shown, represents one of the principal conceptions of art in Cavafy. Art claims to withdraw from the world into its own independent realm created by the imagination. It dissociates itself from life in the pursuit of pure form. It rejects its former representative function. As this discussion has illustrated, however, the segregation of art from life is neither successful nor free from consequences. Art's unwillingness to involve itself in the world results in feelings of inadequacy, irrelevance, and insubstantiality. These in turn undermine the principle of aesthetic autonomy, probably one of the most fundamental assumptions of postromantic art. These poems question the existence of poetry because poetry itself feels guilty for its aloofness. The "poetic idea" is strained; it continues to "come and go" between the trivial and the sublime, between two contradictory conceptions of itself.

It was impossible for Cavafy to escape from this oppositional taxonomy, since the isolation (and worship) of art constitutes one of the central tenets of his poetics. Cavafy failed to overcome this problem because those texts, though attempting to resolve the conflict between life and art, still affirmed the idea of art's essential distinctiveness. If one believes in art's independence, that it somehow constitutes its own sphere of experience divorced from other realms of life, then one is compelled to live with these moral quandaries. Perhaps the only recourse is to question the very idea of art's separation from life, the solution proposed by the historical avant-garde. As Peter Bürger shows in his *Theory of the Avant-Garde*, movements such as dadaism, surrealism, and futurism attempted to deconstruct the institution of art—its material organization as well as the discourse conceiving of it as autonomous—by first bringing attention to its very institutionality. He argues that the avant-garde turned against both the distribution apparatus on which works of art depend and the status of art in bourgeois society as defined by the concept of autonomy (1984: 22). Avant-gardist works such as Duchamp's "ready-mades" reduced the distance between themselves and the social praxis, since they were mass-produced objects of everyday use. In this way the avant-garde strove to desacralize art, to reintegrate it into daily social practice and render it once again a thing among things. Ultimately, the avant-garde failed because it conducted its critique using the language of art and thus was effortlessly integrated into the institution it struggled to subvert.

Cavafy did not share the radical strategies and militant rhetoric of this movement. His work manifests the stage in the development of art when it turned inward and engaged in criticism of itself. Many of Cavafy's poems thematize art's "apartness" from life, its detachment from anything nonaesthetic. The texts examined in this chapter address the consequences of art's autonomy and seek somehow to resolve art's moral dilemma. Cavafy defends art from external censure; he affirms its distinctiveness. Each of the three poems ends with a defense of the absoluteness of art and with a plea justifying its existence. Although Cavafy recognizes the impotence of the artist and the social ineffectiveness of art, he does not see art's moral predicament as the direct result of its self-chosen segregation. As a faithful practitioner of European high modernism, he criticizes his inherited aesthetic conventions and introduces new modes of writing, but he cannot bring himself to

World

question art's alleged independence. Of Cavafy's major concerns art alone escapes his relentless scrutiny.

Yet this does not represent the entire picture. Although aesthetic autonomy constitutes an essential element of Cavafy's poetics, in no way does it define his poetics completely. As demonstrated in Chapters 2 and 3, another theory also informs his poetics, one that stresses the historicity of art and points to the social factors involved in the production of the aesthetic. In this case he sees art as a socially conditioned concept. Unlike the avant-garde, Cavafy does not seek to attack or negate art, but rather to understand it in all its complexity. What runs through his poems, essays, and notes is the pressing need to grasp its meaning.

Afterword

Considering the complexity and many-sidedness of Cavafy's poetics, it would be improper to impose a single view upon Cavafy's productive and creative attempts to comprehend the meaning of art and literature, to incorporate this understanding in his own writing and dramatize it as theme. Thus I cannot conclude with a convenient summary of Cavafy's poetics. Although it would be simple to argue that aestheticism most accurately describes his poetics, that definition would be a violent reduction of his thought. Cavafy struggled with many sometimes incompatible approaches, borrowing ideas from diverse sources in his endeavor to map out a poetic theory; hence his poetics does not easily lend itself to synoptical afterthoughts. The model I proposed is a tool for organizing Cavafy's statements on art and literature. Though Cavafy's principal concern was his poetry and not necessarily the formulation of a coherent theory of literature, the successful manner in which his poetry defamiliarized traditional Greek writing demonstrates that he was a shrewd critic as well. He looked critically both at his own poetry—out of more than the hundred poems he usually wrote in one year he published only a handful—and at the kinship it shared with the Greek tradition and the more general European background. Despite the absence from Cavafy's oeuvre of many prose texts dealing expressly with theoretical issues, his work reveals a profound preoccupation with poetics. This, I think, accounts for Cavafy's current status as one of the great revisionists of modern Greek literature.

I have refrained in this study from discussing Cavafy's relationship to the Greek tradition. This topic deserves a full-length study of its own. Cavafy wrote poetry in the Greek language and in the discursive space designated by Greek literature. I have omitted consideration of this subject simply for heuristic reasons, so as to concentrate exclusively on exploring his poetics, which, I believe, can be best understood in the European context. Cavafy turned to European literature and aesthetics because they presented the most effective vantage point for observing Greek writ-

Afterword

ing. Marginality, as we have seen, is associated in the modern sensibility with creativity and innovation. The writing of poetry, as Cavafy insisted, compels the individual to assume the persona of the outsider. The orientation to Europe at a time of fervent nationalism in Greece permitted this homosexual writer, a petit bourgeois descendant of Constantinople's aristocracy living at the periphery of the Greek world, to acquire the necessary irony toward Greek literature.

At the time that Cavafy was applying modernist techniques to poetry, formulating a self-conscious writing, and exploring the meaning of literariness, Greek society was asking for a patriotic literature that would posit Greece, not art, as the compelling subject of the writer. Greece at the turn of the century was still in search of a national identity and hence expected its poets to participate in its delineation. The principal ideology informing a writer's task was nationalism and not, as in Cavafy's case, aesthetics. Poets celebrated Greekness rather than aestheticism. Greek society was swept up by dreams inspired by the *Megali Idea* (Great Idea) that the newly born nation would rise to the heights established by its classical predecessors and recapture all the territory of the Byzantine Empire. In this context poetry and prose were considered tools in the construction of a national identity. Literary texts were read, understood, and discussed from the perspective of this goal. This does not mean that Greek society was somehow less sophisticated than European society; rather it faced problems different from those of Western Europe. Identity was still a troubling issue. This had to be resolved before poets, novelists, critics, editors, and teachers could direct their attention exclusively to the matter of art.

Living in Alexandria, Cavafy was of course removed from this situation. He did not confront the polemics directly. He involved himself in these debates by criticizing both the contemporary approach to literature and the direction Greek writing had taken. Instead of reassuring his readers with images of fifth-century Athens, Cavafy offered them the decline of Hellenistic power and the "decadence" of Rome. When the majority of poets by the late nineteenth century had accepted the demotic idiom as the literary language of Greece, Cavafy deliberately defied convention

Afterword

by writing in both the demotic and purist registers. He composed a prosaic verse bereft of the traditional features emblematic of lyricism. His poetry, as Timos Malanos complained, walked instead of danced. Cavafy shocked his audience further by his provocative and unambiguous portrayal of homosexuality.

In every way possible Cavafy set his poetry against contemporaneous Greek writing. Perhaps his most daring feat was to posit poetry itself as one of the cardinal concerns of his work at a time when literature had not yet developed in Greece into an autonomous institution and when a professional literary discourse was just nascent. Cavafy asked his readers to become aware of literature as a thing-in-itself when literary texts were still regarded as part of the discussion of national language and identity. This was his challenge to fellow poets and critics. And herein lies perhaps Cavafy's real anomaly—he decided to talk about Art when it did not yet exist in Greece.

In rejecting current trends in Greece, he opposed them with what for Greece constituted a novel approach to the art of poetry. For this and the reasons outlined above his poetry was initially denounced in Greece. Both its style and poetics contravened the dominant conventions for composing and reading poetry. Quite simply, there was no context for either his work or his aesthetic theories. His poetry was eccentric; it had no place in Greek writing and was dismissed as an aberration: D. Tangopulos called it pedestrian; for Malanos it was "antilyrical"; the novelist Theotokas referred to it as a nihilistic dead end. For most contemporary readers Cavafy's work was either inaccessible or a decadent import. He therefore remained a controversial poet for years. As M. Georgiu observes in an article dealing with the hostile nature of early Cavafian criticism, "Up to about 1930 it appears as if Greek criticism was answering the following question in a plebiscite: is Cavafy a poet or not?" (*Epitheorisi Tehnis* 1963: 654). Significantly, the debate was not on whether Cavafy's poetry was good or bad, but on whether it could be considered poetry at all.

The reception of his work became more favorable only after standards of taste altered to accommodate his pioneering poetry. In this respect the intervention on behalf of Cavafy's work of the influential editor and littérateur Gregory Xenopulos played a sig-

Afterword

nificant role. Of more lasting effect were the efforts of critics and poets such as Telos Agras and Alkis Thrilos to establish a favorable context for a modernism in Greece. The changes in literary values brought on by this generation enabled Cavafy's work to move toward the center of critical reference, much in the manner described by Cavafy in his essay "The Reflections of an Old Artist." (Cavafy's own poetry of course also contributed to this transformation of Greek letters.) As a result today Cavafy rates generally as one of the most innovative poets in the Greek canon, whereas his peer and principal opponent, Palamas, once celebrated as Greece's greatest living poet, now suffers from benign neglect.

A close look at Cavafy's poetics offers insight into the course of his work through the hierarchy of Greek literary texts. It also reveals different dimensions of the work itself. Poetics is neither the only subject of his poetry nor the sole access point to it. It simply constitutes one major aspect of his work. In Cavafy, much like the resolute poet of "Dareios," through all the "nervousness" and all the "turmoil . . . the poetic idea comes and goes insistently." Perhaps no Greek poet has explored through his verse the topic of poetry so comprehensively. No other oeuvre of Greek poetry reflects to such a degree on poetics. Few European poets can surpass Cavafy's profoundly dedicated effort to elucidate the groundwork upon which his task as poet is based.

References

WORKS BY CAVAFY:

Cavafy, Constantine P.
1936 "Prota Piimata" [First Poems]. *Nea Grammata* 1:2–12, 104–113.
1963a *Piimata* [Poems] 2 vols. Edited by G. Savidis. Athens: Ikaros.
1963b *Peza* [Prose Texts]. Edited by G. Papoutsakis. Athens: Fexis.
1963c *Anekdota Peza* [Unpublished Prose Texts]. Edited by M. Peridis. Athens: Fexis.
1968 *Anekdota Piimata* [Unpublished Poems]. Edited by G. Savidis. Athens: Ikaros.
1971 *E Skepsis enos yerontos Kallitehnu* [The Reflections of an Old Artist]. Edited by G. Savidis. *Tram* 5:101–104.
1973 "O Kavafis sholiazei ke analiei ta 'Keria' " [Cavafy Comments on and Analyzes "Candles"]. *To Vima* (April 29).
1974 "To Telos tu Odisseos" [The End of Odysseus]. Edited by G. Savidis. *Dokimasia* 6:10–22.
1977–78 "I Sinantisis ton Fonienton en ti Prosodia" [The Meeting of Vowels in Prosody]. Edited by G. Kehayioglou. *Ellinika* 30:353–83.
1979 *Epistoles ston Mario Vaïno* [Letters to Mario Vaïno]. Edited by E. Moshos. Athens: Estia.
1981 "The Unpublished Drafts of Five Poems on Julian the Apostate by C. P. Cavafy." Edited by R. Lavagnini. *Byzantine and Modern Greek Studies* 7:55–88.
1982a *Is to Fos tis Imeras*, Athens: Agra. *In Broad Daylight*. Translated by James Merrill. *Grand Street* 3 (1983):99–107.
1982b "Cavafy's Reading Notes on Gibbon's 'Decline and Fall.' " Edited by D. Haas. *Folia Neohellenica* 4:25–96.
1983a *Anekdota Simiomata Piitikes ke Ithikis* [Unpublished Notes on Poetics and Ethics]. Edited by G. Savidis. Athens: Ermis.
1983b *Ta Apokirigmena* [The Rejected Poems]. Edited by G. Savidis. Athens: Ikaros.

WORKS ON CAVAFY

Alexiou, Margaret
1985 "Cavafy's Drugs." In *The Text and Its Margins: Poststructuralist Approaches to Modern Greek Literature*. Edited by M. Alexiou and V. Lambropoulos. New York: Pella.

References

Beaton, Roderick
1981 "Cavafy: Irony and Hellenism." *Slavonic and East European Studies* 59:516–28.
Bien, Peter
1964 *Constantine Cavafy*. New York: Columbia University Press.
Bowersock, G. W.
1980 "The Julian Poems of C. P. Cavafy." *Byzantine and Modern Greek Studies* 6: 131–56.
1983 "Cavafy and Apollonios." *Grand Street* 3:180–89.
Dalven, Rae
1976 *The Complete Poems of Cavafy*. New York: Harvest.
Dimiroulis, Dimitris
1983 "I Anagnosi tu Kafavi." [The Reading of Cavafy.] *Hartis* 516:574–88.
Epitheorisi Tehnis
1963 Special edition, vol. 108.
Ilyinskaya, Sonia
1983 *K. P. Kavafis. I Dromi pros to Realismo stin Piisi tu 20u Eona* [The Paths toward Realism in the Poetry of the 20th Century.] Athens: Kedros.
Jusdanis, Gregory
1982–83 "Cavafy, Tennyson and the Overcoming of Influence." *Byzantine and Modern Greek Studies* 8:123–36.
1985 "Cavafy and the Politics of Poetry." In *The Texts and Its Margins: Poststructuralist Approaches to Modern Greek Literature*. Edited by M. Alexiou and V. Lambropoulos. New York: Pella.
Keeley, Edmund
1976 *Cavafy's Alexandria: A Study of a Myth in Progress*. Cambridge, Mass.: Harvard University Press.
Keeley, Edmund, and Savidis, George
1971 *C. P. Cavafy: Passions and Ancient Days*. New York: Dial Press.
Keeley, Edmund, and Sherrard, Phillip
1975 *C. P. Cavafy: Collected Poems*. Edited by G. Savidis. Princeton, N.J.: Princeton University Press.
Lambropoulos, Vassilis
1983a "Peri Anagnoseos" [On Reading]. *Hartis* 5/6:658–68.
1983b "The Violent Power of Knowledge: The Struggle of Critical Discourses for Domination over Cavafy's 'Young Men of Sidon, A.D. 400.' " *The Journal of the Hellenic Diaspora* 1/2:149–66.
Lehonitis, G.
1942 *Kavafika Aftosholia* [Cavafian Self-Comments]. Alexandria.

References

Leondaris, Viron
1983   *Kavafis o Englistos* [Cavafy Imprisoned]. Athens: Erasmos.
Nea Estia
1963   Special issue, vol. 872.
Nehamas, Alexander
1983   "Memory, Pleasure and Poetry: The Grammar of the Self in the Writing of Cavafy." *Journal of Modern Greek Studies* 2:295–319.
Peri, Massimo
1979   *Quattro saggi su Kavafis*. Milan: Catholic University Press.
Peridis, Mihalis
1948   *O Vios ke to Ergo tu Konst. Kavafi* [The Life and Work of Const. Cavafy]. Athens: Ikaros.
Pieris, Mihalis
1982   *Efodos sto Skotadi* [Assault into Darkness]. Athens: To Mikro Dendro.
Savidis, George
1966   *I Kavafikes Ekdosis (1891–1932)* [The Cavafian Editions]. Athens: Tahidromu.
Seferis, George
1974   *Dokimes I*. 3d. ed. Athens: Ikaros.
Tsirkas, Stratis
1971   *O Politikos Kavafis* [The Political Cavafy]. Athens: Kedros.

WORKS ON LITERARY HISTORY, THEORY, AND CRITICISM

Abrams, M. H.
1953   *The Mirror and the Lamp: Romantic Theory and the Critical Tradition*. Oxford: Oxford University Press.
1971   *Natural Supernaturalism*. New York: Norton.
1981   "Kant and the Theology of Art." *Notre Dame English Journal* 3:75–106.
Adorno, Theodor
1973   *Negative Dialectics*. Translated by E. Ashton. New York: Seabury Press.
Balakian, Anna
1977   *The Symbolist Movement*. New York: New York University Press.
Barthes, Roland
1968   *Writing Degree Zero*. Translated by A. Lavers and C. Smith. New York: Hill and Wang.
Bate, Walter
1971   *The Burden of the Past and the English Poet*. London: Chatto and Windus.

References

Baudelaire, Charles
1923   *Curiosités Esthétiques: Oeuvres Complètes*, II. Edited by J. Crépet. Paris: Louis Conard.
1925   *L'Art Romantique: Oeuvres Complètes*, III. Edited by J. Crépet. Paris: Louis Conard.

Baumgarten, Alexander
1954   *Reflections on Poetry* [1735]. Translated by K. Aschenbrenner and W. Holther. Berkeley: University of California Press.

Becker, Howard
1982   *Art Worlds*. Berkeley: University of California Press.

Bloom, Harold
1973   *The Anxiety of Influence: A Theory of Poetry*. New York: Oxford University Press.
1975   *A Map of Misreading*. New York: Oxford University Press.

Bradbury, Malcolm, and McFarlane, James, eds.
1976   *Modernism*. Harmondsworth: Penguin Books.

Bürger, Christa
1977   *Der Ursprung der bürgerlicher Institution Kunst*. Frankfurt: Suhrkamp.

Bürger, Peter
1984   *The Theory of the Avant-Garde*. Translated by M. Shaw. Minneapolis: University of Minnesota Press.

Calinescu, Matei
1977   *The Faces of Modernity*. Bloomington: Indiana University Press.

Carlyle, Thomas
1897   *On Heroes, Hero Worship and the Heroic in History: The Works of Thomas Carlyle*, V. London: Chapman and Hall.

Coleridge, Samuel, T.
1975   *Biographia Literaria*. Edited by G. Watson. London: Reeves and Turner.

Comte, Auguste
1880   *A General View of Positivism*. 2d. ed. Translated by J. Bridges. London: Reeves and Turner.

Constant, Benjamin
1957   *Journaux Intimes. Oeuvres*. Edited by A. Roulin. Paris: Gallimard.

Crawford, Donald
1974   *Kant's Aesthetic Theory*. Madison: University of Wisconsin Press.

Eagleton, Terry
1983   *Literary Theory: An Introduction*. Oxford: Basil Blackwell.

Eliot, T. S.
1951   *Selected Essays*. London: Faber and Faber.

References

Emerson, R. W.
1910   "The Poet." In *Emerson's Works*. London: George Routlege & Sons.

Escarpit, Robert
1961   " 'Creative Treason' as a Key to Literature." In *Yearbook of Comparative and General Literature* 10:16–21.

Flaubert, Gustave
1974   *Correspondance*, XIII, *1850–1859*. Paris: Club de l'Honnête Homme.

Foucault, Michel
1972   *The Archaeology of Knowledge*. Translated by A. M. Sheridan Smith. New York: Harper and Row.
1973   *The Order of Things*. New York: Vintage.
1977   *Language, Counter-Memory, Practice: Selected Essays and Interviews*. Translated by D. Bouchard and S. Simon. Edited by D. Bouchard. Oxford: Basil Blackwell.
1980   *Power/Knowledge: Selected Interviews and Other Writings*. Translated by C. Gordon, L. Marshall, J. Mepham, and K. Soper. Edited by C. Gordon. Brighton: Harvester Press.
1982–83 "Sexual Choice, Sexual Act: An Interview with Michel Foucault." *Salmagundi* 58/59:10–24.

Gautier, Théophile
1877   *Histoire du Romantisme*, 3d. ed. Paris: Charpentier.
1981   Preface. In *Mademoiselle de Maupin*. Translated by J. Richardson. Harmondsworth: Penguin.

Gombrich, E. H.
1950   *The Story of Art*. 2d. ed. London: Phaidon.

Greenberg, Clement
1973   "Modernist Painting." In *The New Art*. Edited by G. Battcock. New York: Dutton.

Hazlitt, William
1930   "On Poetry in General." In *The New Art*. Edited by G. Battcock. New York: Dutton.

Huysmans, Joris-Karl
1959   *Against Nature [À Rebours]*. Translated by R. Baldick. Harmondsworth: Penguin.

Jakobson, Roman
1981   "Linguistics and Poetics." In *Roman Jakobson Selected Writings*. The Hague: Mouton.

Johnson, Samuel
1817   "Apology for Apparent Plagiarism: Sources of Literary Variety." In *The British Essayists*, XXV, *The Adventurer*. London.

References

1827   "The Dangers of Imitation—the Impropriety of Imitating Spencer, the Criterions of Plagiarism." In *The Rambler*. Philadelphia: J. J. Woodward.

Kant, Immanuel
1928   *Critique of Judgement*. Translated by J. Meredith. Oxford: Clarendon Press.

Keats, John
1970   *The Letters of John Keats*. Edited by R. Gitings. Oxford: Oxford University Press.

Knox, Israel
1958   *The Aesthetic Theories of Kant, Hegel, and Schopenhauer*. New York: Humanities Press.

Landow, George
1971   *The Aesthetic and Critical Theories of John Ruskin*. Princeton, N.J.: Princeton University Press.

Lehmann, A. G.
1950   *The Symbolist Aesthetic in France, 1885–1895*. Oxford: Basil Blackwell.

Lentricchia, Frank
1980   *After the New Criticism*. Chicago: University of Chicago Press.

Lovejoy, Arthur
1936   *The Great Chain of Being*. Cambridge, Mass.: Harvard University Press.
1975   "On the Discrimination of Romanticism." In *Romanticism: Points of View*. Edited by R. Gleckner and G. Enscoe. Detroit: Wayne State University Press.

Mallarmé, Stéphane
1945   *Oeuvres Complètes*. Edited by H. Mondor and G. Jean-Aubry. Paris: Gallimard.
1959   *Correspondance, 1862–1871*. Edited by H. Mondor. Paris: Gallimard.

Mill, John S.
1897   *Early Essays*. Edited by S. W. Gibbs. London: George Bell & Sons.

Moore, Gerald
1972   *Confessions of a Young Man*. Edited by S. Dick. Montreal: McGill, Queen's University Press.

Morris, William
1948   *Selected Writings*. Edited by G. Cole. London: Nonesuch Press.

Novalis (Friedrich von Hardenberg)
1945   Blütenstaub. In *Gesammelte Werke*, II, Zürich: Bühl Verlag.

Ong, Walter

References

1971   *Rhetoric, Romance and Technology*. Ithaca, N.Y. Cornell University Press.
1982   *Orality and Literacy*. London: Methuen.

Pater, Walter
1901   *Appreciations*. London: Macmillan.
1910   *The Renaissance*. London: Macmillan.

Pierrot, Jean
1981   *The Decadent Imagination, 1880–1900*. Translated by D. Coltman. Chicago: University of Chicago Press.

Poe, E. A.
1899   *The Works of Edgar Alan Poe*, III. Edited by J. Ingram. London. A. C. & Black.

Poggioli, Renato
1968   *The Theory of the Avant-Garde*. Translated by G. Fitzgerald. Cambridge, Mass.: Harvard University Press.

Rimbaud, J.N.A.
1966   *Rimbaud: Complete Works, Selected Letters*. Bilingual ed. Translated by W. Fowlie. Chicago: University of Chicago Press.

Ruskin, John
1893   *Selections from the Writing of John Ruskin*. 1st ser., 1843–1860. London: George Allen.

Schiller, Friedrich
1967   *On the Aesthetic Education of Man*. Edited and Translated by E. Wilkinson and L. Willoughby. Oxford: Oxford University Press.

Schopenhauer, Arthur
1958   *The World as Will and Representation*. 2 vols. Translated by E. Payne. New York: Dover Publications.

Shelley, Percy
1977   *Shelley's Poetry and Prose*. Edited by D. Reiman and S. Powers. New York: Norton.

Steiner, George
1969   *Language and Silence*. Harmondsworth: Penguin.
1978   *On Difficulty and Other Essays*. Oxford: Oxford University Press.

Stephan, Philip
1974   *Paul Verlain and the Decadence*. Manchester: Manchester University Press.

Stevens, Wallace
1951   *The Necessary Angel*. London: Faber and Faber.
1957   *Opus Posthumous*. Edited by S. Morse. London: Faber and Faber.

References

Swinburne, A. C.
1925   *The Complete Works of Algernon Charles Swinburne*. Edited by E. Gosse and I. Wise. New York: Russell and Russell.

Symons, Arthur
1923   *Dramatis Personae*. Indianapolis: The Bobbs-Merrill Co.

Taine, Hippolyte
1887   Introduction. In *The History of English Literature*, I. Translated by H. van Laun. London: Chatto and Windus.

Todorov, Tzvetan
1981   *Introduction to Poetics*. Translated by R. Howard. Brighton: Harvester Press.

Tolstoy, Leo
1930   *What Is Art?* [1898]. Translated by A. Maude. London: Oxford University Press.

Villiers de l'Isle, Adam, Comte de
1925   *Axel*. Translated by H. P. Finberg. London: Jarrolds Publishers.

Weber, Max
1946   *From Max Weber: Essays in Sociology*. Translated and edited by H. Gerth and C. Mills. Oxford: Oxford University Press.

Wellek, René
1955–65 *A History of Modern Criticism, 1750–1950*. Cambridge: Cambridge University Press.
1970   "The Concept of Symbolism in Literary History." In *Discriminations: Further Concepts of Criticism*. New Haven, Conn.: Yale University Press.
1975   "The Concept of Romanticism in Literary History." In *Romanticism: Points of Views*. Edited by R. Gleckner and G. Enscoe. Detroit: Wayne State University Press.
1978   "What Is Literature?" In *What Is Literature?* Edited by Paul Hernadi. Bloomington: Indiana University Press.

Whistler, J.A.B.
1979   "Ten O'Clock Lecture" [1888]. In *The Aesthetes*. Edited by I. Small. London: Routledge and Kegan Paul.

Wilde, Oscar
1945   *Intentions*. London: Unicorn Press.
1974   *The Picture of Dorian Gray*. London: Oxford University Press.

Williams, Raymond
1960   *Culture and Society*. New York: Columbia University Press.
1977   *Marxism and Literature*. Oxford: Oxford University Press.

References

Wilson, Edmund
1931   *Axel's Castle: A Study of the Imaginative Literature of 1870–1930.* New York: Scribner's.

Wimsatt, William, and Brooks, Cleanth
1957   *Literary Criticism: A Short History.* 2 vols. Chicago: University of Chicago Press.

Woodmansee, Martha
1984   "The Interests in Disinterestedness: Karl Philip Moritz and the Emergence of the Theory of Aesthetic Autonomy in Eighteenth Century Germany." *Modern Language Quarterly* 45:22–47.

Wordsworth, William
1966   *Literary Criticism of William Wordsworth.* Edited by P. Zall. Lincoln: University of Nebraska Press.

Young, Edward
1961   *Conjectures on Original Composition* [1759]. Leeds: Scholar Press.

Index

Titles of poems by Cavafy are in quotation marks.

"A Byzantine Nobleman in Exile Composing Verses," 55-56
Abrams, M. H., xiii, xiv, 3, 81, 85n
"Addition," 5
"And I Lounged and Lay on Their Beds," 36, 99-100
"Anna Komnina," 124
"Aristovoulos," 92
"Ars Poetica," 16, 71, 79, 111, 165-67
"Artificial Flowers," 79-80, 159-61

Barthes, Roland, 31, 117
Bate, Walter Jackson, 145
Baudelaire, Charles, xvii, 18, 20, 157
"Before Time Altered Them," 94
Bien, Peter, xvi
Bloom, Harold, 143, 146
Bradbury, Malcolm, xvii, 105-6
Bürger, Peter, 106n, 174

Carlyle, Thomas, 4, 7
"The City," 68
Coleridge, Samuel T., 18-19
"Comes to Rest," 95
Comte, Auguste, 28
"Correspondence According to Baudelaire," 8
Constant, Benjamin, 77
"Coins," 119
"Craftsman of Wine Bowls," 33, 89, 90

"Dareios," 57-58, 172-74
"Days of 1908," 94
"Dimaratos," 130

Emerson, Ralph Waldo, 7-8
"The End of Odysseus," 141-43, 147-48
"The Enemies," 49, 53-54, 62, 113, 151-53
"Epitaph of Antiochos, King of Kommagini," 132n

"The First Step," 6, 43-44
Flaubert, Gustave, 22, 84
"Following the Recipe of Ancient Greco-Syrian Magicians," 86-87, 88-89
"For the Shop," 30, 42
"For Ammonis, Who Died at 29, in 610," 93-94
Foucault, Michael, 57, 96n, 104, 116, 118

Gautier, Théophile, 77, 85n, 157
"Good and Bad Weather," 66
"Gray," 90
Greenberg, Clement, xviii, 106
"Growing in Spirit," 25, 97, 153

"Half an Hour," 16-17, 83, 96
Hazlitt, William, 3
Huysmans, Joris-Karl, 84n, 158

"I Went," 35, 96

Index

"If Actually Dead," 126-28
"Imenos," 133-34
"In Despair," 17
"In the Evening," 91
"In the Month of Athyr," 129-30
"In the Same Place," 20
"In a Township of Asia Minor," 131-32
"Independence," 45-46
"The Inkwell," 9
"Ithaka," 143-44
"I've Brought to Art," 14, 17, 82

Jakobson, Roman, xiv-xv
"Julian and the Antiochians," 101

"Kaisarion," 9-13, 107-8
Kant, Immanuel, 74-76, 163-64
Keats, John, 15
Keeley, Edmund, xii n, xvi, 59, 60, 61n, 91, 93n

Lambropoulos, Vassilis, 130
Lentricchia, Frank, 21, 164
Leondaris, Viron, xi
"Long Ago," 90, 91
Lovejoy, Arthur, xvi

Malanos, Timos, xi
Mallarmé, Stéphane, 40, 41, 78, 84, 85
"Melancholy of Jason Kleander, Poet of Kommagini, A.D. 595," 87, 89
Mill, John S., 39, 40
"Morning Sea," 22, 161-62
Moore, Gerald, 37n, 41, 78
Morris, William, 29

Nehamas, Alexander, 91, 96
"Nous n'osons plus chanter les roses," 66-67
Novalis (Friedrich von Hardenberg), 85n, 13

"Of the Jews (A.D. 50)," 34, 100-101
"On Hearing of Love," 17, 83, 96
Ong, Walter, xvii, 106n, 145n
"Orophernis," 108-10
"Outside the House," 90

"Parthen," 123
"Passing Through," 37, 99
Pater, Walter, 78, 83-84
Peridis, Mihalis, xii n, 59
"Pictured," 46
Poe, Edgar Allan, 13, 32, 77-78
Poggioli, Renato, xvii

"The Reflections of an Old Artist," 49-53, 56, 62, 112, 149-51, 154-55
"The Regiment of Pleasure," 97-98
"The Rest I Will Tell to Those Down in Hades," 119
"The Retinue of Dionysos," 47
Ruskin, John, 29, 74, 101-104

Savidis, George, 59, 60, 63
"The Saving of Julian," 139-40
Schiller, Friedrich, 27, 76-77, 85n
Schopenhauer, Arthur, 88
Shelley, Percy Bysshe, 7, 12n, 39
"Simeon," 169-72
"Since Nine O'Clock," 13
"Singer," 9, 65
Steiner, George, 37, 164n
Stevens, Wallace, 81, 82
Swinburne, Algernon Charles, 78

Index

Taine, Hippolyte, 28
"Temethos, Antiochian, A.D. 400," 25-26, 43
Tennyson, Alfred, 148
"That's the Man," 46
"Theater of Sidon (A.D. 400)," 24, 25, 44
"Their Beginning," 95
"Theodotos," 70
"To Call Up the Shades," 14
"To Sensual Pleasure," 35
Todorov, Tzvetan, xviii
Tolstoy, Leo, 29
"Tomb of Evrion," 93
"Tomb of the Grammarian Lysias," 120

"Understanding," 99

"Very Seldom," 49-50
"Voice from the Sea," 65

"Walls," 23
Weber, Max, 81
Wellek, René, xvi, 15n, 69
"When They Come Alive," 93-94
Whistler, J.A.B., 41, 159
Wilde, Oscar, 41, 79, 85n, 158-59
Wilson, Edmund, 4
"The Windows," 23
Woodmansee, Martha, 81
Wordsworth, William, 3, 7

"Young Men of Sidon (A.D. 400)," 33-34, 123-24, 167-69

Library of Congress Cataloging-in-Publication Data
Jusdanis, Gregory, 1955-
The poetics of Cavafy.

Revision of thesis (Ph.D.)—University of Birmingham, 1984.
Bibliography: p.
Includes index.
1. Cavafy, Constantine, 1863-1933—Criticism and interpretation
I. Title.

PA5610.K2Z726 1987   889'.132   87-3390
ISBN 0-691-06720-1 (alk. paper)

GPSR Authorized Representative: Easy Access System Europe - Mustamäe tee 50, 10621 Tallinn, Estonia, gpsr.requests@easproject.com